Ferraris Chronicle

THE
Ferraris Chronicle
Popes, Emperors, and Deeds in Apulia
1096 - 1228

Translation and Notes by
Jacqueline Alio

Published by Trinacria Editions, New York.

Legal Deposit: Library of Congress, British Library (and Bodleian Libraries, Cambridge University Library, Trinity College Library, National Libraries of Scotland and Wales), Italian National Libraries (Rome, Florence).

Under the title *The Ferraris Chronicle: Popes, Emperors, and Deeds in Apulia 1096-1228* this book was assigned a Library of Congress Control Number on 6 November 2017. Identifying information was registered by the British Library through Bibliographic Data Services on 7 November 2017. Copyright of this work, which was completed on 16 December 2017, was pre-registered with the United States Copyright Office on 11 December 2017 under number PRE000010056 in the class "Literary Work in Book Form."

Some material contained herein previously appeared in other books by Calogera Jacqueline Alio and is used by permission. Except where otherwise indicated, all translations contained herein are by Calogera Jacqueline Alio. Illustrations, maps and photographs by Louis Mendola. The text of this monograph was double-blind peer-reviewed.

ORCID identifier of Calogera Jacqueline Alio: 0000-0003-1134-1217

Printed in the United States of America on acid-free paper.

ISBN 9781943639168 (print)
ISBN 9781943639175 (ebook)

Library of Congress Control Number 2017959982

A CIP catalogue record for this book is available from the British Library.

PROLOGUE

On a clear night in May of 1061, the Normans' sleek galleys, vessels reminiscent of the long ships of their Norse forebears, began transporting men, horses and arms to a place six miles south of Messina, disembarking along Sicily's Ionian coast. Each ship arrived silently, landing in Sicily and then going back across the strait to Calabria to bring more knights and foot men to the island.

Sicily's Arabs expected an attack sooner or later, though from a more northern point directly across the strait at its narrowest, hence their concentration of ships patrolling Tyrrhenian waters on the other side of Cape Faro.

In the event, the undermanned garrison guarding Messina's seaside fortress was taken unawares, being unprepared for a ground assault from the south. By dawn, the Messinians, most of whom were Greek speakers, awoke to find their city, a springboard for trade as an important port, in Norman hands. Indeed, the fighting itself was brief and decisive. Most of the defenders were killed and few attackers injured.

Although the invading force of knights, esquires, foot soldiers and archers consisted of thousands, the fortifications were taken by an initial wave of a few hundred under the command of Roger Hauteville, who advanced and attacked without waiting for additional men to arrive from Calabria with his elder brother, the equally audacious Robert.

The battle was followed by the typical pillaging, along with the occasional rape. At least one Muslim decided to kill his own sister rather than risk her falling into the invaders' hands.

The victory gave the Hauteville brothers a foothold in Sicily and absolute control over ships traversing the Strait of Messina and most of the Ionian Sea. As it happened, the response from the emirs of the other Sicilian cities was unimpressive. Those jealous rulers were too busy nurturing their petty grudges against each other to respond in a serious way to the threat posed by the Normans. Yet their failure to send a large army to take back Messina did not mean they would give up their local emirates without a fight.

It would take the Normans another decade to reach Palermo, the largest, wealthiest city in Italy. By then, chroniclers were writing their story.

Forgotten facts are sometimes the most important facts of all. They enlighten us.

Discovered during the nineteenth century, the *Chronica Romanorum Pontificum et Imperatorum ac de Rebus in Apulia Gestis,* sometimes called the *Chronica Ferrariensis* or, here in Italy, the *Cronaca di Santa Maria della Ferraria,* was written by an unidentified monk of the Cistercian monastery of Santa Maria della Ferraria outside Vairano Patenora, northeast of Teano, near the Volturno River, in the shadow of the Matese Mountains.

Dominated by an impressive medieval castle of grayish stone, the town of Vairano is not without its charm. Little of the squarish fortress remains except the curtain walls and four round towers, but virtually nothing is left of the Cistercian abbey nearby, located along a road to the river, where the cleric composed his minor chronicle during the first three decades of the thirteenth century.

The monastery, in what is now the province of Caserta near Naples, was founded in 1179 as a dependency of Fossanova Abbey, near Priverno, by John of Ferraris, hence its name. It boasted one of the few Gothic churches in southern Italy.

We know the chronicler only through his work. The term "Apulia" in the title refers, rather generically, not only to Puglia, which in medieval times stretched from the heel of the Italian boot northward almost to the march of Ancona, but to regions such as Basilicata, Abruzzi and even parts of Calabria.

Although it recounts public events beginning in 781, those that are most detailed begin in 1096, the year of the First Crusade, just as the Hautevilles were consolidating their power in southern Italy, reaching into the apex of the reign of the Hohenstaufens epitomized by Emperor Frederick II as he arrived in the Holy Land during the Sixth Crusade in 1228.

The chronicler probably met Frederick five years earlier.

Whilst there exist contemporary chronicles of far greater importance, the *Ferraris Chronicle* merits its own niche. The format of its first two chapters is thought to reflect an effort to continue the *Chronica Maiora* of England's Venerable Bede, a prolific, versatile writer who died in the Kingdom of Northumbria in 735, and whose best-known *opus* is the *Historia Ecclesiastica Gentis Anglorum* or *Ecclesiastical History of the English People*. If imitation is the sincerest form of flattery, our Cistercian monk was sincere indeed.

Like Bede, the Italian monk drew his inspiration, and information, from several sources. This is not to suggest that everything told here is merely redundant or even accurate. Each chronicle is unique, and this one occasionally brings us a perspective slightly different from those of others.

There were, no doubt, other minor prose chronicles like this one, some being compendia of earlier works, and there is little doubt that many of them are lost to time.

Chronicles are a very special part of medieval heritage. This one, with its focus on what, in 1130, became the Kingdom of Sicily, speaks to us with the echo of a time and place often overlooked in the study of Italian medieval history, with its emphasis on the likes of Petrarch, Dante and Boccaccio. The chronicle's existence is itself a resounding message.

The manuscript is retained by a library in Bologna, where it reposes in undisturbed dignity. The *editio princeps* was published in Naples in 1888.

The words you are reading are part of a trend that began around a hundred years later as an effort on the part of anglophone scholars to translate the chronicles of the Norman-Swabian Kingdom of Sicily for an increasingly international readership. Today's readers include armchair historians as well as university students, the latter being less familiar with Latin than their predecessors of yore.

To that end, most of the more important chronicles of Italy's Norman and Swabian eras have been translated in recent times. It was time to bring you this one.

INTRODUCTION

Our path to discovery should be a determined trek across the unknown, not a graceless gait down a familiar street.

What is presented in these pages is a precious gift from history. The chronicles of Italy's Norman-Swabian era breathe life into the kings and queens entombed for the last seven centuries in the magnificent cathedrals of Palermo and Monreale: Roger II, William I, Margaret, William II, Henry VI, Constance, Frederick II. King Tancred once rested in the Magione, a splendid church built for the Cistercians near Palermo's Khalesa quarter, but it seems that Henry and Constance had his remains removed when they gave the abbey to the Teutonic Knights.

These kings and queens are a chief focus of the *Ferraris Chronicle*. Translating this record of events was a personal experience, indeed an honour, for somebody having deep roots in the Kingdom of Sicily, somebody who lives in what was once the royal park, the Genoard, between the two magnificent cathedrals that house the pantheons of these monarchs. In these pages is a glimpse of the rulers who shaped a medieval golden age.

Their influence reached far beyond the jagged shores of the Kingdom of Sicily, a realm that consisted of its eponymous island and most of the Italian peninsula south of Rome. The Holy Roman Empire to the north and the Byzantine Empire to the east brushed against the affairs of the Kingdom of Sicily. Zirid Tunisia was an ephemeral, quasi-colonial "Kingdom of Africa" ruled from Palermo, and there was a special relationship with England, whose sovereign, Henry II, betrothed a daughter, Joanna, to William II.

The early reign of Emperor Frederick II, who died in 1250, informs the only "live" part of the chronicle, referring to events that occurred during the monk's lifetime. (This is obvious by the beginning of Chapter 10.)

The *Ferraris Chronicle* was the most recent chronicle of the Norman-Swabian era of the Kingdom of Sicily to be discovered and published, and it was the only one written during the reign of Frederick II that, until now, was not available in English translation. Here it may be noted that the chronicles of "Jamsilla," Saba Malaspina, and Bartholomew of Nicastro were written *after* Frederick's death.

We need not digress into a more generalized discussion except to note that, just as there was no unitary "Italy," despite earnest Lombard efforts to create one, there was no unified "national" Italian chronicle comparable to the *Anglo-Saxon Chronicle,* which complements Bede's work, or the *Primary Chronicle of Kiev.* Perhaps none was needed, as the complex society that was medieval Italy offers us a number of narratives which, if fitted together the right way, form a cohesive chessboard complete with kings, queens, castles, and black and white knights.

Although chronicles are many, there cannot be said to be a surfeit of them for the Kingdom of Sicily before 1250; we find Gervase of Tilbury in Palermo at the court of William II writing very little about his time there.

Authorship

Much as we may like to affirm that any literary work should stand on its own, those written in past centuries usually require at least some explanation as to history and context. In general, the earlier the work, the more explanation is needed. Works from antiquity typically need the most commentary, and modern books the least. Those written in what we call the "Middle Ages" fall, appropriately enough, in the middle of this range.

Who was the chronicle's author? Whoever the monk was that wrote the *Ferraris Chronicle,* he was familiar with the great people and great events of his times and those of the preceding generation. He was a true student of history.

Astronomical events like eclipses are mentioned (and some are confirmed by modern scientific records), and so are calamities like earthquakes and floods. Important meetings like that between King Roger II and Pope Lucius II at Ceprano are not overlooked.

One of the monk's sources was likely a complete version, now lost, of the *Chronicon Beneventanum* written by the chronicler Falco of Benevento, which in its extant form covers the time from 1103 to 1140. The part of Falco's chronicle that is missing in surviving codices of his work is thought to be preserved in the *Ferraris Chronicle,* specifically for the years from 1099 to 1103 and from 1141 to 1146. The text of the earlier period is more succinct not only for the brevity of the time it covers but for the scant detail it offers.

The *Ferraris Chronicle,* like Falco's *Chronicon Beneventanum,* fails to mention the assizes, or constitutions, believed to have been promulgated at Ariano and traditionally dated to 1140.

Even where they are not ignored, certain events, such as the murder of Thomas Becket (see note 301), appear in unexpected places in the text. Others, like the chancellorship of Stephen of Perche, are described only partially and inaccurately.

Though hardly myopic, the chronicler tends to view the world from his own geographical vantage point. This place was, however, convenient to the valleys and roads that led to Apulia, and many travelers passed through the area on their way to Brindisi, Taranto or Bari.

Indeed, Santa Maria della Ferraria was located just a few miles from the road along the Volturno that linked important communities like Capua and Benevento (some segments of the ancient Via Appia were also in use), and not very far from other major monasteries, namely Cassino, Cava and Saint Vincent. (See the first map.)

Thaddeus, the abbot, cultivated a friendship with Frederick II, who visited in 1223, when the chronicler probably met the monarch. (Frederick returned six years later.) Indeed, a charter confirming privileges for the monastery was issued to Thaddeus in Frederick's name in 1205.[1]

Though reflecting a certain respect for Frederick, the *Ferraris Chronicle* is no encomium. It so happens that some of the monarch's greatest achievements were yet to come, after the chronicle ends. He accomplished much during the last part of his reign.

Clearly, the monk is no sycophant of the Normans, but neither does he seem so antipathetic to the Hautevilles as Falco of Benevento, from whose chronicle some of *Ferraris* seems to derive.[2] Nor is the monk so infamously cynical as Hugh Falcandus, who chronicled the intrigues of the Hautevilles' royal court at Palermo.

Whilst writing the chronicle, was the monk himself old enough to remember the Norman reign very well? We do not know.

We may find the views of chroniclers like Hugh Falcandus forceful, but even his partisanship pales in comparison to more adamant perspectives spawned by later political movements like the conflict between Guelphs and Ghibellines during the thirteenth century. Saba Malaspina and Bartholomew of Nicastro were notoriously opinionated.

The *Ferraris Chronicle* does not seem overwhelmingly influenced by any specific movement or sentiment, even if its author is generally sympathetic to Frederick II and unabashedly supportive of the Roman Church against Greek Christians, heretical Cathars, Muslims, and Jews.

Some European monastic chroniclers outside the Greek and Slavic spheres, at first glance, are mistaken for blatantly Papal apologists. That characterization, based on their obvious interest in maintaining Rome's ecclesiastical hierarchy, fails to do clerics justice. The majority of chroniclers, indeed the greater number of learned people, were either churchmen or secular men-of-letters such as court notaries.

An influential knight or courtier, perhaps even a herald, might well have taken notes on events that eventually found their way into a chronicle or annal, but the chroniclers themselves were part of an elite class. It was a class from which women, for the most part, were excluded.

The *Ferraris* chronicler himself would probably tell us that the events are more important than the man writing about them, and yet the two are inextricably linked, reaching out to touch the reader. Yes, chronicles, as they have come down to us, traverse time itself.

At all events, modern scholars' retrospective "psychoanalysis" of medieval chroniclers is seldom a necessary or productive exercise. While points of view certainly color what has been written, chronicles are not gospel, and this one is transparent enough. Most of the time, it is more useful to let the word speak for itself than to attempt to ascertain what is "really" intended.

There is nothing in the text to suggest that the chronicler was born outside the Kingdom of Sicily. His mother tongue was most likely Neapolitan, spoken around Naples and Salerno, or even Sicilian, spoken not only in Sicily but in much of southern Apulia and Calabria. Neapolitan is nearer the Tuscan and Umbrian tongues that emerged in their fullness during the thirteenth century. Middle Sicilian, which flourished at the court of Frederick II when the *Ferraris Chronicle* was being written, brings us such passages as this:

Et incontinentj mandaru per la miragla, lu quali era misser Rujeri di Lauria. Et cumandau lu re di Aragona a mmisser Rujeri chi incontinenti fachissi acconzarj l'armata et andassi a mMissina, et prindissi et ardissi tucti li navili di Re Carlu.[3]

Yes, that is how it was written, with inconsistent orthography and a plethora of double consonants.[4]

A detailed consideration of the significance of Neapolitan and Sicilian in the development of an Italian vernacular lies beyond the purview of this study. It is noteworthy, however, that *Lu Rebellamentu di Sichilia Contra Re Carlu* (quoted above), a source for studying the War of the Vespers of 1282, is the longest narrative text known to us that was composed in an Italian language before 1300, thus predating the earliest Tuscan prose works.

The *Ferraris Chronicle* was written in an age that saw the Sicilian School of poetry emerge as one of Italy's most important literary movements. Had Manfred, the son of Frederick II, not been defeated in 1266 at the Battle of Benevento, the influence of Neapolitan and Sicilian might have come to dominate Italy. Modern "Italian" might well be based on one of these languages rather than Tuscan.

Whatever tongue the chronicler and his contemporaries spoke among themselves, Latin was the written language of most chronicles written in Italy during the Norman and Swabian eras, and indeed for a long time thereafter. The sur-

viving French text of the chronicle of Amatus of Montecassino is a translation of the (lost) original version written in
Latin.

Survival, Discovery, Diffusion

A literary work, obviously enough, is meant to be read, perhaps even enjoyed. Some medieval prose works were published
quite early, during the incunable era, but in Britain, France,
Italy and Germany the greatest impetus to transcribe, translate
and publish chronicles, annals, charters and letters was seen
during the nineteenth century. An early Italian example is the
Rerum Italicarum Scriptores series, begun in 1723 and edited by
Lodovico Antonio Muratori. This movement was a boon to
scholars.

The *Ferraris* manuscript, along with numerous other
codices, was transferred to Bologna, an important depository
in Papal territory, early in the seventeenth century by its archbishop, the young, erudite Ludovico Ludovisi. There it remained, to be discovered by the librarian Antonio Magnani
(1743-1811), a former Jesuit and rabid bibliophile, who left his
collection of some twenty-five thousand items, which included
numerous manuscripts, to the city of Bologna. Although Magnani had written a concise, yet insightful, description of the
work, decades would pass before a more profound examination of it was attempted.

Superficially, *Ferraris* seems unremarkable if compared to
other, more beautiful items in the Magnani collection. It lacks
illuminations, or even an explanatory preface, and its script is
unexceptional.

The body text of the surviving manuscript is written in a
single calligraphic hand throughout, with marginalia added in
another hand later. The penmanship is flowing but simple and
legible, only tenuously comparable to the elegance of the most

refined Beneventan script, although it has been compared to the "Cassino" form of that style used in Campania (the "Bari" variant was popular in Apulia). The extant manuscript was copied after 1300, and much of the writing is quite small.

Augusto Gaudenzi published the *editio princeps* in 1888 as *Ignoti Monachi Cisterciensis: Sancta Mariae de Ferraria Chronica et Ryccardi de Sancto Germano Chronica Priora* in the *Monumenti Storici* series. Issued in a limited edition of two hundred seventy-five numbered copies, this volume printed in Naples included the chronicle of Richard of San Germano previously published by Georg Heinrich Pertz, along with some astute observations by Gaudenzi himself and a number of footnotes indicating which passages were drawn from the chronicle of Falco of Benevento.

A decade later, the historian Karl Andreas Kehr undertook the first extensive analytical study of the text.[5]

If these seem like belated developments, it should be remembered that the earliest known texts of the Assizes of Ariano were discovered, or rediscovered, during the nineteenth century. That was also the case of the *Spinelli Codex,* the oldest extant manuscript of the *Rebellamentu* mentioned above. In 2005, some unpublished letters between Frederick II and his son, Conrad, were rediscovered in a library in Austria.

Some codices meet a more dire fate. In 1943, when German troops deliberately set fire to the manuscript collection of the state archives of Naples, we lost the *Catalogus Baronum* (the "Domesday Book" of Italy's Norman era) and a number of unpublished charters issued by Frederick II; the former, fortunately, had already been photographed and partially published.

Was the *Ferraris Chronicle* in some way "suppressed" following the fall of the Hohenstaufens? Did the monks of Santa Maria della Ferraria consciously elect to secret it away lest they be seen as apologists for the deposed dynasty should the Angevin kings in Naples learn of the chronicle? This we cannot know, but works about the Normans and Swabians were, at least to a degree, marginalized during the fourteenth century and into the nascent Renaissance as Italy's literary focus shifted northward. The few exceptions to this trend were chronicles by people like Saba Malaspina that reflected an obviously anti-Hohenstaufen bias, thus influencing the views espoused by Dante and Boccaccio.

In view of this, it is perhaps unsurprising that we find the first publication of the chronicle of Hugh Falcandus being undertaken not in Italy but in France (in 1550).

Being published for the first time only in the late nineteenth century, *Ferraris* came to be regarded by scholars as something of an "open secret." Admittedly, the work of the monk of the Ferraria abbey is less important than the chronicles of Falco of Benevento and Richard of San Germano, yet even today it is all but ignored by historians.[6]

In fact, *Ferraris* is the only chronicle besides Richard's *Chronica Regni Siciliae* that was written about Frederick in the Kingdom of Sicily during his reign, rather than afterward.

There is no evidence to suggest that *Ferraris* influenced subsequent chroniclers who wrote during the end of Swabian rule, beginning their works with Frederick's death. The *Jamsilla Chronicle* (from 1250 to 1258), with its Ghibelline orientation, was probably written by a courtier of King Manfred, the son of Frederick II. Saba Malaspina (whose *Rerum Sicularum Historia* spans the years from 1250 to 1285), who entertained blatantly Guelph sympathies, was a cleric from Rome. Nothing in the work of these two chroniclers can be identified as a specific borrowing from *Ferraris*. Neither "Jamsilla" or Malaspina even recounts much about the life of Frederick except in perfunctory commentary in what is essentially a concise preface.

Details

Chronicles and annals bequeath us something rarely found in other sources. *Ferraris* is a chronicle of narrative prose. However, one part of it, consisting of concise entries arranged by year, owes something to the format of annals like that of Cassino (an obvious influence), while another, with its focus on a succession of pontificates, is reminiscent of early chronologies.[7]

Each chronicle expresses itself through a few features that make it unique and many that place it firmly into the socio-cultural milieu of its era. A chronicle is nothing if not a product of its time, a reflection of zeitgeist.

A certain writing form and particular details lend a specific prose style to *Ferraris,* and we may readily discern traces of the work of Falco of Benevento, and probably other chroniclers as well. In several instances the monk even copies Falco's errors, as when he writes *Florida,* instead of *Richenza,* as the name of the consort of Lothair of Supplinburg, the Holy Roman Emperor.

Not every event or detail found in the chronicler's account of the twelfth century can be attributed to a single source.

Leaving aside purely linguistic and calligraphic nuances, and possible copying errors by an amanuensis, the "editorial" details pertain, for example, to the famous address of Bernard of Clairvaux before King Roger II in 1137 and the oft-repeated tale of the "wandering Jew."

Bernard's profound influence shaped the great political currents of his times, rivalling that of pontiffs and monarchs. His role was instrumental, even decisive, in everything from ending a schism that divided the papacy to promoting the Second Crusade. In the text, Bernard of Clairvaux is revered not only as a leader (and reformer) of the chronicler's own order, but as a key figure in events throughout southern Italy and beyond.

That, of course, is nothing less than the truth.

The story of the Jew is a generally unflattering trope that arrived in Italy with pilgrims returning from the Holy Land, and the *Ferraris* author was one of the first Europeans of his time to write about it, in 1223. It is subsequently mentioned by Roger of Wendover in 1228 and repeated by Matthew Paris in 1240. This tale is one of many stones that, over time, formed the foundation of an increasingly virulent anti-Semitism. However, its inclusion in the chronicle belies the fact that the Jews, like the Muslims, were an integral part of the complex mosaic that was the Kingdom of Sicily, something confirmed (after the period covered in the chronicle) with the Constitutions of Melfi issued by Frederick II in 1231.

Most of what the chronicler recounts reflects the common threads running through the medieval tapestry of his time rather than any opinion on his part. True, the monk is inclined, often stridently, to side with Rome against her opponents, but the fact that pontiffs saw themselves as kingmakers was not a policy of the chronicler's doing. In the greater number of cases, he is simply reporting what he has seen, read or heard.

He refers to Frederick II, his contemporary, in flattering terms, never criticizing him.

There is nothing in the chronicle to imply that the monk condones the poor treatment that Frederick received at the hands of Pope Gregory IX. This pontiff was elected in 1227. The following year, he infamously invaded the Kingdom of Sicily while Frederick, in a state of excommunication, was away from Europe on the Sixth Crusade. Gregory was abetted by John of Brienne, Frederick's father-in-law. Richard of San Germano, whose chronicle extends to 1243, is sympathetic to Frederick. Unfortunately, the account of the monk of Ferraria ends shortly after Frederick's departure for the Kingdom of Jerusalem, and before his return in 1229. Nonetheless, he does mention Frederick's excommunication, while his carefully-worded commentary about Gregory, "an eloquent man of letters who showed an alert intellect," hardly constitutes unbridled praise.

The chronicles and annals that contributed so greatly to the retrospective parts of *Ferraris* are considered in Appendix 4.

Significance

We should not permit style to overshadow substance, the content of the chronicle being its paramount element. Yet some consideration of its format is necessary insofar as it reflects the work's importance.

Given its varied literary form, which in some places conforms to that of an annal (or even a history) and others a conventional chronicle, and its absence of a prefatory note, *Ferraris,* considered *in toto,* does not enjoy a great uniformity to give its content what might be termed "cohesion." Whereas some chronicles, such as those of Hugh Falcandus and Romuald of Salerno in the twelfth century and Richard of San Germano and "Jamsilla" in the thirteenth, are based principally on the personal observations of an author as a witness to unfolding events (hence covering a comparatively brief span of time), the same can be said only of the last three decades of *Ferraris.*

There is nothing novel in this theory. In his introduction to the first print edition, Gaudenzi remarked that some of the chronicler's references to Frederick II, unlike those to his predecessors, are written in the present tense; the monk's vivid descriptions of the eclipses of March 1197 and July 1208 (confirmed by Gaudenzi in Teodor von Oppolzer's *Canon der Finsternisse* published in 1887) likewise suggested to the publisher direct observation rather than a secondhand account.

Some parts of *Ferraris,* particularly the listing of popes and Longobard kings near the beginning of the text, are written in the unequivocal fashion of a "biblical" chronology.

Certain sections, such as those recounting events from the First Crusade through the reigns of the Norman rulers (from around 1072 to 1194), form what is essentially a "dead," or retrospective (non-contemporary), "third-person" chronicle, although some passages are very similar to what one encounters in a narrative history like the one written by Anna Comnena.

A few passages, recounting events very succinctly by year (from 1105 to 1111), are presented in the rather perfunctory, neutral mode of an annal, lacking much explanatory detail.

Only the final part (from around 1195 to 1228) is a "live," or synchronous (contemporary), "first-person" chronicle comparable to those of Falcandus and Romuald.

The monk, therefore, is both continuator and originator. Yet, despite its change in form from annal to chronicle, and its change in tense in the final chapters, *Ferraris* is presented in a single, clear authorial voice.

As a first-person record, the greatest value of *Ferraris* lies in its contemporaneous account of the first half of the reign of Frederick II. This, however, cannot be said to be uniquely revelatory, since we have an ample number of contemporary chronicles that focus on Frederick, chiefly that of Richard of San Germano, who knew the sovereign personally and (later) the chronicle of Salimbene di Adam. Another distinguished chronicler, Peter of Eboli, wrote during the reign of Frederick's father, Henry VI. Here one would be remiss to overlook letters, such as those of Peter della Vigna.

Nevertheless, the *Ferraris Chronicle,* whatever its biases, serves to confirm what were then the prevailing perceptions in the Kingdom of Sicily of the essential, quasi-current events of Frederick's reign whilst reiterating the past events (recent history) of the Hauteville era into the reign of Henry VI and his consort Constance, the daughter of Roger II.

Through fortunate happenstance, it includes a few pieces of text believed to be excerpted from what may be a lost copy of the chronicle of Falco of Benevento (but not present in the surviving copies), thus extending the span of that work forward and backward in time.

Like those snippets, a few other unique details within the body of the *Ferraris* text may have been drawn from a source that is now lost. Here an example that comes to mind is the reference to Ranulf of Alife having a concubine whilst married to Matilda, the sister of Roger II. Matilda herself probably did not regard this as a mere detail, yet Alexander of Telese, whose chronicle was written at her request, does not mention it. (Perhaps Matilda did not wish to focus on her husband's infidelity?) In any case, *Ferraris* owes far less to the chronicle of Alexander of Telese than it does to Falco's work.

Another example is the siege of the large fortress at Bari by Lothair III, the Holy Roman Emperor, in 1137. Like *Ferraris,* the surviving text of Falco's chronicle states that the Bariots surrendered quickly, but it does not mention the garrison of the seaside castle resisting for another month or so.

Neither Falco nor the monk of Santa Maria della Ferraria mentions the Assizes of Ariano, although Falco notes the introduction of the unpopular ducat coin at Ariano in 1140. The extension of (what is thought to be) his text in *Ferraris* takes us into the middle of the 1140s, and by then the legal code was certainly introduced, so we might expect it to be mentioned there.

A detail that stands out is the physical description of King William I, particularly his black beard, something not noted elsewhere.

The presence of twelfth-century details in *Ferraris* that are not mentioned in other (known) chronicles of the Norman era may tempt the reader to conclude that these pieces of information lack historicity, that they are little more than the fruit of the monk's imagination. The other possibilities are that such details were preserved over time as an oral tradition, or that they were indeed recorded in a source (known to the chronicler) extant in 1228 but subsequently lost. Here certainty is elusive. This phenomenon, however, reminds us to consider historical sources critically and collectively.

Except for a few succinct forays into the realm of spirituality or legend, and then only to repeat stories that were prevalent at the time, *Ferraris,* despite some errors typical of medieval chronicles, does not present much that is whimsical or preternatural. The monk who wrote it cannot be said to be particularly imaginative for the age of frequent miraculous events in which he lived, certainly not much more than Falco of Benevento or Richard of San Germano. That is good, for we don't want a chronicler's writing to be too creative any more than we would want a journalist's reporting to be too imaginative.

A theory little explored until now would place the *Ferraris Chronicle* into a literary category of its own, or at least a niche distinct from those of most other writings of its era. Arguably, with its format embracing more than one medieval genre, its lengthy topical range (essentially from 1096 to 1228) covering the span of several lifetimes, and its content aggregated from sundry sources, the work could well be classified as the first *history* of the Kingdom of Sicily.

Yet *Ferraris* is not altogether unusual as an aggregation drawn from various sources if we consider that, writing in the same era, Roger of Wendover begins a narrative with the story of creation and uses the work of Bede, among many others, in his *Flores Historiarum,* or *Flowers of History,* completed by 1235. (More widespread use of the neologism by historians would add *aggregator* to *continuator* and *originator* as a way we categorize the practical functions of medieval chroniclers and annalists.)

Considering the particular relevance of its "live" account of the reign of Frederick II, *Ferraris* finds its place in an elite clique of chronicles forthrightly sympathetic to the Hohenstaufens, and therefore relevant to the study of that Swabian dynasty. It is part of a "Ghibelline Trilogy," complementing the chronicles of Richard of San Germano and "Jamsilla."

However the modern historian chooses to classify or define *Ferraris,* the fact that widely known, if lengthier, chronicles like those of Falco of Benevento and Richard of San Germano were more likely to be copied and distributed ensured a greater chance of their survival. In terms of survival, the abbey of Santa Maria della Ferraria did not fare so well as the chronicle written in its scriptorium.

The Abbey

Despite what is sometimes depicted of it in modern literature, monastic life in western Europe was anything but an isolated vacuum. Monasteries were constantly visited by all kinds of travelers, be they couriers, knights, pilgrims or merchants, and monks themselves often traveled from one monastery of their order to another. Like the vast patchwork of baronial estates and the numerous commanderies of knightly orders (the Templars and Hospitallers), abbeys were part of a *de facto* network spanning Europe and reaching into the westernmost part of Asia. As we have said, Santa Maria della Ferraria, despite what the visitor may perceive as its remote location, was positioned along the lines of greatest communication.

Monasticism was not a monolithic institution. Besides its fragmentation into religious orders like the Cistercians and Benedictines, it bore the mark of both the Latin and Greek traditions. There were, at best, just a few small Byzantine (Orthodox) monasteries left in the *Regnum Siciliae* by the time the *Ferraris Chronicle* was written, but for a tangible vestige of Orthodoxy's enduring legacy we need look no further than the icon fresco (shown on this book's back cover) preserved at Santa Maria della Ferraria, with its strikingly Byzantine style, and of course the stunning mosaics in Monreale Abbey.

The history of the monastery of Santa Maria della Ferraria is a long one. The lands upon which it stood were donated to the monk John of Ferraris by Richard del Sangro in 1171, and construction was essentially complete at its consecration eight years later. Its splendid church was a rare, early example of the true Gothic in southern Italy.

In 1190, the abbot supported King Tancred of Sicily against the claim to the throne made by his cousin, Constance Hauteville, consort of the Holy Roman Emperor Henry VI. Tancred, in turn, granted the abbey many privileges and made it, in effect, a royal protectorate.

This special status granted by Tancred was later confirmed by his successor, Henry VI, ruling in Constance's name. Constance and Henry were succeeded by their son, Frederick II.

The friendship of this distinguished monarch with Thaddeus, the abbot from 1201 to 1227, when the chronicle was being written, facilitated the acquisition of lands far afield, in Apulia and the small region called *Molise*.

Frederick's falconer, Malgerio Sorel, retired to the abbey, where he is commemorated in a fresco depicting his friend Peter da Morrone, the future Pope Celestine V, said to have attended Sorel's funeral here.

During the fifteenth century the monastery fell to the jurisdiction of the Archbishop of Capua. Later, Cardinal Ludovisi, who we have already met, sought to conserve its assets, of which it had been largely despoiled by a succession of absentee administrators. In 1807, when a few monks were still living in it, the abbey was confiscated with other ecclesiastical property during the Napoleonic occupation.

The Translation

The chronicle's prose style is generally consistent throughout, its ideas uniformly expressed in a Latin typical of monastic writers, reflecting influences somewhat more medieval than classical. This subtlety is lost in its translation into a modern, Germanic language like English.

Subjective as such opinions can be, most scholars, particularly those of us having a native fluency in Italian (which derives directly from the vulgate), would concur that the Latin of the thirteenth century is less cumbersome than the language of Tacitus. This is certainly the case of *Ferraris,* whatever classical idioms and usages occasionally color it.

Compared to some works, the Latin we find in *Ferraris* boasts a splendid clarity. Nevertheless, each translation, like the language of each chronicle, has its own idiosyncrasies.

As our chief objective is a translation for the benefit of historians, rather than a linguistic study, this work does not dwell on such subtleties beyond occasional questions of diction (what a specific word means).

Scholars compare the surviving codices of the same chronicle to discern linguistic nuances or copying errors that constitute differences between the texts and, implicitly, distinctions in meaning. That is not a consideration for the *Ferraris Chronicle,* with its single known (and fairly early) codex. In comparing the original manuscript to Gaudenzi's publication, there are a few ambiguities, but none were deemed important enough to justify anything more than a succinct note.

A number of factors determine the way chronicles and other medieval texts are translated and interpreted (evaluated) in the context of their time and place, and this is certainly true of *Ferraris.* The most obvious, commonplace questions concern philological details rooted in history, bringing us, to cite a typical example, *serf* in the Middle Ages and *slave* in antiquity for the same noun, *servus*. To the Romans *militis* was a *foot soldier,* but to medieval kings it was a *knight.*

Some terms are defined by *sui generis* usages; *familiaris* and *amiratus* have particular meanings, as in the Kingdom of Sicily each word referred to a specific high-ranking position, not simply a *friend* or *admiral.* The chronicler sometimes refers to Lombard governors of cities as *comes* (count) where *gastald* might be more accurate.

This aspect of our study implies a certain paradigm of prosopography but, far more prosaically, the necessity for the translator's knowledge of the institutions present in the Sicilian monarchy, not only in view of their statutory (legally defined) status but in actual, everyday practice. Even the word *Sicilia* is potentially deceptive; sometimes it denotes the *island* of Sicily but often it refers to the entire *kingdom*, with medieval writers presuming the reader's understanding of which meaning is intended, the *insula* or the *regnum.*

The modern translator must know that *procurator* meant something different in the thirteenth century than in the third.

Filius and *frater,* and *filium* and *fratem,* are sometimes interchanged through simple errors in copying.

Therefore, some of the words and phrases we encounter are mere errors in transcription, but *sic erat scriptum* or (if one prefers) *così era scritto.* Because it is intended chiefly for scholars, the translation in these pages is rather literal. There was no need to embellish it.

There is, admittedly, some subjectivity in the translation of proper nouns, where the intent is accuracy and understandability. The gentilic *Arab* (which may refer to Aghlabids, Kalbids, Zirids or Fatimids) is more modern than the Latin cognate for *Saracen* favored by medieval writers; likewise *Africa* may be more appropriate than *Barbary* (for the *Berbers* who lived there). Modern toponyms are more accurate than *Romania* or *Macedonia* for the Balkan region of the Byzantine Empire, or *Babilonia* for the hinterlands of what are now Syria and Jordan. As an ethnonym, *Lombard* is preferred to *Longobard* after the tenth century, and the medieval Greeks are usually referred to as *Byzantine Greeks* or *Byzantines*. Some names are best rendered in English or Italian, others in Latin. Some Latin forms of common nouns are anglicised in certain cases, giving us *palliums* instead of *pallia*.

In the anglophone academy today's Latinists are divided into vaguely identifiable "schools" of translation style. More than a mode of interpretation, however, it is the analysis of a chronicle's content that seems to divide scholars studying the history of the Normans and Swabians in Italy. This book seeks to set forth details that supplement the text whilst avoiding the most arcane, contentious (often useless) debates.

The chronicles of Norman-Swabian Italy translated into English thus far have been published, for the most part, as sole editions. We do not find many instances of two anglophone scholars effecting their own translations of the same chronicle, nor rival publishers willing to issue competing editions of works having a rather small market.

A fine English translation of the sections of *Ferraris* thought to be taken from the chronicle of Falco of Benevento was first published in 2012.[8]

Historiography

Concordance is important. The primary sources that confirm or refute the accuracy of what has been written by our chronicler are, firstly, charters and letters issued by the personages he mentions (usually pontiffs, prelates, nobles or monarchs) and, secondly, contemporaneous chronicles and annals. In studying these, we find the author of *Ferraris* to be generally reliable in recounting the facts. Most of the dates he gives are years rather than specific days or even months (and some are based on a calendar year that begins in March), but most are accurate.

In the case of *Ferraris,* the fact that concordance with events in Italy is confirmed by charters and chronicles is most important for the reign of Frederick II (who was crowned King of Sicily in 1198) because this is when the monk's account is "live," pertaining to his own times and to things he, or people he knew, may have witnessed. It may be hearsay, but it is contemporary hearsay.

Archival research is scholarship pared down to its essentials.

There exist, in addition to this documentary record, supplementary sources, often unknown to scholars working outside Italy, such as architectural artefacts. Here one is reminded of an inscribed plaque conserved in Palermo that was installed in a church, now destroyed, dedicated to Saint Peter near the Fatimids' sea castle by Robert Hauteville and his wife, Sichelgaita, in 1081.

Many edifices have vanished but others are simply hidden from view. An arched medieval bridge spanning Sicily's San Leonardo River is now submerged by a man-made lake (although there is talk of a plan to dismantle the structure for transfer to another site in the manner of the Abu Simbel temples which guard the Nile). Most of Palermo's Punic walls are now incorporated into buildings erected during the Middle Ages or later.

Beyond this are general considerations of environmental context to bear in mind. For example, much of Apulia and Calabria, and certainly Sicily, was more lushly forested in the reign of Frederick II than it is today. The average mean temperature was lower. There was greater precipitation, and certainly more snowfall. Deer and boar roamed the land, and streams teemed with fish. Such factors influence, for example, the precise identification of topographical features like woods.

Where stone has been quarried, rocky knolls such as Hagar Sàrlu (Arabic for "Serlo's Rock"), near Nissoria in Sicily, have disappeared from the landscape.

A medieval chronicler can be forgiven for not knowing that a certain mountain was higher than another. The modern scholar, on the other hand, should do her best to identify the site of a village or settlement, long extinct, that a chronicle mentions.

Thankfully, we understand much more than our forebears could about physical maladies. One would not expect somebody living in the thirteenth century to know the precise cause of death of a ruler who died naturally and perhaps suddenly, especially where symptoms are generic or unobservable. Malaria and dysentery were ubiquitous and identifiable, other conditions much less so.

Superstition was widespread. An event like an earthquake or the appearance of a comet might be considered an omen. The interlude of legends recounted in Chapter 3 is sufficient proof that medieval minds were often given to belief in supernatural events beyond the miracles espoused by the church.

As if the supernatural were not difficult enough to grasp, certain physical details are sometimes omitted from the written record. Here an interesting example is the analysis of the remains of Henry Hohenstaufen (1211-1242), the son and one-time heir of Frederick II, which suggests he was suffering from leprosy. This, perhaps as much as the "insolent" behavior so resented by his father, may explain Henry's exclusion from the line of succession.

Physical evidence sometimes validates accepted facts. Phylogeography helps us to link places and populations. Sicily is the world's most conquered island, and the presence of certain haplogroups confirms what has always been written about its history.

The times and visibility of the lunar eclipses mentioned in

Ferraris were confirmed by data available from NASA.

In the telling of history, anything less than a multidisciplinary approach is a disservice to the reader.

Be it agreed that our study of the past must make use of every method available to us, several phenomena ascribed less importance by an earlier generation of scholars have risen to prominence in historical studies over the last few decades. At least two of these topics are relevant to a very general discussion of the views of the monk who wrote the *Ferraris Chronicle* and therefore merit consideration, even if this succinct commentary falls short of anything like a complete exposition or sociological analysis.

Eurocentrism

There is nothing to suggest that the Cistercian monk who wrote the *Ferraris Chronicle* ever set foot in the foreign lands he describes, even those in Europe. Most of his references to abbeys other than his own are to those in what are now Italy and France, and they are Cistercian and Benedictine.

Perhaps a chronicler based in Sicily, rather than the Italian peninsular heartland, would have entertained a slightly more tolerant, if not inclusive, view of Muslims and Greek (Orthodox) Christians. Here, however, the modern term *Eurocentric* would not be an entirely suitable adjective, for the perspective of Sicily's Normans and Swabians, like that of the Phoenicians and Romans before them, generally considered the Mediterranean *in toto* almost as a world unto itself. The people of the *Regnum Siciliae* knew where, from their own vantage point, Asia and Africa began but not precisely where these continents ended.

The chronicler's view is devoid of sympathy for the Orthodox Christians whose monasteries were to be found in Asia Minor, Kievan Rus, Armenia and Egypt, and even (albeit in ever diminishing numbers) in Calabria and southern Apulia. To his way of thinking, the "Saracens" of Asia, Africa, Iberia and Sicily, be they Sunni or Shia, were almost beneath contempt.

Yet defining the chronicler as a fanatical "Romanist" would be something of a simplification. It may be more accurate to consider him to be no more or less than a product of his time, place and education. In this he was scarcely unique; medieval chroniclers the world over cultivated instinctively localized biases that favored their own faith, people, culture and region.

Opinions rooted in religious belief were often presented as fact, and the monk does not shirk expressing criticism of fellow Catholics. Writing about William II, his presumption that the late king's lack of heirs was a punishment from God is hardly an exceptional view for the Middle Ages.

Religious zeal was the order of the day. This was an age of crusades, even when some of those crusades were prosecuted against fellow Europeans like the Cathars. One of the things that made Roger II and his grandson Frederick II so exceptional was their familiarity with the various Mediterranean languages and peoples of their multicultural kingdom; during his pacific Sixth Crusade, the oft-excommunicated Frederick spoke to the Ayyubids in Arabic.

Following the fall of Frederick's dynasty, true multiculturalism vanished in the Italian dominions he had ruled. In 1300, the Muslims of Lucera who were not killed or expelled were forced by the Angevin monarchy to convert to Catholicism. In 1493, Judaism in Sicily fell victim to Spanish policy.

Only in the last two decades of the twentieth century, with the arrival of immigrants from Africa and Asia, was a true multiculturalism reintroduced here in Italy, which inherited a Fascist legacy of xenophobic racism.

More than a Eurocentrist, the chronicler of the Ferraria abbey was a rather opinionated, Catholic conformist. What is far more troubling than his opinion of those who did not share his beliefs is the fact that religious bigotry flourished for so many centuries, surviving into our own times, and not only as the exclusive province of the more zealous proponents of a single religion.

Feminism

It would be inaccurate to characterize the chronicler as being much less feminist than most men of his era. Here history should be our guide.

By the time the chronicle was written, three strong women had been regents for their young sons destined to become kings: Adelaide for Roger II, Margaret for William II, Constance for Frederick II. It is difficult to imagine that the monk knew nothing more of these women than what he reveals; indeed, he goes so far as to disparage Stephen of Perche, named by Margaret as chancellor during William's minority, and it was generally known that Stephen was Margaret's cousin. Then again, the monk refers to the Norman Stephen as "Spanish" so, in reality, he may have been less than assiduous about certain details.

As we have observed, the chronicler fails to mention the Assizes of Ariano (of 1140), which outlawed rape (though chiefly for nuns). He could not have known that in 1231 the Constitutions of Melfi were destined to confirm this law whilst permitting divorce and instituting female inheritance of property.

However, the monk overlooks the Assizes of Capua of 1220 even whilst acknowledging that laws were changed in that city in that year. The Assizes of Messina enacted the following year are ignored completely. Both of these legal codes were precursors to the Constitutions of Melfi implemented a decade later. These Norman-Swabian legal codes of the Kingdom of Sicily were rooted in an inspired interpretation of the *Codex Justinianus.*

That the statutes on divorce and rape fell into disuse following the end of the Hohenstaufen era partially explains why these laws were all but forgotten for centuries. This meant that, unlike the English, who enshrined (and perhaps even exaggerated) the significance of the Magna Carta, we Italians ignored important developments in our own juridical history.

In effect, the laws that protected women's rights were banished from the social landscape; divorce was again legalized in Italy only in 1970 and rape became a major crime, as a form of physical assault rather than a minor offense against public decency, in 1996 (sic).

One of the few laws guaranteeing female rights that remained in force from Frederick's reign until modern times was the freedom of daughters to inherit feudal property from their fathers. This "Sicilian Succession" was abolished after the Kingdom of the Two Sicilies was annexed to the nascent Kingdom of Italy in 1860.

Returning to the Middle Ages, it is interesting that (as noted earlier) the chronicler mentions Matilda, the sister of Roger II, being the victim of adulterous betrayal. Unless it is merely a pretext for criticizing Matilda's husband, Ranulf of Alife, who was a notorious opponent of Roger II, this seems to imply the monk's disapproval of such behavior.

Matilda, of course, was not just any noblewoman, but the sibling of an important ruler. The chronicler might well have ignored her plight were she a lady of lesser social status. Another characteristic that makes this case unusual is that, unlike most women confronted by an unfaithful husband, Matilda actually left her spouse; here again, she enjoyed this right because her brother was king and therefore could offer her protection and even punish Ranulf.

Here in Italy, where the philandering husband is something of a social trope, it is worth noting that a medieval woman like Matilda refused to tolerate such treatment.

The chronicler of Ferraria, like others, mentions the disrespect shown Adelaide, King Roger's mother, through the bigamy of Baldwin of Jerusalem, to whom she was betrothed (see note 266). Again, however, the monk was being selective insofar as this was a matter involving royalty rather than the nobility. Like the infidelity of Ranulf of Alife, who seems to have been as disloyal to his king as he was to his own wife, this concerned matters of state. In this case, it made Roger unreceptive to the idea of sending knights to defend Jerusalem.

The chronicler also mentions another affront from the east regarding marriage that resulted in resentment at the Sicilian court. This was the failure of Maria "Porphyrogenita" Comnenus, betrothed to William II, to arrive in Apulia (see Appendix 5) as planned. The culprit here was not Maria herself but her father. A fate worse than marriage to William befell Maria when she was murdered in 1182, an event mentioned in *Ferraris*.

We know far more about the regency of William's mother, Queen Margaret, than about those of Adelaide and Constance. It is remarkable that the most vociferous, defamatory opposition to her (as reported by Hugh Falcandus) did not emanate from the Muslims, Greeks or Jews of the Kingdom of Sicily but from a jealous feudal baronage consisting almost exclusively of Roman Catholics. This observation is not meant to be an indictment of Catholicism, but a simple recognition of the circumstances which then prevailed.

To the extent that it can be surmised, and employing contemporary norms, the monk's general view of women seems not to be one of overt misogyny but of simple indifference.

Environmentalism

A topic more relevant to the time during which the chronicle was written than to the writing itself is nature, specifically ecology.

Frederick II considered the state of the environment, at least in terms of human safety, in his Constitutions of Melfi (see this book's epilogue). His lengthy treatise on falconry addresses, among other things, the health and care of birds of prey. Frederick seems to have enjoyed falconry more than hunting for deer and boar. Following the Sixth Crusade, he brought back to Italy several African creatures given to him by Sultan al Kamil. Among these were panthers, camels, elephants, and what was probably the first giraffe ever seen in Europe.

Francis of Assisi is not mentioned in the chronicle but he was present at the crusaders' siege of Damietta, which is mentioned. Canonized just two years after his death, he was long the patron of animals, and in the Catholic Church (since 1979) he is the patron of those who defend the environment. To quantify this in medieval terms, one imagines Francis gently reproving a man he might encounter who was kicking a dog. Although he was not a lifelong vegetarian, Francis refrained from eating lamb.

The monk who wrote the *Ferraris Chronicle* almost certainly knew of Francis of Assisi and the religious orders he founded. However, there is no evidence that Francis and Frederick ever met, interesting as such a meeting would have been.

Hybrid

Would that we could discern in the *Ferraris Chronicle* a single style, theme or approach beyond generalities. A uniformly applicable definition, as we have said, is elusive.

As a literary work, the chronicle defies simple categorization because it straddles a chasm dividing several shifting worlds. As we say in Italian, *non è né carne né pesce,* "it is neither meat nor fish." Perhaps it is both, a kind of surf and turf, which Italians call *mare e monti,* "sea and mountains."

Ferraris is at once an annal and a chronicle, with some characteristics of a history. It is both "live" and "dead," and even its tenses change. Like the deeds it recounts, it is tranquil and then tempestuous. Some of its words and ideas are original, others much less so. Its geographical viewpoint is often provincial yet sometimes strikingly cosmopolitan. Its pragmatic sobriety is punctuated by strange, if interesting, interludes of whimsy that are little more than supernatural tales drawn from the fey reports of tired pilgrims. On the other hand, the monk seems to distinguish between astronomy and astrology; at the very least he takes the former seriously.

There are clichés but occasional flashes of insight, even wisdom. The chronicle offers the reader an eclectic, inconsistent cascade of information that is surprisingly accurate in obscure details yet astonishingly inaccurate in banal facts that are more widely known. Simplicity is juxtaposed with complexity, one tempering the other but never quite nullifying it.

By the time we have read *Ferraris,* we know little more about the chronicler than we did when we began (and maybe that is his intention). All we really know about him is that his philosophy, or perhaps just his mentality, was that of the typical thirteenth-century Catholic monk.

Here there is no prescient modernism, only medievalism, but that is quite enough.

Legacy

The Battle of Benevento, as we have seen, was a turning point that signalled the demise of the Hohenstaufen dynasty. This triumph of Guelphs over Ghibellines set the stage for the language and culture of northern Italy to assert themselves as the most quintessentially "Italian."

As if that were not sufficient, some six centuries later, with the unification of the Italian peninsula, along with Sicily and

Sardinia, into a nation, histories of most of the former kingdoms that comprised the new state were suppressed in the public mind in an attempt to focus on Italy as a whole.

This subtle but real censorship did not impede the publication of medieval chronicles like *Ferraris* and specialized scholarly studies appearing in esoteric journals, but it discouraged the wide distribution of biographies of monarchs like Roger II and his grandson Frederick II. The trend only worsened under the Fascist dystopia.

Into the first half of the twentieth century, the greatest appreciation for the Norman Hautevilles and the Swabian Hohenstaufens was to be found (respectively) in France and Germany, hence the works by Ferdinand Chalandon and Ernst Kantorowicz.

Freedom of expression finally arrived in Italy in 1943 with the Allies, who granted Italian women the right to vote just in time for the referendum that ousted the defeated nation's tainted, dysfunctional monarchy in 1946.

In succeeding decades it became possible, for the first time since national unification, to publish books and papers about southern Italy's medieval golden age as a sovereign kingdom without, in the process, risking the censorship that poisoned intellectual life in the erstwhile dictatorship.

Even so, it took a few more decades for a generation of Italians educated in an era of Risorgimentalist and Fascist propaganda to recognize Roger and Frederick as "native sons" born in Italy and worthy of serious consideration; the chief biographies about them published in Italian before the present century are translations of works from German, French and English.

English editions bring medieval works like *Ferraris* to a wider readership. That is their raison d'être.

The heritage of humanity knows no borders. Medieval chronicles are part of a universal patrimony.

Redaction

Like many chronicles, the *Ferraris* manuscript is essentially one long block of uninterrupted text. In this book the text has been divided into chapters, presented in the order in which it appears in the manuscript, with only minor editing. The Latin titles are intended to aid the reader searching for a corresponding passage in the original text.

As this is the translation and commentary of a primary source, it would have been invidious to correct errors in the original text, although many of these are explained in the notes. The objective was to express the chronicler's words, not to censor his thoughts. Like any source, this one should be read critically.

The first two chapters are not particularly insightful, but they do bring us nuggets such as the *filioque* controversy which placed some distance between the churches of east and west. The precise lengths of pontificates (years, months, days) given by the chronicler are not always correct.

Some twelfth-century dates are skewed by the chronicler's occasional use of March, rather than January, as the beginning of the calendar year. This was a common practice around Benevento that the monk writing *Ferraris* imitated from Falco of Benevento, whose chronicle he consulted. The notes cite some specific references that are drawn from Falco's text.

The greatest usefulness of the chronicle as a resource begins with its third chapter, where we find the Normans firmly established in Italy and Pope Urban II preaching the First Crusade.

Except for the Backstory, which is intended to introduce readers to the geography and general history of a region with which they may be unfamiliar, the Timeline (chronology) was chosen over a lengthy historical summary in narrative form.

In general, specific notes refer to original sources only

where this is clearly required or where the chronicler has made an affirmation of historical fact very obviously at variance with what may be considered to be scholarly consensus. This was thought to be less necessary for the first two chapters, where (for example) the reigns of Roman pontiffs, Longobard kings and Holy Roman Emperors are now common knowledge.

As this monograph is a translation with notes, rather than a "critical edition," the Latin text is not included except for explanatory purposes in excerpts. For detailed comparisons of the *Ferraris* text to those of various chronicles and annals, the reader is referred to studies (mostly in Italian or German) cited in the Sources.

A sincere attempt was made to render this work as understandable and useful as possible.

MAPS

IGNOTI MONACHI CISTERCIENSIS

S. MARIAE DE FERRARIA

CHRONICA

ET

RYCCARDI

DE SANCTO GERMANO

CHRONICA PRIORA

Repperit in codice ms. bononiensi atque nunc primum edidit

AUGUSTUS GAUDENZI

adiectis ejusdem Ryccardi chronicis posterioribus

EX EDITIONE GEORGII PERTZII

NEAPOLI

EX REGIO TYPOGRAPHEO FRANCISCI GIANNINI & FIL.

Mdccclxxxviii

*The first edition of the chronicle was published
in Naples in 1888 in only 275 numbered copies*

MOLISE

N.

PAPAL STATE

+ St. Vincent

Ferentino

VOLTURNO

A P U L I A

Cassino

Lucera

Ceprano +

Terracina

* Ferraria

Matese
Mountains

Teano

Benevento

OFANTO

Gaeta

Capua

Ariano

Melfi

Acerra

Avellino

Ischia

Naples

Cava

Irpinian
Mountains

Capri

Salerno

Eboli

LUCANIA

Cilento
Mountains

T y r r h e n i a n

S e a

C A L A B R I A

Sila
Mountains

Cosenza

* Abbey of Santa Maria
+ Other Major Abbey
● Fortified City or Town

Regnum Siciliae: The Norman-Swabian Kingdom of Sicily

PAPAL
STATE
Spoleto

March
of
Ancona

A B R U Z Z O

Pescara

ADRIATIC
SEA

Rieti

Aquila

Ferentino

M O L I S E

Cassino
Ceprano

Ferraria

Loritello

Mount
Sant'Angelo

Lucera

Benevento

A

Gaeta

Capua

Ariano

Mandra

Barletta

Avellino

Trani

Acerra

P

Troia

Naples

Terra di Lavoro

Melfi

A

Nocera

N

Lucania

Andria

Bari

I

Salerno

Eboli

Gravina

A

Montescaglioso

Taranto

Brindisi

Lecce

Otranto

TYRRHENIAN
SEA

Crati
Valley

Cosenza

A

Sila

R

Catanzaro

B

IONIAN
SEA

Mileto

A

Bagnara

L

Gerace

Stilo

C

Reggio

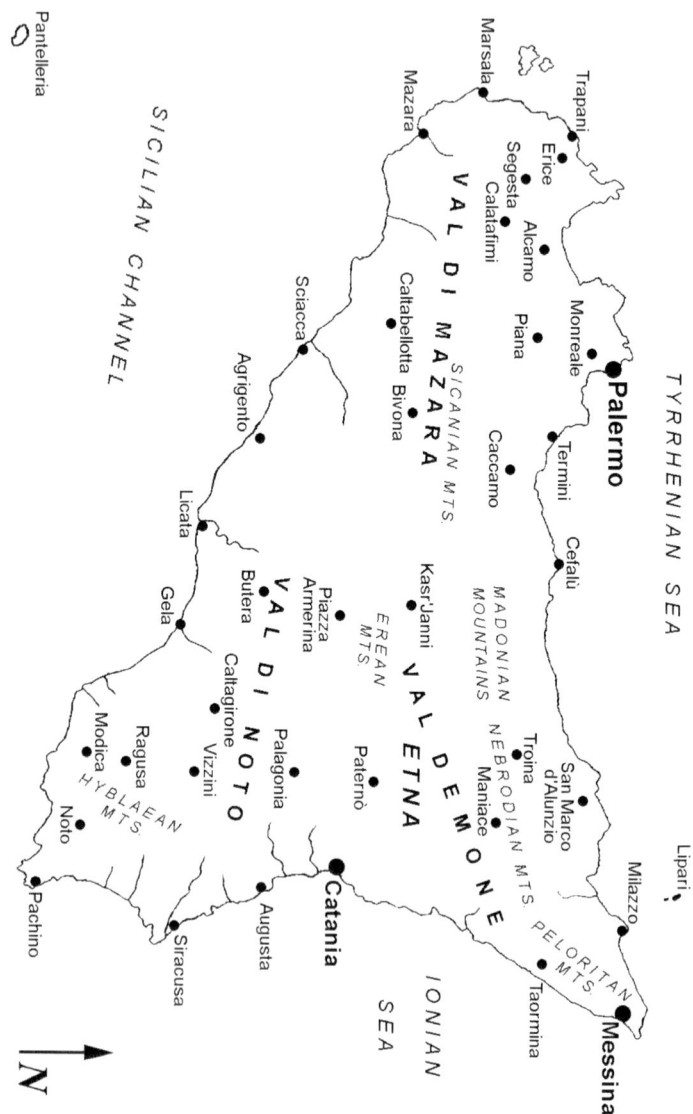

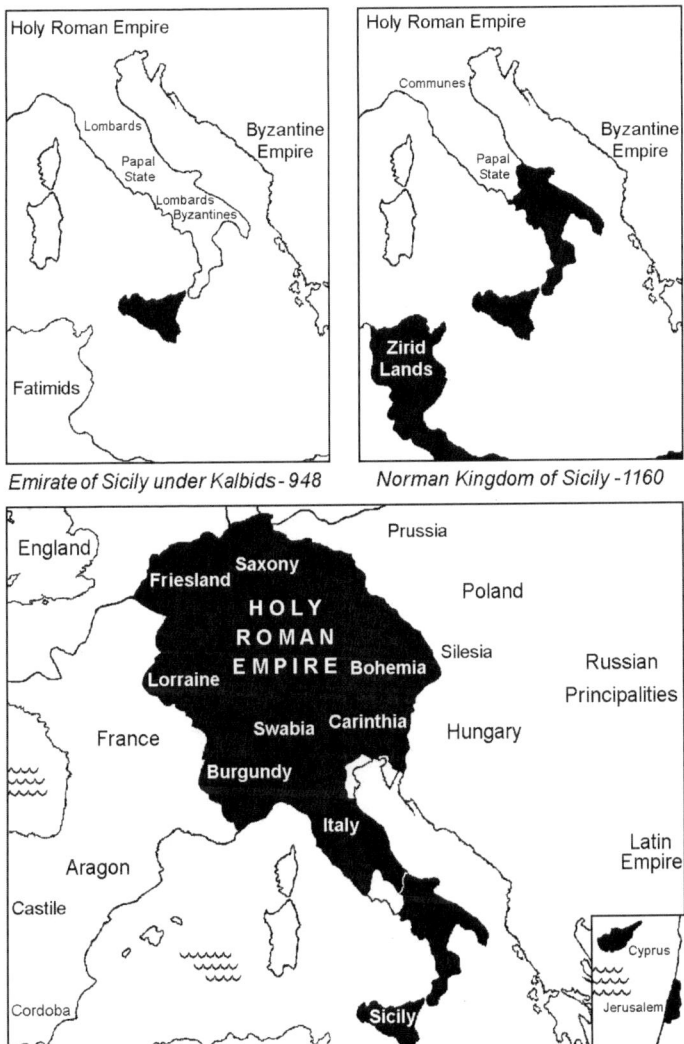

Emirate of Sicily under Kalbids - 948

Norman Kingdom of Sicily - 1160

Greatest extent of Hohenstaufen dominion under Frederick II - 1229

39

Shifting Borders: Principal European and Mediterranean states and regions in 1200

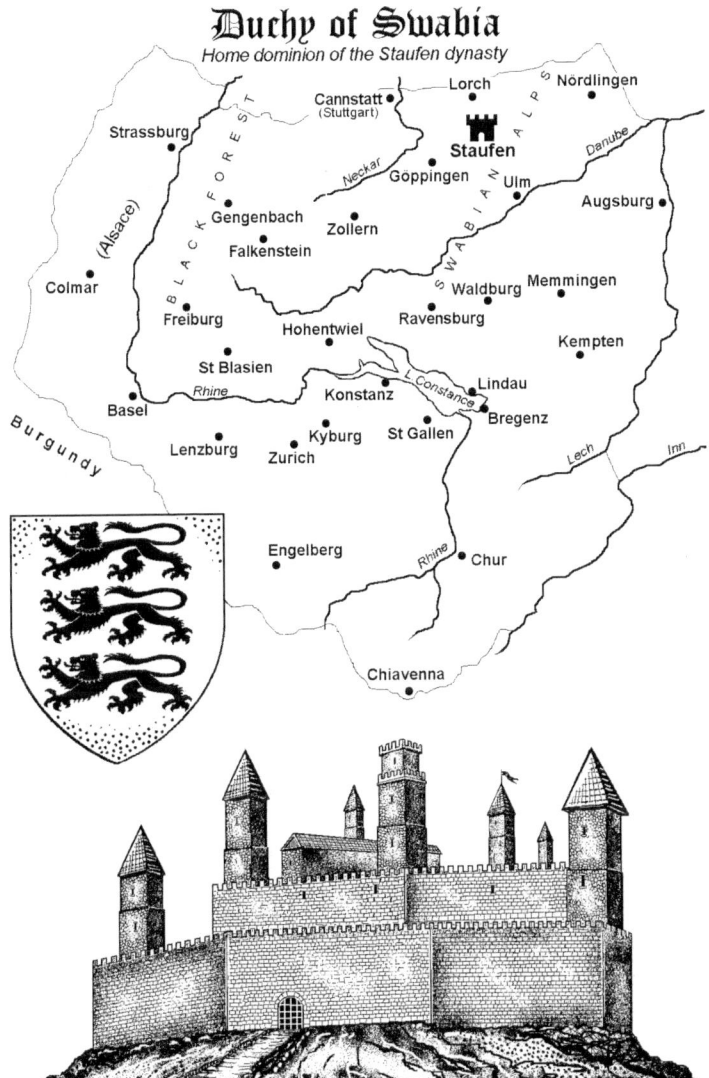

Duchy of Swabia
Home dominion of the Staufen dynasty

Hohenstaufen Castle in the 13th century

41

Italian states in 1859: The kingdom described in the chronicle flourished until Italian unification

PHOTOGRAPHS

Fresco in the church at Santa Maria della Ferraria

The cloister was similar to Saint John of the Hermits

The church of Santa Maria della Ferraria was vaguely similar to Gothic structures like Pamplona's cathedral (this book's author is standing near the royal crypt)

The crown of Constance of Aragon, consort of Frederick II, shows Byzantine influences

Some Coins of the Norman-Swabian Era

˝Scyphate˝ ducat of Roger II

˝Lion's face˝ follaris of William II

Fatimid tarì   *Tarì of Roger II*

Canterbury Cathedral: Thomas Becket's death is mentioned in the chronicle, and his nephews were given refuge in Sicily during their exile

The author in a Romanesque corner of the abbey at Canterbury little changed since the days when Thomas Becket lived there

Apse and cupola of the Palatine Chapel

Norman-Arab architecture in the capital: The royal palace (top) in Palermo and the Zisa in the Genoard park

Built for the Cistercians, the Magione was the resting place of King Tancred and then a church of the Teutonic Knights

*Transept, towers and apses of Palermo's cathedral,
where Frederick II and Henry VI were both crowned*

Porphyry tombs of Roger II (top) and Frederick II

Sarcophagi of Constance (top) and Henry VI

Mosaic icon of Thomas Becket at Monreale

BACKSTORY

To refer to it generically as "southern Italy" is to err on the side of conformity, for the lands known to the author of the *Ferraris Chronicle* once formed *Magna Graecia*. The temples standing at Segesta, Paestum and elsewhere in this region are a silent but salient testament to this classical legacy.

The Place

In 1130 these dominions were consolidated by Roger II of Hauteville to form the Kingdom of Sicily. Later, following occasional separations of the mainland from Sicily after 1282, they were reunited as the Kingdom of the Two Sicilies, a state that existed until Italian unification in 1861.

The realm boasted its own culture and languages. By 1200, we find the origins of the tongues that became Neapolitan and Sicilian which, contrary to a misplaced belief, are not dialects of Tuscan.

The entire *Regnum Siciliae* of the Normans and Swabians covered around 112,000 square kilometers (43,243 square miles) which, as a point of reference, was slightly smaller than

England's 130,000. The peninsular part of the kingdom extended over an area of approximately 85,000 square kilometers; for comparison, Scotland encompasses around 80,000.

At 26,711 square kilometers, the island of Sicily is larger than Wales and slightly smaller than Massachusetts, but more mountainous than either.

The most northern point of the mainland territory was just north of Pescara on the Adriatic side and Terracina, in what is now Lazio (essentially the ancient Latium) on the peninsula's Tyrrhenian side.

Except for a few notable plains, such as the area around Lecce in southern Apulia in the heel of the Italian boot, most of this part of Italy is ruggedly mountainous.

There are a number of impressive chains, like the Sila of Calabria and the Gran Sasso of western Abruzzi, that are part of the Apennine range for which Italy is famous. The highest peak in the peninsular part of the former Kingdom of Sicily is Corno Grande near Teramo in Abruzzi, at 2912 meters (9,553 feet). Of course, the most famous mountain in the southern part of the peninsula is Vesuvius, the ominous volcano that casts its shadow over Naples. It is 1281 meters high. Like Etna, it boasts a very long recorded history useful to geologists.

Majestic Mount Etna, Europe's largest active volcano and greatest natural wonder, rises to a variable 3,329 meters above sea level. Sicily's next highest peak is rocky Pizzo Carbonara at 1,979 meters, in the Madonian Mountains visible from the environs of Palermo; like Etna, it is covered by snow for part of the year.

The People

The centuries-long saga of what became the Kingdom of Sicily is very much the story of conquerors and colonizers, peoples and cultures, and that is what defines the region's history.

A number of civilizations are identified in the chronicle, and the haplogroups revealed by genetic (DNA) testing, something unavailable to historians until two decades ago, confirm that all are the forebears of today's Italians.

Let us cast a quick glance over the ancient and medieval foundations that gave rise to the kingdom ruled by the Hautevilles and Hohenstaufens. This abridged journey shall take us to the eleventh century, when the essential narrative of the chronicle begins.

The Bronze Age

The inception of Greek Italy's Bronze Age, characterized by the use of copper tools, can be dated to around 2500 BC (BCE).

By 2000 BC, Mycenaean and Late Minoan (Cretan and Aegean) cultures were present in isolated eastern localities of Sicily, especially near the Ionian coast, and by this time Malta's last temple builders, identified with the Tarxien Culture, had left Malta, with some perhaps settling in southeastern Sicily, in effect returning to the land of their ancestors. The Ausonians, an Italic people, traded with the Aeolian islanders and other communities around Messina.

It was probably the Mycenaeans or Minoans who planted the first domesticated olive trees in Sicily, and a Kalamata cultivar from this era has been genetically identified.

The Greek conquest of the southern part of the Italian peninsula was gradual and, for the most part, peaceful. In most instances, the indigenous peoples assimilated quite readily. The situation in Sicily was more complicated, and its complexities would impede the Greeks' westward expansion.

Greeks and Phoenicians

The Phoenicians, who are identified with the Biblical Canaanites, founded Carthage around 840 BC (BCE). Within a few decades, the Phoenicians and Greeks began to colonize Sicily as part of their burgeoning empires.

Of course, there were Phoenician influences long before this. Their alphabet, the basis for the lettering systems of Greek and Latin, is the most obvious example. Some of the art they left in Sicily bears Egyptian motifs.

The Phoenicians established emporia in the island's west, especially at Motya (Mozia), Zis (now Palermo) and Solunto. The Greeks founded colonies at Naxos (near Taormina), Agrigento, Catania, Selinunte, Hymera, Messina, Gela and, most importantly, Syracuse (Siracusa).

Sicily's native Elymians, Sicanians and Sikels, like the indigenous peoples on the peninsula, were absorbed into the conquering populations.

When Phoenicia fell to the Chaldean (Neo-Babylonian) Empire in 612, Carthage, in what is now coastal Tunisia, became the Phoenicians' major city. With the emergence of Carthage as perhaps the wealthiest and most powerful metropolis in the Mediterranean, the Greeks turned their attention to this potential adversary. What followed was a complex series of wars over several centuries involving a tangled web of alliances with participants as far away as Persia.

In 480 BC the Carthaginians – exhorted to fight the Greeks by Xerxes of Persia who had won victories in Greece – were defeated by Gelon of Syracuse at the first Battle of Hymera, east of Palermo. The Persians, meanwhile, were defeated at the Battle of Salamis.

A few years later, in 474, the Syracusans won a decisive naval victory over the Etruscans at Cumae, but the Etruscans' Latin successors, the Romans, would one day pose a far greater threat to Greek hegemony. Visiting Syracuse some eight decades later, Plato suggested Sicily as a potential model for his utopian society, an idea that must have flattered the proud *Siceliots,* as Greek Sicilians were known.

Raging from 431 to 404, the Peloponnesian War was particularly bitter, leading to the Athenians' invasion of eastern Sicily where, fortunately, the Syracusans defeated them in 413.

Another Carthaginian war broke out in Sicily, lasting from 346 to 341. Following an ephemeral peace, there was a Carthaginian incursion into a few Greek-controlled areas in 311. Not without reason, the Siceliots were tiring of incessant problems with their contentious Punic neighbors.

In 310, the Greeks under Agathocles invaded some Carthaginian territories of the African coast. A peace concluded in 306 established the Halycos (Platani) River as the Greco-Punic boundary in Sicily.

The Greeks of antiquity endowed civilization with a priceless body of literature, philosophy and law. Greek culture has given us Sophocles, Aristotle, Plato and others.

After a few centuries, the Italic peoples challenged Greek power. Fending off the Etruscans was not too difficult, but the society of Rome, in Latium, eventually posed a greater threat.

The Romans

Rome's conquest of the southern part of the Italian peninsula reflected a natural expansion of their territory. Having subdued peoples such as the Samnites on the peninsula, they were soon eyeing Sicily. Here was their trial by fire, the proving ground that would make or break the Romans' control of the central Mediterranean. Their greatest initial obstacle was the empire of Carthage ruled by Phoenician descendants in northern Africa.

On the pretext of curtailing the Carthaginians' influence in northeastern Sicily, the ambitious Romans invaded in 264 BC (BCE). The Punic Wars, which would continue for another century, were essentially a territorial power struggle rather than an ideological conflict, but the enmity was real.

The Siceliot city of Syracuse, perhaps the largest metropolis in what became Italy, made a tenuous peace with Rome. However, during a successive Punic War the Syracusans reneged on this agreement by siding with the Carthaginians. This decision provoked an invasion by Rome. When Syracuse fell in 212 BC, Archimedes, the greatest scientist and engineer of his age, was killed. Much of Sicily's Greek culture died with him, yet Greek remained the island's chief vernacular language.

Although the Romans imposed heavy taxes, Sicily, as a Roman province, flourished. Public order was occasionally punctuated by slave revolts, but the long Roman period was essentially a peaceful and prosperous one for Sicily. Indeed, the island emerged as an important crossroads in the sprawling Empire. Yet historians' references to it as "the bread basket of the Roman Empire" may manifest a slightly exaggerated perception, even though the Romans deforested many areas to make room for wheat cultivation.

In the southern part of the peninsula, the *Bellum Sociale,* a rebellion by the Samnites and Lucanians that broke out in 91 BC, lasted just a few years.

In 70 BC, Cicero prosecuted Verres, Sicily's corrupt governor, who fled following the great orator's opening argument.

Lasting from 27 BC until AD (CE) 180, the *Pax Romana* was a prosperous interlude, yet it saw Jesus put to death around AD 33.

Paul of Tarsus preached in Syracuse *en route* to Rome to stand trial around AD 59. At this early date, the Romans generally viewed Christianity as little more than a nuisance, an eccentric sect of Judaism.

Before long, the new religion came to be viewed as something more troublesome, at least from what was then the prevailing Roman point of view. Christians were regarded with raw contempt. Saint Agatha was martyred in 251 and Saint Lucy suffered the same fate some fifty years later during the rule of infamous Diocletian, who excelled at persecuting Christians.

Lucy's death in 304 came at the end of a long and wicked trend. Armenia, at the Empire's eastern fringe, had made Christianity its official religion three years earlier, and the Emperor Constantine, whose rule began in 306, brought about a more tolerant treatment of Christians. In 313, his Edict of Milan legalized the open practice of the new religion. In 325 the Council of Nicaea established a uniformity in the faith's fundamental precepts, and it was the Empire's official faith by 380. Over time, even some foreign peoples beyond the Empire's frontiers began to adopt Christianity. This included the Vandals and Goths.

In 395, following the death of Theodosius I, the Roman Empire definitively split into Western ("Latin") and Eastern ("Byzantine") administrations. Sicily began in the West but would vacillate between the two, while most of peninsular Italy was firmly Western. Seven years later, the capital of the Western Empire was transferred from Rome to Ravenna. Eastern administration was based at Constantinople, the former Byzantium.

Myriad influences combined to weaken the mighty Empire, whose decline cannot be attributed to just one or two factors. In the event, Sicily was one of the last provinces to fall to external elements.

Vandals, Goths and Longobards

In 378, a Roman army was defeated at the Battle of Adrianople, now Edirne in European Turkey, by the ravenous Goths, a Germanic people that had been forced into Roman territory by the migrating Huns. Clearly, circumstances were changing, even if Roman bureaucrats were initially reluctant to acknowledge the political implications of the debacle that took place at this outpost.

When the Vandals, Sueves, Burgundians and other tribes crossed the Rhine in 406, the "Great Invasion" had well and truly begun. Alaric's Visigoths sacked Rome four years later.

In 429 the Vandals occupied the Roman province of Africa, within striking distance of Sicily. An invasion in 440 led to mass raids in Sicily, but the Vandalic incursions were halted by the Byzantines in 441.

What followed was a series of migrations and invasions. Attila's Huns invaded northern Italy in 452. Following the pattern established by the Visigoths, the Vandals sacked Rome in 455, returning to Sicily in a long series of raids in 461. By 468 they were masters of the island. The Christianized Vandals left most of the existing administration in place but destroyed the synagogue of Syracuse.

Odoacer deposed the last Western Roman Emperor in 476, and the beginning of the Middle Ages is usually dated from this time. The Vandal king Genseric, meanwhile, concluded a "perpetual" peace with Constantinople.

In 491 the Ostrogoths achieved complete control of Sicily, ousting the Vandals, who retreated to their kingdom in Tunisia.

While most of the peoples who conquered ancient and medieval Sicily left something of value behind, the legacy of the Vandals and Ostrogoths is more difficult to quantify, apart from some genes for blondish hair and blue eyes. Their rule defined a brief interlude bridging the gap between what are now identified as the ancient and medieval epochs.

The Ostrogoth leader Theodoric the Great managed to keep his people unified against the Byzantines. His death in

526 brought an end to decades of peace.

Ascending the Byzantine throne as "Roman" Emperor in 527, Justinian already had his eye on Italy. Nobody in Constantinople seemed willing to assent to a jewel, and a territory of strategic importance to commercial shipping, like Sicily remaining in Ostrogoth hands.

In a series of bloody battles from 533 to 535, the Byzantine Greeks under Belisarius defeated the Vandals in Tunisia and the Ostrogoths in Sicily, annexing both regions to the Byzantine Empire and assimilating these aggrieved Germanic peoples into it.

The Byzantine Empire could afford such campaigns. A vestige of this prosperity is the grand basilica dedicated to Saint Sophia, erected in Constantinople in 537. The world's largest church epitomized Byzantine wealth and culture.

Back in Italy, the tenacious Goths did not succumb easily. The Ostrogoth leader Totila raided Sicily in 550 in an attempt to reclaim it for his people. This was little more than a lengthy incursion. Totila's defeat by Byzantine forces at the Battle of Taginae two years later signalled the end of Ostrogothic influence in Italy.

Following the Byzantine victories over the Ostrogoths in the bloody Gothic War, another Germanic people, the Longobards, invaded Italy *en masse* in 568, eventually reaching the south.

Coming to be called *Lombards* (and lending their name to a region of northern Italy), they handily confiscated rural areas, where they introduced something vaguely resembling rudimentary feudalism. The Byzantine Greeks, for their part, were generally content to rule the more important centers, leaving the rest for the Lombards, but over the next few centuries there were occasional conflicts.[9]

What soon emerged in southern peninsular Italy was a complex checkerboard of manorial and ecclesiastical dominions. Bari remained essentially Byzantine, while Salerno became the seat of a Lombard principality. Rome was held by the popes as the cornerstone of what eventually became a pontifical state. The Greek influence was greatest in Apulia and Calabria; major Latin monasteries like Cassino and Cava answered to Rome.

Christianity was soon to lose its monopoly on the western world. Mohammed, the founder of Islam as its Prophet, was born in Mecca in 570.

The Byzantine Greeks

In 660, the Byzantine Emperor, Constans II, established his court at Syracuse with a view to crossing into Calabria and invading the Lombard lands. This plan never materialized, and by the end of his reign eight years later Constantinople had, for the time being, given up any hope for such a conquest.

Now Latin, which appears never to have been the chief spoken language in the majority of Sicilian communities during the Roman era, was almost completely eclipsed by Greek, which was also the language of liturgy. Christianity would openly split only much later, with the Great Schism in 1054, but by the seventh century, with the distinctions between East and West little more than an arcane nuance, subtle differences were already growing between the two spheres of influence, namely Rome and Constantinople. (These would eventually provoke the Iconoclast Controversy.) For the present, however, there were greater differences between Christians, on the one hand, and Muslims on the other.

The Byzantine Empire, which was the medieval Greeks' continuation of the Eastern Roman Empire, survived in some form until 1453, when the Ottoman Turks finally took Constantinople. Though there were inspired pockets of learning in Europe's monasteries as far afield as Ireland, until the eleventh century the greatest flowering of Christian culture was to be found in the Byzantine world.

Whilst peninsular regions like Apulia and Calabria were divided by Lombards and Byzantines, a new culture flourished in Sicily.

The Arabs

Mohammed's death in 632 signalled a new onslaught. Despite divisive differences within Islam between what came to known as the Shia and Sunni factions, the Muslim Arabs conquered Carthage in 698, working their way westward and invading Spain in 711, seizing islands like Pantelleria. An Arab force was defeated by Charles Martel at Tours in 732, but this did not impede the general expansion of Islam. Syracuse, still Sicily's largest city, was attacked in 740 and again in 752.

Internecine disputes characterized the expansion. The Berbers, in particular, often resented the Arabian leadership. By 800 there were Berber traders in Sicily, particularly at Sciacca, Marsala and Mazara.

In 826, Euphemius, a Sicilian general disgruntled with the Byzantine Emperor Michael II, offered control of Sicily to the Aghlabids, the regnant dynasty of Ifriqiya (Tunisia), in return for political asylum. They accepted, but in the event Euphemius, who lent military support to the Aghlabids, was killed by Byzantine loyalists.

In July of the following year, the first major Arab-Berber incursion arrived under Asad ibn al-Furat, the general appointed by Emir Ziyadat Allah I ibn Ibrahim of Ifriqiya. It consisted of at least ten thousand troops, including some Persians, sailing from Tunisia. Mazara was the first city to be occupied.

The facile first stage of the conquest belied difficulties to come. In September 831 Bal'harm (Palermo) was finally conquered by the Aghlabids following a year-long siege. This city was destined to become the capital of the Emirate of Sicily, but it took the better part of seventy years for the Aghlabids to bring all of the island, including the Greek areas of the east, under their control.

Peninsular Italy was not overlooked. During the second half of the ninth century some Aghlabids briefly established themselves at Bari and Taranto.

By 900 there was a small Arab trading settlement at the mouth of the Garigliano River on the Tyrrhenian near the town of Minturno. Lying near the Papal domain, this was, arguably, Lombard territory, but Rome took an interest in it as the settlement grew in size over the next decade.

Meanwhile, in 909, the Fatimids had succeeded the Aghlabids in Tunisia and Sicily. It was to this new dynasty that the settlers on the Garigliano answered. In the spirit of Fatimid zeal, the settlers began to raid small towns in the immediate vicinity. At first they did so with impunity, exploiting the fact that the Lombards' dominion was little more than a loose federation of baronial estates lacking a large standing army. By 915, the Papacy could no longer tolerate this nuisance. In that year, in a rare expression of unity, a joint army of Papal, Lombard and Byzantine troops attacked the Muslims and expelled them.

As recently as 964, a battle was fought at the fortified Greek town of Rometta, near Messina, against a large force sent from Constantinople to bring Sicily back into the Byzantine fold, and this was a costly victory for the Arabs.

In medieval times, the ethnonym *Arab* came to refer to speakers of Arabic generally, and by the ninth century Islam was inextricably linked to Arab culture. The Koran was written in Arabic, and to this day translations into other languages are regarded as "interpretations" because the word of God was revealed to the Prophet in the Arabic language.

The arrival of the Arabs portended great changes in society. The Arabs instituted a period of religious tolerance, though giving precedence to Islam and converting a number of churches, including the cathedrals of Syracuse and Palermo, to mosques. They founded numerous towns, introduced Hindu-Arabic numerals and paper (from China), superior irrigation systems, and schools for girls as well as boys.

Mathematics and various sciences flourished under the Arabs; the word *algebra* itself comes to us from Arabic. While some of these ideas originated in India, China or Greece, it was the Arabs who refined and propagated them.

Agriculture was revolutionized. Sugar cane, rice, mulberries (for silk making as well as consumption), citrus fruits, cotton and various crops were cultivated. The basis of much of Sicilian cuisine was formed during this era. Halal and kosher dietary observances made their influence felt, a fact which may account for the dearth of traditional pork recipes.

Bal'harm became a marvelous city rivalled in its beauty only by Baghdad and Cordoba.[10]

The Fatimids ruled Sicily until 948 when, moving their center of power eastward to Egypt, they entrusted the island to the Kalbid dynasty in a kind of suzerainty.

Like the Fatimids, the Kalbids were Shiites. The Aghlabids, conversely, were Sunnis who had introduced principles of the Maliki school of law in Sicily. It has been suggested that this may have influenced English common law in the twelfth century when contact between Palermo and London was frequent.[11]

Jawhar al-Siqilli, thought to be a Sicilian, founded the Fatimid city of Al-Qahira (Cairo) in 976. Significantly, the Fatimids brought Sicily into a wide orbit of trade and prosperity extending from the Iberian peninsula to what is now Pakistan.

The Lombards

The southern part of mainland Italy, meanwhile, was shared between the Byzantine Greeks and the Lombards.

The Lombards, whose forebears are commonly known as *Longobards,* originated as one of the many Germanic tribes to the north of the Roman Empire, their population being concentrated in the Elbe Valley in what is now Saxony. Like the Vandals and Goths, they migrated southward. The Longobards arrived in Italy later, in the aftermath of the devastating Gothic War between Byzantine Greeks and Ostrogoths, which ended in 554.

By 570, they were the masters of northern Italy, where they established what eventually became a kingdom. Under Liutprand, who reigned until 744, most of southern Italy was conquered from the Byzantine Greeks with the exception of Calabria and part of Apulia, and the area around Rome was given to Pope Gregory II by the Donation of Sutri.

The Lombards' Kingdom of Italy forged alliances with the Franks and the popes. Unfortunately, it was not destined to last very long.

The monarchy effectively ended in 774 when the Lombard lands of northern Italy were confiscated by Charlemagne as an appendage of the Holy Roman Empire. He surpassed the generosity shown with Liutprand's Donation of Sutri by granting the entire Lombard territory of central Italy to the Pope as the Papal State.

However, a few prosperous southern cities, notably Salerno, Capua and Benevento, remained in Lombard hands as principalities into the eleventh century; the dominion of Guaimar III, who died in 1027, extended into parts of Apulia and Calabria that he confiscated from the Byzantines. Like many Lombards, the chronicler and judge Falco of Benevento overtly resented the Normans.

By the eleventh century, the Lombards of southern Italy, save for a few vestiges of their ancestral language, were Germanic in name only, having intermarried with the local population for generations.

They introduced a precursor of the manorial (feudal) system. This differed in certain respects from the Norman system; for example, a Lombard estate might be inherited in moieties equally among a lord's sons instead of being transmitted to the eldest according to the principle of male primogeniture.

Such practices were rooted, albeit sometimes tenuously, in longstanding Longobardic legal principles, such as those enshrined in the Edict of Rothari of 643, which enumerated traditional Germanic tribal precepts, rather than the Code of Justinian that (at least in theory) governed life in Papal and Byzantine Italy.

Certain elements of what we now call "common law," such as trial by jury, trace their origins to Germanic practice, which in Italy survived for a time under Lombard and Norman rule.

By the eleventh century, the greatest conflicts between Lombards and Byzantines owed more to simple hegemony than to substantial differences in jurisprudence or government. Most often, these were struggles between two adversaries for control over territory and wealth. Nonetheless, a certain coexistence prevailed.

Try as they might, the Lombards could not dislodge the Byzantines from Italy. Before long, however, they would be forced to contend with more formidable adversaries.

The Normans

In July 982, Otto II, the Holy Roman Emperor, led a force of Germans and Lombards against the Kalbids of Sicily at the Battle of Stilo, in Calabria. Otto's army was defeated.

The chronicler Amatus of Monte Cassino tells us that by 999 the Lombards of Salerno were paying tribute to the Muslims. Witnessing this extortion, some visiting Norman knights chased off the Arabs collecting it. Soon, this story goes, the grateful Lombard leader, Guaimar III, was employing Norman mercenaries.

Other accounts of the Normans' arrival in Sicily complement this.

In 1016, a band of Normans was employed by Melus, a Lombard lord who was trying to recapture the city of Bari, which he had seized from the Byzantines but then lost. Augmented by other Norman knights, this company joined the Lombard campaign.[12]

Following early victories against the catepan Leo Tornikios Kontoleon in the spring of 1017, a combined Norman-Lombard force suffered a decisive defeat at the hands of the catepan Basil Boioannes in the autumn of the same year.

Among Basil's troops were knights of the Varangian Guard, Norsemen (Vikings) in the service of Constantinople. The Normans were themselves the descendants of Norsemen who had settled on the Cotentin Peninsula, marrying women of the region that came to be called *Normandy*. Although they spoke a brand of French, the Normans in Apulia knew of their link to these distant Scandinavian cousins.

As knights errant, the Normans served the highest bidder. At Troia they briefly manned the garrison of the Byzantine catepan against whom they had fought.

Holding on to Apulia was one thing, but the Byzantine Greeks were seriously considering a reconquest of Sicily. With this objective in mind, they launched an invasion in 1038. These ambitions were quashed four years later, but not before George Maniakes occupied parts of eastern Sicily. His army was composed of Byzantines as well as Normans, Lombards and the Norse Varangian Guard under Harald "Hardrada" Sigurdsson, who went on to glory as King of Norway and defeat as defender of Saxon England. The Normans, more than the others, viewed Sicily as a place they might like to possess for themselves.

By now, the island was beset by the rivalries of jealous emirs. Separating it into four *qadits,* or administrative districts, in 1044, seemed not to help matters. In 1053, following the death of Hasan as-Samsam and the extinction of the Kalbid dynasty, three emirs divided control of Sicily's more important districts, but growing discord led to the eventual establishment of several minor emirates around the island over the next few years.[13] At least one emir decided to seek help further afield, and not necessarily from fellow Muslims.

The Normans established themselves at several towns in parts of Calabria, Lucania (Basilicata) and Apulia that were essentially Byzantine. Melfi was an important stronghold. Mileto, in Calabria, became the dominion and base of the many sons of the lord of the small Norman town of Hauteville.

From Calabria, the Hauteville brothers began to eye the large island across the Strait of Messina. Its capital, opulent Palermo, the richest city of what is now Italy, was the jewel in the crown. The Normans wanted it.

So did Pope Nicholas II, a Frenchman.[14] In 1059 he invested Robert "Guiscard," the eldest of the Hauteville brothers, as the *de jure* lord of Apulia, Calabria and Sicily. Rome, obviously enough, wanted the Muslims christianized, but she also wished to see Sicily's Greek "Orthodox" Christians under the Papal yoke rather than Constantinople's ecclesiastical jurisdiction.

If the military conquest enjoyed Papal support, the interests of the Hautevilles were more worldly than spiritual. The Normans wanted Sicilian territory as much as the Papacy wanted its souls. Both would get what they wished for.

*Roger II depicted as a Byzantine basileus crowned by Christ
in engraving based on mosaic in Martorana church, Palermo*

CHRONICLE

I

CORPUS MARIE MAGDALENE REPERTUM

In the Year of Our Lord 781 the Byzantine Emperor Constantine V had ruled for thirty-five years and the body of Mary Magdalene was found by Gerard, Count of Burgundy. During the pontificate of Pope Zachary, Carloman, the brother of Pepin, King of the Franks, took the monastic habit and went to live at the Abbey of Monte Cassino.[15] This monastery enjoyed many privileges and endowments granted it by the Holy See. In those times, the monastery dedicated to Saint Vincent depended upon that of Monte Cassino, assisting in its support.

Pope Zachary reigned for ten years, three months and fourteen days. To this pontiff we must attribute the ultimate fall of Rome's empire to Greeks and Germans.

Succeeding Zachary was Pope Stephen II, whose pontificate lasted but five years and twenty-nine days. Persecuted by Astulf, King of the Longobards, Stephen found refuge in France, where he reconsecrated Pepin, son of King Charles Martel, and his two sons as Kings of the Franks.[16]

Accompanying Pope Stephen to Italy, Pepin seized Ravenna from Astulf, who he forced to submit to Papal authority along with twenty-two cities. Following this event the Roman patriciate was established.

Succeeding Pope Stephen was Paul I, whose pontificate lasted ten years and one month. Following Paul I was Stephen III, whose pontificate lasted three years, five months and twenty-seven days. Then followed Pope Constantine, who reigned for one year and one month (sic).[17]

Following Constantine was Pope Adrian I, whose pontificate lasted twenty-three years, ten months and seventeen days. During Adrian's reign was convoked a synod at Rome attended by a hundred and twenty-three bishops.[18]

Under this pontiff, Charlemagne, the son of Pepin, came to Italy and besieged the Longobards at Pavia, capturing King Desiderius and his wife and taking them to France.[19] Having restored to the See of Saint Peter all the possessions formerly given to the Pope by his father, Pepin, with the addition of Benevento and Spoleto, Charlemagne was accorded the honour of a Roman patrician.

The Longobard Kings

This era saw the end of the reign of the Longobard kings, who had invaded Italy during the pontificate of Pope Benedict I, when Emperor Justin II ruled in Constantinople.[20] The Longobards came from Pannonia, a province in Germany.[21] They established their Italian capital at Pavia, with principalities at Benevento and other cities. They also founded duchies at Troia and in various cities in Apulia and chartered for themselves the first laws.[22]

The following were their kings.[23]

The first, Alboin, reigned for three years and six months (sic).[24]

Cleph reigned for five years.[25]

Authari, called "the Long-haired," ruled for two years and nine months.[26] He subdued Benevento, where he installed Zotto as duke.

Succeeding Authari was Agilulf, who reigned for twenty-five years.[27] During his reign the abbey of Saint Benedict was destroyed.[28]

Agilulf's successor was Adaloald, who reigned for ten years.[29]

Arioald then reigned for twelve years.[30]

Agilulf and Arioald both maintained their capital at the Julian Forum[31] whilst Gisulf[32] governed Benevento as its duke.[33]

Gisulf's nephews, Paldo, Taso and Tato, reconstructed the abbey of Saint Vincent, near the source of the Volturno River, that had been destroyed by the Muslims.[34] This abbey was endowed with many lands.

Rothari ruled for sixteen years and four months.[35]

Rodoald ruled for five years and seven months.[36]

Aripert [I] reigned for nine years.[37]

Grimoald ruled for nine years.[38]

Perctarit then reigned for twenty-four years.[39]

Cunipert ruled for fourteen years.[40]

Liutpert reigned for two years and six months.[41]

Aripert [II] ruled for twelve years.[42] In his times the monastery of Saint Vincent was erected.[43]

Ansprand ruled for three months and one day.[44]

Liutprand reigned for thirty-one years and one month.[45]

Hildeprand ruled for eight months.[46]

Ratchis reigned for five years and six months.[47] Aistulf ruled for five years and six months.[48] Wishing to persecute Rome, they sought to invade Papal territory, extorting money from individual citizens.

Desiderius ruled for eighteen years, two months and ten days. He was the last of the Longobard kings.[49]

The Longobard Dukes of Benevento

Meanwhile, the Longobard dukes[50] who governed Benevento were the following.

Zotto ruled for twenty years.[51] Arechis [I] reigned for one year.[52]

Arechis [II] erected the monastery of Saint Sophia at Benevento, and the nunnery of the Holy Savior at Alife.[53] Arechis was a very Catholic prince who died in the Year of Our Lord 787.[54]

His son, Grimoald [III], reigned for twenty years.[55] He donated the entire estate of Santa Maria dell'Oliveto to the abbey of Saint Vincent.

Grimoald II (sic) reigned for twelve years, one month and ten days.[56] Falling prey to an ancient error of the Gentiles, he worshipped a golden viper and communicated to his soldiers whatever he interpreted from fragments that fell from a piece of leather tacked to a pine tree, consecrated to demons, pierced by the frequent loosings of arrows. In a private room he assembled a silver apparatus that resembled stars in the heavens, from which he suspended the sun, moon, twelve constellations and seven planets fashioned of precious stones, along with other astronomical details, and from this he divined false messages.[57]

But the Lord Almighty, who does not desire that any souls be lost, but wishes that all of those redeemed by his blood be saved, sent against him Constans, the Emperor of Byzantium.[58] With a large army, Constans besieged Benevento, forcing Grimoald to seek the intervention of the Blessed Barbato[59] with a promise to mend his ways if the saint would spare the city. Following a fast of three days by the duke and the people, the prayers of God's servant Barbato were answered. Inspired by this, the emperor wed the sister of the Duke of Benevento.[60]

The saint uprooted the pine tree mentioned earlier. Grimoald ordered that the golden viper be smelted to make a splendid chalice, and that the astronomical apparatus be adapted to ecclesiastical use. In this way, heretical Grimoald became a Catholic prince.

Grimoald [IV] was succeeded by Sico, who governed Benevento for sixteen years and two months.[61] His son, Sicard, ruled for six years and ten months.[62]

Radelchis [I] reigned for thirteen years.[63] Under him the Principality of Salerno was separated from Benevento.

Radelgar, the son of Radelchis ruled for three years and three months.[64] Adelchis, the brother of Radelgar, reigned for twenty-four years and six months.[65]

Gaideris, son of Radelgar, ruled for two years, eight months and twenty-one days.[66] In his time the monasteries of Saint Benedict and Saint Vincent were set afire by the Arabs.[67]

Radelchis [II], son of Adelchis, ruled for three years, eight months and twenty-one days.[68] His brother, Aiulf, reigned for six years.[69]

Ursus, Aiulf's son, ruled for a year.[70] In the second year of his reign the strategos Sybbaticos, with a multitude of Greeks, conquered Benevento and held it for three years, nine months and twenty days. After this two delegates, George and Barsacius, governed the city. Then the margrave Guy[71] came to the aid of the Beneventans, expelling the Greeks, who shamefully returned to their homeland. Guy governed the city for two years and six months until he was defeated by the count Atenulf [I] of Capua, who had just rebuilt his own city. The following year[72] Atenulf established that his son, Landulf, would govern on his behalf; he did so for ten years and six months.[73]

So ended in Italy the reigns of the Longobards and Greeks over the course of two hundred and fifty years, until the time of Charlemagne, King of the Franks.[74]

The Carolingian Kings

With the Longobards and the Byzantine Greeks subdued in Italy, the Kings of the Franks abolished the very name of the Roman Empire. That is to say, it was abolished by Pepin the Elder, who reigned for twenty-seven years.[75]

Charles reigned for twenty-seven years.[76] Pepin, the son of Charles, ruled for twenty-seven years.[77]

Charlemagne, the son of Pepin, reigned for forty years.[78] His sons were Charles, who was crowned Roman Emperor (sic) by Pope Leo [III], Carloman (Pippin), who inherited the Italian lands, and Louis, who inherited Aquitaine.[79] Louis succeeded Charlemagne as Roman Emperor.

After the death of Louis[80] his sons succeeded him. These were Lothair, Louis and Charles.[81]

Upon the death of Lothair, his lands were inherited by his three sons. Louis [II] succeeded to the Italian lands.[82] Lothair [II] held Lotharingia.[83] Charles received Saxony (sic).[84]

Whilst Louis ruled Italy, the Apulian city of Bari was occupied by Sawdan, an Arab emir.[85] From this city the Arabs set forth to raid and pillage all of Apulia and Calabria, as well as Salerno, Benevento and other places.

Apprised of these facts by the abbots of Saint Vincent and Monte Cassino, the Emperor Louis made his way to Bari with a large army.[86]

The Saracen Menace

In his incursion, Sawdan, leading a great number of men, had pillaged the Benevento region by the sword, with fire and by besieging cities, laying waste to Telese, Alife, Supino, Boiano, Venafro and other towns.[87]

The Arabs sacked the monastery of Saint Vincent on the Volturno, where they extorted three thousand gold coins[88] in exchange for their pledge to refrain from burning the premises. They behaved in a similar manner with the monks of Monte Cassino.

These ransoms served no purpose, for the abbeys were set

aflame anyway as soon as the payments were made.

The Arabs were reinforced by more men following the death of the saintly Emperor Louis.[89]

They occupied Apulia and Sicily.[90] They attacked Capua, Nola and other cities, raiding the Papal lands as far as Spoleto, destroying monasteries and pillaging cities.

In those times Athanasius, the Bishop of Naples[91] who had been excommunicated by Pope John III (sic) for having reached a truce with the Muslims, commanded Neapolitan troops. Athanasius had imprisoned his own brother, Sergius.[92] He thus took control of the city and granted full rights to its port to the Arabs.

At Saint Vincent, the betrayal of some heretics revealed to some Arab invaders the presence of around ninety monks, who were killed. They had come from many places to the abbey of Saint Vincent in the Year of Our Lord 881.[93]

It was not possible to expel the Arabs from the Italian cities until the arrival of Charles, brother (sic) of Louis, who succeeded him as Holy Roman Emperor.[94]

Whilst the Greeks rose up and the Lombards fought among themselves, the Franks let their dominion of Italy slip away. Patricians sent by the Emperor of Constantinople became judges and governors.

II

SED PROPTER REGRESSUM EQUIDEM KAROLI

There is no doubt that the withdrawal of Charles to his dominions beyond the Alps left the Arabs unchallenged in Sicily, which they dominated until the arrival of the Normans. The Arabs oppressed and greatly devastated Apulia, Calabria and the coast of Campania.[95]

Otto III, King of the Germans [and Holy Roman Emperor], visited Benevento in 999. In August of the following year, the Arabs reached Benevento and occupied Capua, Naples and the surrounding lands.[96]

The Coming of the Normans

Following the arrival of the Normans, Robert Guiscard, by a concession of the Roman Pontiff, became Duke of Apulia and of Terra di Lavoro.[97] He crossed the strait into Sicily and conquered the Arabs of that dominion, and in northern Africa.[98] Guiscard and his brothers subjugated all of Sicily, which the Arabs had dominated for nearly two hundred years.

Following this, Sicily, Calabria, Apulia and the Principality of Capua were ruled by Robert and then his son, Roger.[99]

After Roger, they were ruled by William.[100]

When William died without male heirs, he was succeeded by Roger [II], son of the count Roger [I] who was the brother of Robert Guiscard. Roger [II] inherited all of Sicily, Calabria, Apulia and Terra di Lavoro as far as Campania and Amiterno.[101] Therefore, in time all of these lands comprised a single kingdom.

By the grace of the Roman Pontiffs, the same Roger [II], nephew of Duke Robert Guiscard, was crowned king of this dominion. Succeeding him as king was his son William [I] and following the death of that king, William II.

William II betrothed Constance, daughter of his grandfather Roger [II], to Henry, the illustrious lord of Tuscany and Liguria, son of Frederick the Great, Roman Emperor.[102]

From this marriage between Constance and Henry was born Frederick [II], who succeeded William II, who died without male heirs, on the basis of hereditary rights through both his parents. Frederick thus inherited both the Kingdom of Sicily and the Holy Roman Empire.[103]

In this way, the Kingdom of Sicily has been united to the Duchy of Apulia and the Principality of Capua for around two hundred years (sic).

We have thus set forth the events that led to the dissolution of the Roman Empire, Italy thence passing from [Byzantine] Greeks to Franks and Longobards and finally to the Holy Roman Emperor. We have likewise explained the way that the Principality of Capua and the Duchy of Benevento passed to Capua after Charlemagne ceded the city of Benevento to the Papacy, keeping its dukedom for himself. Furthermore, we have seen how the duchy and [later] the principality of Benevento was divided from Salerno through the efforts of the Prince of Benevento, who placed his son on the Salernitan throne as prince.[104] Let us now return to the roll of Roman Pontiffs.

Pontificates

Leo III was Pope for twenty years, five months and twenty-seven days.[105] At a synod attended by three hundred and five bishops (sic) he affirmed that the Holy Spirit proceeds from the Father and the Son.[106] During a procession in Rome, whilst reciting the litany of Saint Peter, Pope Leo was attacked, blinded and his tongue cut out.[107]

Finding refuge at the court of Charlemagne, King of the Franks, the Pope was accorded every honour and returned to Rome with the same sovereign. There he refuted the crimes of which he was accused by his enemies, who were punished according to the law. He then crowned Charlemagne Roman Emperor.

Stephen IV was Pope for seven years (sic).[108] He anointed Charlemagne with holy oil during his last days[109] and confirmed his son, Louis, as Roman Emperor. From the time of Saint Gregory to this Pope there elapsed two hundred and sixty three years and two months.[110]

Paschal I was Pope for seven years and seven days.[111] Eugene II was Pope for seven years, seven months and twenty-three days (sic).[112] Valentine was Pope for ten months and forty days. Gregory IV was Pope for sixteen years. Sergius II, who was Pope for three years, crowned Louis[113] Roman Emperor. Leo IV was Pope for eight years, three months and five days. Benedict III was Pope for two years, three months and ten days. Nicholas I was Pope for nine years, six months and twenty days. Adrian II was Pope for five years. John VIII was Pope for ten years and two days.

Boniface VI was Pope for fifteen years (sic).[114] Stephen VI was Pope for one year and three months. Romanus was Pope for three months and twenty-two days. Theodore II was Pope for twenty days.[115] John IX was Pope for two years and fifteen days. Benedict IV was Pope for two years, six months and fifteen days.

The Arabs conquered Sicily.[116]

Pope Leo V reigned for forty days. The cardinal-priest Christopher took him prisoner and usurped the Papacy, keeping the office in his hands for seven months. He was then deposed and became a monk.[117]

Sergius III was Pope for seven years, three months and sixteen days. Anastasius III was Pope for two years and two months.

Lando was Pope for seven months and six days. During his pontificate the Hungarians devastated Apulia in the Year of Our Lord 9—[118]

John X was Pope for fourteen years, two months and three days. Leo VI was Pope for seven months and fifteen days. Stephen VII was Pope for two years, one month and thirteen days.

John XI was Pope for four years and ten months. He was the son of Pope Sergius III.[119]

Leo VII was Pope for three years, six months and ten days. During this time the Hungarians devastated much of Campania.[120]

Stephen VIII was Pope for three years, four months and fourteen days. Martin III[121] was Pope for three years, six months and thirteen days. Agapetus II was Pope for ten years, seven months and ten days.

John XII was Pope for nine years and three months. Benedict V was Pope for two months and five days. Leo VIII was Pope for one year and two months.

John XIII was Pope for six years, eleven months and five days. Arrested by Peter, the Prefect of Rome, he was imprisoned in Castel Sant'Angelo and then exiled to Campania. Once freed, on the orders of Emperor Otto I, he took reprisals against those who had persecuted him.

Benedict VI was Pope for one year and six months. Arrested by Crescentius the Elder, [grand]son of Theodora, he was imprisoned and strangled in Castel Sant'Angelo.

Boniface VII was [anti]Pope for one month and seven days.

Benedict VII was Pope for nine years.

John XIV was Pope for eight months. For four months he was imprisoned in Castel Sant'Angelo, where he died of starvation or poison. Boniface VII then returned and acted as Pope for eleven months.

John XV was Pope for ten years, three months and ten days. Gregory V was Pope for one year and five months (sic).[122]

John XVI was [anti]Pope for ten months.[123]

Sylvester II was Pope for four years, one month and nine days. He became Pope through a pact with the devil that he could meet his death only if he ever celebrated mass in Jerusalem. Yet he died in the Lateran, buried where a cart drawn by oxen happened to stop.[124]

John XVII was Pope for ten months and twenty-five days. John XVIII was Pope for one year (sic).[125] Sergius IV was Pope for four years.

Benedict VIII was Pope for thirteen years. He was forced to flee Rome for a time.

The next Pope was John XIX. Following him was Pope Benedict IX.[126]

Benedict IX, initially reigning rather briefly, was deposed and Sylvester III was elected Pope to replace him. After one month and twenty days (sic) Benedict offered the Papacy to [his godfather] John [Gratian], archbishop of Saint John Before the Latin Gate, who took the name Gregory VI. This Gregory was deposed by the Emperor Henry III and exiled to Germany.

Sylvester III was Pope for fifty-six days.[127] During this time, the Normans continued their conquest of Apulia begun in 1017, when a comet had appeared.[128]

Gregory VI was Pope for two years and seven months.

Clement II was Pope for nine months and seven days. Damasus was Pope for twenty-three days.

Leo IX was Pope for five years, two months and seven days. Noble, attractive and erudite by any measure, he led an army into Apulia against the Normans. There he was defeated because an angel had prophesied that the Normans would prevail and that those who died in this war would go to a greater glory in death than they could ever have enjoyed in life.[129]

In 1053, on his way to Rome following his [lost] campaign against the Normans in Apulia, Pope Leo stayed in Benevento, where he consecrated Olderic archbishop. He died in Rome on the twenty-ninth day of April the next year.[130]

Victor II was Pope for two years, three months and ten days. Stephen IX was Pope for seven months and twenty-nine days. Nicholas II was Pope for two years, seven months and twenty-four days. Alexander II was Pope for eleven years, six months and twenty-two days.

III

GREGORIUS ANNIS UNDECIM

Gregory VII was Pope for eleven years. During the fifth year of this pontificate [1078], Robert Guiscard besieged Benevento for three months and twenty-one days following the death of its last prince, Landulf VI [in 1077].

Jerusalem

In October 1083, Robert Guiscard crossed the sea for the Balkans and defeated the Venetians who had occupied that region.

Whilst a prisoner at Castel Sant'Angelo [in 1084], Pope Gregory VII was restored by Robert Guiscard, who entered Rome with a great army to liberate the pontiff and bring him to Salerno.[131] Being in that city for eleven months, the Pope consecrated the oratory of Saint Matthew.

Pope Gregory died at Salerno during 1085, the same year that Robert Guiscard, Duke of Apulia and leader of the Normans, died.

Robert Guiscard was succeeded as Duke of Apulia by his son, Roger [Borsa]. Having assembled a multitude of men-at-arms, Roger (sic) traveled beyond the mountains to Antioch, to take it from the Muslims, who had held it for sixteen years.[132]

Following the brief, year-long pontificate of Victor III, Pope Urban II reigned for twelve years.

Pope Urban convened a synod at Benevento, followed by similar synods at Troia and other Italian cities.

Largely at the urging of a religious man named Peter[133] who was from Burgundy, Urban adamantly encouraged the reconquest of the holy city of Jerusalem, which the Muslims had occupied for sixteen years.[134]

The Muslims, Peter claimed, had turned the Church of the Holy Sepulchre into a stall for horses.[135] The priest further asserted that Christ had appeared to him as he prayed before the tomb, ordering him to tell the Pope to raise a holy army to undertake a crusade against the Muslims.[136]

Pope Urban enlisted the support of many, even King Philip of France.[137] The pontiff thus assembled a multitude of armed men who took up the cross and were willing to die for their love of God and for the liberation of the Holy Sepulchre. Joining this great number were dukes, princes and counts of royal blood from Germany, Britain and Spain as well as Italy.

Present also were Roger [Borsa], Duke of Apulia, son of the late Robert Guiscard, and his half-brother Bohemond, who was destined to conquer Antioch and become its sovereign. Joining them was Bohemond's nephew, Tancred, the bravest of all.[138]

And so, with innumerable pagans subdued, some violently, and after confronting a great many perils, such as the dearth of victuals, the crusaders managed to reconquer Antioch and many other lands in the Year of Our Lord 1098.

The following year, with God's help and with valorous effort, the crusaders defeated the Muslims at Jerusalem and established themselves there as kings who had arrived from beyond the mountains. The city valiantly repulsed the Muslims for eighty-eight years.[139]

And so Jerusalem was reconquered by the Christians in the year of Our Lord 1099 on Friday, the fifteenth day of July, during the pontificate of Urban II, reigning in Germany King Henry, in Greece Emperor Alexius, in France King Philip, and in Apulia Duke Roger, son of Robert Guiscard.

Legends

God answered the prayers of the faithful, and in those times he revealed many miracles. An emir in a place to the east of Jerusalem doubted that the lamps in God's church are lit by divine light until he saw them light themselves when unlit iron rods, of the kind used for torches, were placed near them.

A glorious God brought forth a more impressive miracle to confuse the Muslims. A certain apostate archbishop from Bari had been expelled from Jerusalem with some others. This man sought a way to please an emir by justifying the killing of Christian ambassadors being sent to his city. To this end, he suggested that the Christians move a mountain as Christ had promised [in Matthew 17:20 and Mark 11:23]. If they could not perform this feat, all would perish or at least abandon Christ as a liar and seducer.

With this, the Muslims taunted the Christians, who feared for body and soul. Now, however, God kindled the spirit of a certain European monk in the ambassador's party named William, who was poor in appearance but endowed with abundant faith and eloquence, to comfort and convince the Christians with him to believe the word of Jesus Christ, whose boundless truth never fails those who have faith.

Instead of trying to reason with the doubters, William fasted for three days and confessed himself. Then, on the designated day, he went to an open place that had been established with the emir, attended by a large crowd gathered for the occasion. Having divided Christians from pagans, William stood on a mound and commanded a mountain visible in the distance to move from its present position to one that he indicated.

Hearing this, the Christians shouted, "So shall it be done!" With this, a blinding light descended upon the Christians accompanied by the sound of thunder, and they feared being killed by a bolt of lightning. Everybody present fell to the ground, remaining prostrate for an hour for fear of standing.

Finally, William arose and helped the emir to stand and pointed out to him and the others that the mountain had indeed moved. Then the apostate bishop began writhing in an epileptic fit, foamed at the mouth and died instantly.

The emir freed the Christians. He sent with the ambassadors silk robes, precious stones and other gifts for the European monarchs lodged with the army in Jerusalem, seeking peace with them.

Vicissitudes in Italy

Pope Urban II died the same year, 1099. On the thirtieth of July he was succeeded by Paschal II, who was Pope for nineteen years.

In August of 1100 (sic), he held a synod at Melfi in Apulia. The next year, Roger [I] of Sicily died, and Pope Paschal met Roger [Borsa] of Apulia in Calabria.[140]

In 1101, returning with a great army, Pope Paschal besieged Benevento as far as its walls. For that reason, [the rector] Anso, who governed the city against Papal will, panicked and decided to flee. The citizens of this city then received the Pope with the honour he deserved. After this, Rosman was installed as rector and the Papal party departed.[141]

The next year, 1102, Roger of Apulia, Herbert [of Ariano] and other nobles reached Benevento and encircled it so that provisions from the outside could not be delivered. Tormented by hunger and fearful that Roger and his barons would sack the city out of their malice towards John of Cito, who was then rector, the citizens chased this man out of Benevento. The people implored God to deliver them of their hunger and the threat of the besiegers.[142]

In 1105 there was extensive flooding of rivers due to an unusually high level of snowfall. Following this, Pope Paschal visited Benevento for three days.

In 1106, Henry of Germany died.[143]

The year 1107 saw the death of Roffred, the Archbishop of Benevento.

Pope Paschal came to Benevento for a synod in 1108. This year, there was a bad grape harvest and a pestilence that killed many animals.

In 1110, another Henry came to Rome and imprisoned Pope Paschal through deception.

The brothers, Roger [Borsa] of Apulia and Bohemond of Antioch, died during the same month in 1111.[144] Under the pretext of an agreement with certain bishops, cardinals and other honest men, Pope Paschal was long deceived by the German king, Henry, until, with an accord finally established, he crowned him Roman Emperor.[145]

In this same year, during the eleventh year of the pontificate of Paschal and the fifteenth year of the Cistercian constitution, Saint Bernard, then aged twenty-two, who was later to become the abbot of Clairvaux, established a Cistercian monastery with thirty followers from the university at Paris.[146]

In March of 1112, Pope Paschal held a synod at Rome. Here he broke the pact he had stipulated with Henry.[147] During the same year, the oratory of Saint Bartholomew[148] in Benevento was erected. The Beneventans, suffering every kind of robbery from every quarter, sent messengers to beg the Pope's help, that the pontiff might deign to help the city, which was otherwise destined for ruin.[149]

In March of 1113, during the fourteenth year of his pontificate, Paschal II visited Benevento [where he held a synod] to find the Papal city oppressed by conspiracies and persecutions from every part due to machinations by the Normans, who had failed to maintain their promises. He convened a council of the citizens, appointing a constable named Landulf of Greece, a man in equal parts brave and tenacious, before returning to Rome. In truth, this constable opposed his enemies for an entire year. However, the Archbishop of Benevento, who could not tolerate Landulf's severity, set the citizens against him. This led Landulf to resign as constable. Seeing this situation, the Pope deposed the archbishop.[150]

After some time had passed, the Beneventans made peace with Count Jordan of Ariano, his barons, and with Prince Robert of Alife and Airola [in 1114] following the deaths of Roger of Sicily and Bohemond of Antioch. Under fear of excommunication, the Pope's enemies sought peace.[151]

Around this time lived an exceptionally intelligent man named Bruno, Bishop of Segni and Abbot of Cassino.[152]

In these years [1116-1117] there were many terrifying events, such as great earthquakes that caused the collapse of walls, towers and churches, causing numerous deaths. Waters grew rough, and the hanging lamps in churches swayed without being touched by people or by the wind.[153] One of the worst earthquakes occurred at the hour of vespers.

The seas rumbled unnaturally. Water erupted from wells and springs. In Milan, it rained blood for several days.

In 1117, Henry V came with his wife to Rome, where he was acclaimed by great crowds. Having donated of his own will, he was crowned in the Lateran on Pentecoste[154] and then departed the city happily.

In that same year there were two lunar eclipses, on the first of July (sic) and on the eleventh of December. On the sixteenth of December parts of the sky seemed afire, in the north as well as the south.[155]

Pope Paschal II died on the twenty-second day of January [1118] in Rome, and the cardinal deacon John Caietani was elected in that same place on the twenty-fifth of the month with the name of Gelasius [II].

There was a lunar eclipse on the twenty-third of January (sic).

It irritated Henry V that a new Pope was elected without his knowledge or approval. Angrily, he came to Rome in great pomp and placed in the Holy See [Maurice] Bourdin, Archbishop of Braga.[156] Gelasius was forced to flee.[157]

Knowing the vindictiveness of the Emperor, Pope Gelasius stealthily made his way along the Tiber, to the sea and thence by ship to Gaeta at night. There he met with the cardinals and dignitaries who supported him.

Gelasius then departed for Britain.[158] There he was received honourably. He then went to France, where he convoked a synod of bishops from that country and from Germany and other regions north of the Alps. There he formally annulled Henry's nomination of Bourdin.

Feeling very ill, Gelasius reached the abbey of Saint Peter at Cluny knowing he was dying. He gathered together the cardinals, who elected the archbishop Guy of Vienne with the name of Callixtus II.[159] Pope Callixtus was an exceptionally sage, honest man, beloved by the cardinals and by the people of Rome.

Pope Gelasius died at Cluny on the twenty-ninth day of March in 1119. He had been Pope for one year and one month. Callixtus II was destined to be Pope for six years and eight months.

During the pontificate of this Pope, Count Ranulf of Alife and Airola fought a war against Count Jordan of Ariano.[160]

When Robert [Drengot], the Prince of Capua, died [in

1120]. He was succeeded by his son, Richard, who died ten days later. This Richard was then succeeded by his own uncle, Jordan [Robert's brother].[161]

In many areas there were earthquakes strong enough to destroy castles, and other edifices also collapsed.[162] During the month of May in the second year of the pontificate of Callixtus, three days before the feast of Saint Eustace (sic), the Calore River rose above its usual level and flooded the surrounding country.[163]

Pope Callixtus died in the Year of Our Lord 1124. Lambert, Bishop of Ostia, was elected and took the name Honorius [II]. His pontificate lasted five years and two months. He went to Apulia, where he gave that duchy to Roger [II], Count of Sicily upon the death of William, his cousin, that is to say the son of Roger [Borsa] of Apulia.[164]

During the night of the eleventh of October in 1125 there was a great earthquake around Benevento. The frightened people sought refuge at the Saint Sophia monastery. Pope Honorius, who was in the city, immediately abandoned the sacred palace and went to the basilica of Saint John. There the pontiff prostrated himself before the altar, tearfully imploring God's mercy.

The night before, a single tremor was sufficient to frighten everybody. There were more tremors for the next fifteen days. But even as his prayers went unheeded, the Pope continued to pray, barefoot, in the Lord's church, assisted by a congregation of men and women, mothers and children who sang litanies between screaming and sobbing.[165]

In March 1126 (sic) the Holy Roman Emperor Henry [V] died.[166]

The Rise of Roger II

In 1127 Duke William, son of the late Roger [Borsa], died

at Salerno without male heirs.[167] Hearing of his nephew's death, Count Roger [II], immediately readied seven galleys and set sail for Salerno, where he soon arrived.[168]

For ten days Roger remained in port on his flagship. He summoned the Salernitans' leaders, who listened to his words of peace and accepted his claim to the succession.[169] Within a few days, Roger brought the Duchy of Amalfi into his dominion.[170]

He then set out for Apulia, bringing Troia, Melfi and other cities of that region under his rule, accordingly being called Duke of Apulia.[171] He made generous donations to the Pope, who was at Benevento. Roger asked for the pontiff's confirmation of his right to the duchy of Apulia but the Pope refused.

Therefore, on Roger's command, Romano of Fraineta, Hugh the Infant and other barons besieged the Papal city of Benevento. These men attacked more zealously than what was ordered, mercilessly killing many Beneventans. This prompted the pontiff to go to Capua, where he anointed Robert [Drengot] as the Prince of that city.[172] There a crowd of some five thousand gathered for the solemn ceremony. Present was Count Ranulf of Alife, who swore fealty to the Pope.[173]

The Pope explained the promises made by Count Roger in order to obtain Papal approval of the Duchy of Benevento; even so, the pontiff did not wish to subject so many nobles of the region to Roger's power.

Hearing these words roused the newly-anointed prince, the counts and the barons to resist the Count of Sicily with all their might.

Upon returning to Rome, Pope Honorius raised a force of two hundred knights[174] and a great number of armed foot men. Seeking to avoid a pitched battle against such a large force, Count Roger stayed in mountainous terrain for the month of July [1128].[175] In truth, Prince Robert, being frail, and Count Ranulf, losing interest in the campaign, pulled up their tents and returned home to Capua.

Finding himself abandoned by Robert and Ranulf, the Pope sought and received assurances from the Count of Sicily that the city of Benevento would be undisturbed, its Papal status respected. The Pope thus agreed to recognize Roger as Duke of Apulia. He returned home after having appointed a certain William as rector of Benevento.

The Beneventans soon rose up against William. During a riot, the rector sought refuge behind the altar of Saint John in the chapel of the curia, where in those times the holy mass was celebrated. This did not save him. William was attacked there with knives by an angry crowd. His corpse was then dragged across the square as far as the abattoir of Saint Lawrence, where it was left.

Then the angry mob destroyed the houses of the dead man's friends, these being Poto Spitameti, John Quisliccio, the judges Transo and Lawrence, and the physician Louis. Fearing still further reprisals, these men fled to Mount Fusco.

The citizenry organized itself as a commune, declaring that the men whose homes had been destroyed could not return to the city for seven years and forty days.

The Pope, upon learning of the death of the rector and the exile of his friends, and not obtaining a satisfactory response from the leaders of the commune, who refused to permit the exiled judges to return, personally asked Roger to act in reprisal against the Beneventans. This attack by Roger was to take place in May.[176] Nonetheless, along his route returning to Rome the Pope attacked and sacked the fortified town of Ceppaloni.[177]

Pope Honorius II died in Rome in February 1130.

IV

DISSIDENTIBUS IN INVICEM CARDINALIBUS

Following much discussion (sic), the cardinals unanimously elected Innocent II at the third hour of daylight. Already being vested, they immediately consecrated him Pope.

The Papal Schism

Other cardinals, led by Peter, Bishop of Porto [a diocese near Rome], elected Peter Pierleone as Pope Anacletus II.

This contestation found the people of Rome divided into two parties. One was led by Leo Frangipani. The other was led by Leo Pierleone, brother of Anacletus.

The party of Leo Frangipane supported Pope Innocent II, who had been elected by the greater number of cardinals.[178]

The opposing party [led by Leo Pierleone], made corrupt by bribes, supported Anacletus II.

This led to many violent feuds within the city of Rome. In March of 1130, Anacletus, emboldened by his own riches and the wealth of his brother Pierleone, as well as his friendship with Roger, ensconced himself at Benevento, whose citizens swore loyalty to him.

Birth of a Kingdom

Speaking with Roger at Avellino, Anacletus promised to crown him King of Sicily. To that end, he sent to Sicily a cardinal named Conte[179] to crown Roger on his behalf. Accompanied by Robert of Capua and many other Papal supporters and nobles, he crowned Roger King of Sicily on Christmas Day in the Year of Our Lord 1130 in the city of Palermo.

During the same year, Pope Innocent, forced to confront ever more civil unrest among the Romans, heeded the advice of his counsellors and traveled beyond the mountains to seek the support of the King of France[180] and the other faithful of the Roman Church. At a synod convened in Rheims with a hundred and one bishops, he condemned and excommunicated Anacletus and all who supported his claim to be Pope.[181] At Rome, meanwhile, Anacletus consecrated Landulf as Bishop of Capua.

Now Roger, having assumed all of the perquisites that appertain to the title of king, began courageously to force all of the duchies, principalities and counties of Apulia and Terra di Lavoro to firmly submit to his authority. He first went to Salerno, which was among his possessions, and to Amalfi.[182]

Next he brought a large army and various siege engines to Bari, which he encircled for fifteen days. He captured rich, pompous Grimoald [Alfaranites], sending this prince, accompanied by his wife and children, to Sicily as prisoners. He meted out the same punishment to Geoffrey of Matera and many others, thus subduing the greater part of Apulia.

Roger's sister, Matilda, was the wife of Ranulf of Alife, who had taken a concubine.[183] Matilda much lamented her husband's comportment. Learning of this situation, Roger rescued his sister, along with her son by Ranulf, from the unfaithful husband.

For this reason, Ranulf was ever more indignant about the

king and grew ever nearer Roger's adversaries.

Robert of Capua, who Pope Anacletus had sent to Roger's coronation, was fearful that the king might use the same tactics with him that he used with Ranulf. With this in mind, and seeking allies, Robert solicited the Pisans and Genoans, offering them gifts. The citizens of these important mercantile cities then sent a large fleet of galleys to Naples against the King of Sicily.

In the meantime, Roger pillaged Capua, Aversa and many other dominions where the people supported Prince Robert of Capua and Count Ranulf of Alife.

In the month of March in the Year of Our Lord 1132, the moon lost its splendor, turning blood red in color. Observing this phenomenon made men believe it was an omen.[184]

The same year, Pope Anacletus went to Salerno to meet King Roger. The pontiff asked the king to return Matilda and her son to Ranulf but Roger refused to grant this request.

Therefore, Robert and Ranulf mustered nearly three thousand knights and around forty thousand foot men to fight Roger.[185] They made it known to Roger through ambassadors that he must return to Ranulf the wife and son he had taken away.

Roger replied that first he desired to know why the two men were acting against him in this way, and to that end he offered to meet with them. Instead, Robert and Ranulf responded that if the city of Avellino, along with Matilda and the boy, were not restored to Ranulf there would be no explanation forthcoming, only combat.

What more can be said? In fact, the king came to learn that the Beneventans now sided with Robert and Ranulf, to whom the citizens gave their support.

Roger arrived at the city with a great army, where he waited for fifteen days in the plain beyond the Valentine Bridge.[186] Here the king promised the Beneventans that if they supported him he would exempt them from the excise duties and all the taxes the Normans had imposed upon them.

Cardinal Crescenzio, the rector of Benevento, who took the side of Pope Anacletus [who supported Roger], who he wished to please, made the city's leaders sign oaths of allegiance to the sovereign. Consequently, some prominent Beneventans who opposed this act told the rest of the populace that the cardinal and his accomplices wanted to submit the [Papal] city to the dominion of the King of Sicily. With this, the agreement stipulated with the king was annulled.

Nocera

King Roger saw that the enemy army gathered on the plain before Montesarchio was enormous. He realized that the Beneventans, as well as the inhabitants of the towns around the city, were loyal to his adversaries rather than to him. He regretted that matters had developed differently from what he had hoped for, and during the night he ordered his army to break camp.

The royal army marched into the territory of Salerno. Here the king besieged a well-fortified town of Robert called Nocera, posting arbalesters and longbowmen along the main road leading to it to avoid a surprise attack by the enemy. Robert and Ranulf, who wished to reach the castle early in the morning, found these roads, and the bridge across the Sarno River, blocked and impassable, so they pitched camp farther along the river, where they erected a wooden bridge.

They thus crossed the river, and here a fierce battle began.

But the king's men fought back the first wave of attackers, forcing them to retreat back over the bridge, where they crowded together, many plummeting into the river. Others were killed by arrows. Had Ranulf himself not come to their aid with reinforcements, this engagement would have been won by the king's troops.

Ranulf fought bravely alongside his men. No longer able to offer resistance, the king's troops retreated, hotly pursued by the attackers. Seeing so many of his men fleeing, and unable to block their retreat, filled the king with anger. He ordered a march to Salerno.

Robert, Ranulf and the commander of the Neapolitan soldiers, along with the other counts and barons who had pursued the royal troops, acquired a vast booty of arms, horses and innumerable other loot. They then returned to their homes.

Apart from numerous vases of gold and silver that they stole, twenty barons were captured, along with seven hundred knights and numerous foot men of the king.[187]

This battle took place on the vigil of Saint James's Day in July 1132.[188] Ranulf of Alife went on to reconquer the various Apulian cities the king had confiscated from him, and as a result he was placated. Meanwhile, the king returned to Sicily [in December].

Innocent and Lothair

The following year, in 1133, Pope Innocent returned to Rome with Emperor Lothair[189] accompanied by two thousand knights. They were received by the populace with joy and great honour. The Pope went to reside in the Lateran and the emperor stalwartly encamped with his army at the monastery of Saint Paul.

It is said that Lothair, having consulted theologians, invited Anacletus to meet with him personally, hoping that, with the intercession of the Holy Spirit, an end could be brought to the killing and to a great error. Anacletus refused this proposal that he renounce his pontificate.

Meanwhile, Prince Robert of Capua and Count Ranulf of Alife, learning of Pope Innocent's long-awaited arrival, went immediately to the pontiff with Cardinal Gerard [rector of Benevento] and around three hundred knights to recount the events that had transpired recently at Benevento and Nocera.

Listening to this news, Emperor Lothair did not respond to their wishes for help, for he had come to Rome in the interest of his own affairs rather than those of others. Without remaining in the city very long, he departed for Tuscany.[190]

Whilst visiting the Pope, Robert and Ranulf learned that King Roger had returned to Apulia with sixty galleys[191] and was now devastating the hinterland. Ranulf immediately took an army to Troia, where he wanted to find out if the citizens were still keeping the agreement they promised to him and Prince Robert. Out of fear of the king, the Troians reneged on the agreement. After remaining in the region for forty days, Ranulf departed.

He then went to Benevento, where he made a pact with the citizens before returning to his own lands.

Robert left his principality [Capua] in Ranulf's care and accompanied the Pope to Pisa, where they solicited the help of the Pisans and Genoans against King Roger in return for three thousand silver pounds.[192]

Upon returning to Capua, Robert explained the conditions of this treaty to Ranulf, the Neapolitan militia master Sergio, and all their supporters. All agreed to what had been negotiated.

King Roger Returns

Whilst Robert, Ranulf and their allies collected the money needed to pay the Pisans and Genoans, who were preparing for the campaign, King Roger returned to Apulia with sixty galleys and a great army, ferociously attacking his adversaries with the sword, with fire, with iron and with famine. Some were hanged, others simply stabbed to death, and still others dismembered. Some were sent to Sicily as prisoners. He depopulated cities, castles and monumental places.

The city of Bari was sacked, along with Troia, Matera and other coastal localities. Reaching the lands of the Principality of Capua, Roger deprived Prince Robert of Nocera, Sarno and Lauro. He set Aversa afire. By that time, however, Robert had returned to Pisa.

By distributing money, the king attracted to his sphere the greater part of the more important baronage that had supported Robert and Ranulf.

Knowing to be abandoned by those in whom he had placed the greatest trust, Ranulf dared not attack the king despite having fifteen hundred knights and many foot men and archers at his disposal. He knew that this comparatively paltry force could achieve nothing.

In pain and fear, he bowed his head and submitted to the king, swearing fealty. The king was full of joy at having reined in the power of Count Robert. Having also occupied the Principality of Capua, he confiscated it from Robert and returned to Sicily.

Sustained by the king's power, Pope Anacletus went to Benevento. where he asserted his own authority. Then he ordered the destruction of those who supported his rival, Pope Innocent.

In March of the year 1135, during the sixth year of Innocent's pontificate, Prince Robert of Capua returned, having been received honourably by the Pisans and the Pope. On the sixth day of April he reached Naples with a fleet of twenty galleys. He took Aversa and Cucculo during an excursion and then returned to Naples, remaining there with the Pisans.

That same year, Count Ranulf joined Prince Robert at Naples with four hundred knights.

In June, King Roger landed a large army at Salerno and attacked Aversa, razing the town with sword and fire, destroying its residents' property.[193]

Along his route back to Salerno, he besieged Naples for nine days. Finding he could not take that city, he returned to Aversa, which he rebuilt.

With the arrival of another twenty galleys, the Pisans attacked Amalfi, destroying much in the city. Then they returned home to Pisa with Robert and their booty.[194]

After Robert and the Pisans had withdrawn from Naples, King Roger again assaulted the city by sea. Whilst attempting to engage the Neapolitan fleet on what happened to be the feast of the Nativity of Mary, the Mother of God [8 September], the royal fleet was damaged by a sudden tempest. Faced with such conditions, and believing some galleys to be lost, the king narrowly survived by taking his ships to the port of Pozzuoli nearby.

Apart from the weather affecting a sea battle, he considered that this was not the opportune moment to initiate campaigns on land. He ordered the ships to return to Sicily and the army to be divided. The king immediately departed for Sicily.[195]

Machinations

After having consulted with Pope Innocent and Cardinal Gerard, and also with Ranulf's brother Richard, Robert of Capua went to Germany to see Emperor Lothair. Sobbing, but in a voice worthy of evoking compassion, he explained how he had been divested of his property by the King of Sicily. In the humility of a supplicant, he asked if Lothair might deign to come with help as soon as possible.

Lothair kindly acceded to this plea, promising to come the same year (sic) with a great army to liberate Robert as well as the Church of Rome.

Having received Lothair's letter, along with generous gifts for the Pope, Robert returned to Italy, where he explained these developments to Innocent.

In the same year, the militia master [Sergio] went from Naples to Pisa to seek the help of Pope Innocent and the Pisans.[196] He was received by them with great courtesy, and in view of their meeting he was at first promised every assistance. Yet those hostile to him ensured that this decision was not acted upon. Realizing this, the military master returned sadly to Naples, where he fortified the city as best as his resources permitted.

Whilst these events were occurring, in 1136, the seventh year of the pontificate of Innocent II, Emperor Lothair sent letters to the Pope and Prince Robert of Capua notifying them that he would arrive in Italy on the feast of Saint James [25 July]. Receiving this news, Robert departed Pisa with five ships and shortly arrived in Naples. There found the militia master and the entire populace on the verge of starvation for the lack of food.

As soon as he learned the emperor was in Italy, Robert made haste for Pisa. At Cremona he met the emperor and his army. Prostrating himself at the monarch's feet, Robert, who had been deprived of his birthright, implored him to come as soon as he could. Now the emperor sent letters with his own envoys to the Pope and the militia master. He addressed the populace with conciliatory words, asking the people to maintain their loyalty until, with God's help, he would liberate them at the earliest possible moment.

Before long, Lothair's legates arrived at Naples, where they showed the people the letters bearing the imperial seal, affirming that they had witnessed the emperor issue these in their own presence at Spoleto.

Lothair in Apulia

A few days later, similar letters bearing like words of en-

109

couragement arrived with other envoys, who affirmed that these were issued by the emperor at Pescara on Easter [22 March]. They confirmed that the emperor would be in Apulia[197] before long. Learning of this, the Archbishop of Naples[198] and some Neapolitans went with Ranulf to meet the emperor, returning to tell the people that he was already in Apulia. Despite fear and famine, the Neapolitans rejoiced at this news. They awaited the emperor's arrival.

In the eighth year of the pontificate of Innocent II, during the month of March 1137, the Pope departed Pisa and went to Viterbo to speak with the emperor.[199] The emperor sent to the pontiff his son-in-law, Henry, his heir, with three thousand German knights. Henry[200] had orders to make an incursion into Roman territory, submitting all in it to the authority of the Pope whilst restoring to Robert the entire Principality of Capua.

With the Pope, Henry subdued the area around Albano[201] and all of Campania. To avoid becoming embroiled in local difficulties with the Romans, Innocent avoided entering the city.

The emperor, meanwhile, advanced through the Marches, occupying all the lands of that region.

From Pescara, where he celebrated Easter, he went to Termoli. From there, he reached Siponto, occupying Mount Sant'Angelo on the eighth of May. Then he headed south to Bari, whose citizens immediately submitted.

During the course of the next forty days the strength of Lothair's war machines besieged the well-defended fortress that King Roger had erected there. Of the knights and soldiers who defended it in the king's name, some were taken prisoner, some were tossed into the sea, and others were simply stabbed to death.[202]

And so, all the provinces of Apulia, Taranto and Calabria, and their coasts, fell to Emperor Lothair.[203] The people thanked God for their deliverance from a terrible king.

Meanwhile, the army of Pisans and Genoans, fulfilling the promise they made earlier, arrived at Naples with a hundred galleys full of armed men. Following the emperor's orders, they attacked Amalfi, laying siege to it. But the Amalfitans, by paying tribute to the invaders and swearing loyalty to the emperor, avoided the worst fate. Instead, the galleys went to Ravello and Scala, where the invaders sacked and destroyed with fire and sword everything they found there. They captured men, women, children, animals and all they could carry. So enriched, they returned joyfully to their ships.

At the same time, the Pope and the emperor left Melfi, which they had besieged, making their way to the lands around the city of Potenza, where for thirty days they camped along a river near Lagopesole.[204]

Prince Robert of Capua, Count Ranulf of Alife and the Pisans blatantly attacked and besieged the city of Salerno. The emperor supported this effort by sending a thousand German knights, who surrounded the city walls. In the city were four hundred of the king's troops who responded day and night by attacking the Pisans and the men with Robert and Ranulf.

Although a few of the defenders were captured beyond the walls, day by day the resistance grew ever fiercer. Seeing this resistance, the Pisans erected an exceptionally high siege engine that they took to the wall.

The citizens, seeing this kind of mobile "castle," grew fearful and immediately sent emissaries to the emperor and the Pope to sue for peace. An agreement was stipulated and the city surrendered to Lothair. Some of the king's knights were granted safe conduct and permitted to leave the city.

In truth, a few knights took refuge in the citadel at Torre Maggiore[205] on high ground overlooking the city, happy to be free from the threat of the enemy.

The Pisans were angered to learn that the city had submitted to Lothair, and was therefore taken from their control, without their being consulted first. In fury, they set their great timber siege tower afire and returned to their galleys ready to depart for Pisa. Their departure was averted only by the Pope's entreaties.

With Salerno and its environs subdued except for Torre Maggiore, which was left unconquered for the dispute with the Pisans, Innocent and Lothair set out for Avellino.

From there, they decamped to Benevento. There, on the second day of August [1137], they pitched camp near the church of Saint Stephen. For nearly thirty days, ever since they had left Avellino, pontiff and emperor had disagreed about questions of dominion, with the latter wishing the region to come under his rule rather than Rome's.

Disagreeing with the emperor's proposal, the Pope undertook to place a duke and defender in Apulia in the name of Saint Peter, Prince of the Apostles.[206] Divine clemency saw to it that the differences in the papal and imperial points of view were obviated through the sage counsel of wise men. To the emperor's pleasure, and with the unanimous approval of his men, the Pope chose as Duke of Apulia Ranulf of Alife, a prudent and wise man. Following this announcement, the Pope and the emperor together invested him, bestowing upon him in front of everybody the banner of his duchy for loyalty to Saint Peter.

Three days later, the empress, who was named Florida (sic), arrived at Benevento with a hundred knights.[207] There, in Saint Bartholomew's church, she made the offering of a pound of silver and a pallium before returning to the army.

Following this by three days, Pope Innocent arrived, entering in great honour, and consecrated the archbishop-elect Gregory.[208] Attending in great reverence was the Patriarch of Aquileia[209] with many other archbishops, bishops, abbots and prelates.

After the consecration, the Pope entered his palace and tried to comfort with kindness the citizens who had been afflicted by a series of mistreatments. With the consent of the emperor and the baronage, he abolished forever the existing taxes on estates, roads, common lands, labor, produce, vines, olives, pastures, hunts and livestock exacted in the Beneventan territory by the Norman counts, barons and lords. This was confirmed with the golden imperial seal.

The pontiff then received an oath of loyalty from the Beneventan citizens, who went to their homes happily and contentedly. Then Innocent and Lothair departed, visiting Capua with Prince Robert before returning to Rome.

In Rome [November 1137] they were received by the populace with great honour. The Pope returned to the Lateran Palace. Lothair marched to Tuscany, setting forth for his lands as quickly as possible.[210]

V
REX ITAQUE ROGERIUS

Learning that the imperial troops had departed, Roger raised an army and went immediately to Nocera.[211] Having forced that city to submit to royal authority, he broke camp and subjugated some lands of Count [now Duke] Ranulf.

Roger's Revenge

Then the king marched on Capua, which he conquered with great rage and violence. Here he commanded the brutal destruction of some houses. Church ornaments were pillaged. Even ladies and nuns were treated harshly.

He then went to Avellino, placing the lands between that city and Benevento under his rule. The king brought into his alliance Sergio, the Neapolitan militia master.

Outside Benevento, the city's judges, acting out of concern for the citizens, went to the king and swore loyalty to him. They abandoned their fealty to Pope Innocent, passing to Pope Anacletus, to whom they submitted their city. They took no account of the oath they had sworn to Innocent.

In the middle of October the king, having gathered his army, passed by the highest gate of Benevento and rapidly marched to Mountsarchio, which he conquered. From there, he went to the city of Count Richard.[212] Richard quickly fled, going to his brother, Ranulf.

Then the king subjugated the town of Monte Corvino, which he ordered destroyed by sword and fire, giving the plunder to Ranulf's enemies.

Learning of the king's presence in Apulia, Ranulf recruited an army that included fifteen hundred knights from Bari, Melfi and Troia. With this force, he set out to meet the king. Ranulf vowed that it would be better to die than to bow to royal power.

Ranulf

The venerable Cistercian abbot, Bernard [of Clairvaux], a man saintly and prudent, was sent by Pope Innocent to King Roger in the hope of bringing an end to the damage caused by the great conflict between the monarch and Ranulf. As a result of differences over many issues, such a peace was not achieved.

This led to a confrontation outside Ariano on the second day (sic) of October in the year 1137.

Confident in the numerical superiority of his army, and not wishing to humble himself to consider this holy man's advice, Roger divided the ranks of his force in preparation for an attack. Ranulf, instead, placed his faith in God and the prayers of Catholic men, who he trusted absolutely. He too drew up his troops.[213]

The first side to charge was the army of the king, which penetrated the duke's line. There, however, the royal troops routed and defeated by Ranulf's men who, conversely, were reinforced and gave pursuit to the king's fleeing men.

As soon as he saw his knights routed in this way, the king grew afraid and he was the first on his side to turn and beat a hasty retreat. Not far behind, indeed with dizzying speed, his men followed, abandoning their tents and all the gold and silver objects of immeasurable value they had recently plundered.[214]

Ranulf and his men-at-arms, having defeated the enemy and enriched themselves with spoils, returned to their own lands. Some three thousand died in the battle. Among the fallen were Eterno [Iderno] of Monte Fusco, Gerard of Lanzulino, Sarolo del Tuffo, [Sergio] the Neapolitan militia master, and many others.

The king fled in the night. The next day he reached the fortified town of Paduli. From there he went to Salerno.[215]

The abbot Bernard had foreseen Ranulf's victory in the battle and Roger's flight. During the battle he went to the nearest city he could reach. Later, whilst Bernard was deep in prayer, he heard the sudden noise of those who were fleeing and those being pursued; in fact it was Ranulf's men chasing Roger's. When one of Abbot Bernard's monks approached a knight to ask what had happened, the knight responded, "I saw an impious man taller than a cedar of Lebanon, but when I got near him there was nobody there."

Then Ranulf passed by whilst chasing Roger's men and saw the monk. Even though he was suited in armor, the duke dismounted and fell at the monk's feet, saying, "I give thanks to God and to his faithful servant that this victory has been bequeathed us not through force of arms but through the force of faith." Then he mounted his horse and continued chasing the enemy knights.

At all events, the state of the king's spirit was unmoved despite heaven inflicting this defeat upon him. Nothing could alter the storm brought forth from a perverse mind.

Yet later, reunited with those who managed to escape, Roger feigned enthusiasm, donning royal robes to address his knights and demanding that the envoys of both Anacletus and

Innocent come before him. It had been established that, to determine what motivated both sides, three cardinals of Innocent and three of Anacletus would meet. By hearing their arguments, the king might make the better choice for the grandeur of his realm.

Two Popes

The king was well aware that the greater part of the faithful supported Pope Innocent and that now only he and his Kingdom of Sicily supported Anacletus. Pope Innocent sent his chancellor, Haimeric, and Gerard, a cardinal, with Bernard of Clairvaux. Pope Anacletus sent his own chancellor, Matthew, Gregory, a cardinal, and Peter of Pisa, a cardinal and expert in canon law.[216]

Thinking that Peter, the jurist, would take their side, both King Roger and Pope Anacletus were hopeful of a favorable outcome.

The king first ordered Peter, who he knew to be amply briefed and highly enthusiastic in view of the promise of lavish compensation, to present the case of Anacletus. Above all, Peter sought to show that the election of Anacletus was indeed canonical. To that end, he bolstered his thesis by citing many civil laws and canons.

But [Bernard] the venerable man of God, knowing well that the Kingdom of God is to be found not in words but in deeds, explained:

"I know, Peter, that you are a wise and learned man, and heaven itself could not have found one more honest or less corrupt than you! I only wish that heaven had enlisted you for a nobler cause! Your great eloquence would surely convince us were your position logical. We rustic men, being more accustomed to heaving the hoe in the field than to uttering great words at court, would remain silent were it not for our faith.

But now the charity of the word compels us to speak, remembering that neither Gentile nor Jew dared tear the robe worn by Our Lord, yet, bolstered by the king, Peter Pierleone [Anacletus] tears it and denigrates it. There is but one faith, one Lord and one baptism. We do not say that there are two Lords, two faiths or two baptisms. Beginning with the ancients, in the time of the great flood there was only one ark, which saved eight souls whilst the others who were not on it perished. Who can doubt that this ark represented the church? But another ark has been constructed. Since there are now two arks, one is necessarily false and must be sunk in the profound depths of the sea. The ark guided by Peter, if it be God's ark, will be saved. The ark guided by Innocent, if it is not God's ark, of necessity will be destroyed, and in that case will the eastern church forfeit the entire west, losing France, Germany, Ireland and England? Should the barbary kingdoms be submersed beneath the sea? Should this ark, bearing the monks of Camaldoli, Chartreuse, Grandmont, Cîteaux, Premontré and innumerable other orders of the servants of God, both men and women, fall into the abyss for just a single tempest? Must the stormy sea swallow up bishops, abbots and princes simply because the church is tied by its neck to a burdensome millstone? Roger, alone among the world's princes, has chosen Peter's ark, but if all the others have abandoned it, will Roger alone be saved? It cannot be that the religion of the entire world should perish for the ambition of Peter [Pierleone], who alone obtains the Kingdom of Heaven!"[217]

Hearing these words, those present could no longer restrain themselves but abandoned Peter of Pisa and the case he advanced.

Bernard took Peter by the hand, and as both men rose, said to him, "If you believe me, we will enter the safer ark."

Agreeing with Bernard's reasoning, set forth with kindness and with the help of God's grace, Peter reconciled with Pope

Innocent upon returning to Rome.

The king still refused to agree with Bernard because, having zealously occupied some Papal lands [around Benevento], he wished to leave the matter unresolved to press his advantage to obtain more privileges from the Papacy. He proposed holding a meeting with the bishops of Sicily and those of the entire kingdom to determine how to rule in a question of such great importance. He asked the cardinals who had been present to write an account of what had been said, which the cardinals going with him to Sicily could bring along.

Cardinal Gerard responded that he did not wish to write anything. "You have heard the affirmations and rebuttals," he said. "What do you want to do? Do what you must. We have to return to Rome."

In those days the physicians seeking to cure a certain nobleman of Salerno failed in their efforts. Everybody knows that the city's medical school is held in great esteem.[218] Yet in view of the doctors' failure to cure him the aristocrat became skeptical. One night this patient dreamt that a pious man had arrived in the city who could cure [miraculously] all manner of maladies. Believing the dream to be true, the ill man began searching for the saintly visitor. Finding him, the patient asked to drink the water with which the visitor had washed his hands. Drinking it, the nobleman was immediately cured. News of this spread around the city, reaching the ears of the king and many nobles.[219]

Of those involved in some way in the Papal schism, only the king remained unconvinced by the recent discussions. Abbot Bernard was comforted by the approval of the people, and by the support of Peter of Pisa and others now united with Pope Innocent. With Cardinal Guy, who supported Innocent, and another cardinal, supportive of Anacletus, King Roger returned to Sicily.[220]

In the same year[221] Anacletus died on the seventh day of

January, the eighth year of the erroneous pontificate that was the fruit of his confusion. He had been ill since the twentieth of November and then bedridden for three days. Catholics ignored his funeral.

However, the party of the late Anacletus chose another Pope, not out of the arrogance typical of schism, but rather to be in a better negotiating position with Innocent II for a while. The newly elected pontiff, a laughable figure named Gregory [Conti][222] who the schismatics called Victor [IV], went in the night with the Pierleone brothers of the late Anacletus to see Innocent. There Gregory divested himself of the insignia of office he had worn unlawfully and begged forgiveness at the feet of Pope Innocent, asking to be pardoned for his error. The brothers of the late Anacletus likewise apologized to Innocent.[223]

With this, the city of Rome rejoiced that Innocent's authority was now universally recognized. All Romans saw Innocent as their lord and shepherd.

Three Fountains

Bernard of Clairvaux was held in great esteem. All considered him the to be bringer of peace and the father of the Papal country. Recognizing this, Pope Innocent ceded to him the monastery of Saint Anastasius of the "Three Fountains" at Aquas Salvias[224] which had belonged to the Papacy but was no longer inhabited.

There he restored the churches, brought people to live in the houses and cultivate the fields and vineyards. The Pope asked Bernard to send a religious community, and this was done.

The first abbot was a man named Bernard, who had been subdeacon of the diocese of Pisa. He eventually became Pope as Eugene III, during a time that the Cistercian Order was rather prosperous.

The same year, Emperor Lothair III died in Tuscany on his way to Germany.[225] He was succeeded by Conrad [Hohenstaufen] in 1138, the ninth year of the pontificate of Pope Innocent II.[226]

Roger Strikes Back

Not long afterward, the Pope gathered an army and went to Albano, from whence he planned to assist Ranulf in Apulia. Feeling ill, however, the pontiff cancelled this expedition.

King Roger, meanwhile, mustered an army and went to Apulia to take back all of the lands that had been occupied by Emperor Lothair. Ranulf likewise raised an army to contest the king, which he did for two months.

At the same time, Roger recognized Innocent as Pope and ordered the Beneventans and all of the realm's subjects to honour the pontiff as their spiritual father and ecclesiastical lord.

With Ranulf forced to withdrawal to a small area of Apulia in the cities of the Adriatic coast, the king returned to the mountainous regions around Benevento, burning and pillaging Alife, Venafro and many other towns.[227] He then stopped at Benevento before returning to Sicily for the winter.

On April eighth of 1139, Pope Innocent opened a synod [the Second Lateran Council] in Rome[228] attended by many bishops, archbishops and abbots. King Roger and his followers were excommunicated.

Ranulf reached Troia on the thirtieth day of April in the same year. Struck by a high fever, he died there, greatly mourned by that city and all of Apulia.

On the twenty-eighth day of June in that year the volcano at Pozzuoli, near Naples, was seen to emit terrible flames. People in the nearby castles and villages feared for their lives. From the eruption was released coarse black ash that arrived as far as Salerno, Benevento and Capua. The ash covered the ground for thirty days.[229]

During the same year, Roger made his son, Roger, Duke of Apulia, granting him the rights to all of the coastal cities except well-fortified Bari, whose leader[230] had four hundred knights and the support of the fifty thousand inhabitants.

Young Roger, the new duke, realizing that Bari could not be subdued, left its environs and went with his army to consult with his father, the king, who was in the area near Troia, to discuss how it could be taken. There he saw that Roger of Ariano and his seven hundred knights resisted a royal siege.

Soon it was announced to King Roger that Pope Innocent was at San Germano. The king immediately sent envoys to negotiate peace, promising to maintain the pontifical prerogatives. Having received these envoys with honour, the Pope sent them with two of his cardinals to Roger bearing a written peace treaty. If this pact were to the king's liking, he must go at once to meet the pontiff at San Germano to ratify it.[231]

Having reached a peace with the citizens of Troia, the king and his son the duke [Roger], along with his younger son [Alfonso], who had been named Prince of Capua, broke camp. With the entire army, they hastily set out for San Germano.

There Pope Innocent asked that Capua, which had been taken by force from Prince Robert, be restored to this man faithful to the Papacy. This Roger flatly refused to do, and for eight days king and pontiff debated the matter without reaching an agreement.

With this, both parties departed. The king marched into the County of Molise, where he took some lands belonging to the Borrello family.[232] The Pope went with his army to besiege Galluccio. Learning that one of his cities was under attack, the king went there in alacrity. News of Roger's arrival traveled quickly.

This king's sudden presence alarmed the pope, Prince

Robert of Capua, and the Roman troops. In view of the danger, the Papal army immediately struck camp and went to pitch their tents in a more secure place. Roger, the king's eldest son, surmised the direction they were taking. Leading nearly a thousand knights, he ambushed the Papal army.[233]

In the face of such an attack, and finding themselves trapped, the Papal knights turned and fled in various directions to places unknown. Some managed to escape, but others were captured. Prince Robert of Capua and Richard of Ravacanina saved themselves, along with some foot men. Many men, however, fell into the Garigliano River and died.

A large number of men were taken prisoner along with Pope Innocent, who had been following the main host without fear. On the tenth of July the pontiff and his chancellor, Haimeric, along with the other cardinals, were accommodated in a tent set up for them in the royal camp.

But what a terrible affront to their dignity it was to be prisoners! The Pope tried [unsuccessfully] to negotiate the cardinals' release, as if such a thing were even possible. Meanwhile, amidst what had been the Papal train, sacrilegious and excommunicated men pillaged precious, sacred objects. The souls of the faithful were filled with sadness to learn what had happened to the pontiff.

Now, though, those who had recently persecuted pacific men were the first to seek peace. Firm pacts were stipulated.

What more can be said? On the twenty-fifth of July, the king and his sons prostrated themselves at Innocent's feet, swearing to accept his authority and to keep their loyalty to him and his successors according to canon law. Further, they swore to uphold the very model of fealty.

With this, the Pope granted them absolution and benediction. He recognized Roger as King of Sicily and his sons as heirs to that kingdom as (respectively) Duke of Apulia and Prince of Capua.[234] Liturgy was celebrated as a sign of peace.

In this way sadness became joy and fear became safety, and all praised God.

The pontiff and the king then traveled together, secure in their peace, like father and son, to Benevento.[235] There prisoners were freed and compensated with gifts.

The Beneventans received both Innocent and Roger in happy spirits. The squares were cleaned, and the churches and monasteries were visited by the king.

The ordinations and other acts of the late Anacletus were annulled as if they had been the work of a heretic. Rosman, who had been ordained by Anacletus, and consecrated by him as Archbishop of Benevento, was deposed. Pope Innocent consecrated Gregory[236] in his stead.

Even the castle erected by Rosman was destroyed, down to its foundations. Rosman was expelled from the city and taken to Sicily by King Roger.[237]

The pope celebrated the Assumption of Mary, Mother of God, and then the feast of Saint Bartholomew.[238] He happily and peacefully left the city of Benevento on the second day of September[239] for Rome, where he was welcomed with the greatest honour by the Romans. They prevailed upon the pontiff to break the treaty he made with the king under duress, which was thereby illegal. This Innocent refused to do, explaining that, "Brothers, it has been established by the will of God that my imprisonment should lead to peace for His church. For that reason, I do not wish to break the peace accord through my own action. A merciful God saw fit to bestow this peace upon His people."

VI
REX VERO LICENTIA

Having obtained Innocent's blessing and granted to the Beneventans the freedom they desired, Roger set out for Troia. There he refused the citizens' invitation to enter until the cadaver of Ranulf, his erstwhile arch-enemy, was removed from the city. The people were frightened to hear such a severe request from so great a king.

Absolute Power

But what more can be said? The people chose to obey their earthly king rather than their heavenly King. They ordered a man named Gallican, who had been a friend of Ranulf, to break the tomb, where the corpse still emitted a foul odor. He tied the body to a rope and dragged it out of the cathedral to a place beyond the city walls that was muddy and swampy. Frightened and pained as he was, Gallican was coerced into doing this as if he were happy.

Duke Roger, the king's son, witnessed this, and found himself dissatisfied with the order his father had issued. He immediately reproved his father most courageously, obtaining permission to reinter the corpse in the church with the appropriate ceremony. The city's bishop[240] and clergy obeyed this command. The king still did not wish to enter the city.[241]

From Troia, King Roger went to besiege the city of Bari for two months.[242] So hungry and thirsty were the Bariots that they butchered horses for meat.

Advised of the disaster, the Pope sent a cardinal as an envoy to negotiate peace between the citizens and the king. The Bariots were too arrogant to listen to the cardinal.[243]

The king therefore erected thirty siege towers around the city. He demolished not only the outer walls but some houses within the city. This provoked a revolt among the citizenry not only for their hunger but for the destruction of their homes.

At this point the city's leader, Jaquinto, sent as emissaries to the king Roger of Sorrento and others.[244] They offered to surrender Bari if the city's nobles were freed and granted safe conduct. As part of the agreement, the king would return the Bariots he had taken as prisoners whilst the city would free the captives the Bariots had taken. King Roger accepted these terms.

With peace established by both sides, the city returned to the king's authority.[245] He then left Bari for Salerno.

At that city, Roger met with the local aldermen. Some enemies he punished [by confiscating their property]. Others he permitted exile if they swore never to return to the kingdom without permission. A few were hanged and a few mutilated. Roger of Ariano and his wife were sent as prisoners to Sicily. Having concluded these matters, and with his ships prepared, Roger returned to Palermo.[246]

The same year, a terribly powerful earthquake destroyed many houses in a wide area.[247]

During the month of March in 1140, the eleventh year of the pontificate of Innocent II, King Roger sent his son, Alfonso, Prince of Capua, into the province of Pescara to subjugate it with a large army. This led to the destruction of many fortified towns.[248] Some were destroyed by flame, then plundered with great effort.

After a few days, Alfonso's brother, Duke Roger reinforced him in Pescara with a thousand knights and a great number of foot men. The two princes subdued not only that province but certain lands bordering Papal territory.

Learning of this disturbing news, Pope Innocent met in council with the Romans and sent the two brothers a message borne by a cardinal. It said that the princes should refrain from invading the lands of others, and that they were not to appropriate Papal territory by force.

In their response to the pontiff they said, "We do not aspire to take the lands belonging to others. We merely wish to take back the lands belonging to the Principality of Capua, which is our right."[249]

All the provinces comprised a sole kingdom, delineated on most sides by the sea. In the east is the great sea beyond Sicily. In the south is the Tyrrhenian uniting the kingdom, Africa and Mauritania. In the north is the Adriatic between the kingdom, Greece, Slovenia and Hungary. To the west the frontier borders the province of Campania, the Duchy of Spoleto and the March of Ancona.

The king fortified this last [land] frontier so that nobody could enter against royal will. In fact, the same Kingdom of Sicily is bordered either by impassable rivers accessible only by bridges, or by mountains whose valleys are blocked by walls.

The coasts are protected by towers on rocky cliffs or overlooking beaches. In this way, ships transporting an army can be identified as soon as their flag is visible, permitting sentinels to ward of their location and number.[250]

In 1142, the thirteenth year of the pontificate of Innocent II, that Pope notified King Roger of Sicily that the sovereign lacked the prerogative to appoint the pastors of churches and that he must therefore cease his pretension to that authority.

The king replied in these terms: "Since the time of Duke Robert Guiscard, and in the time of Duke Roger [I] and Duke (sic) William until this moment that law has been our practice. In no way shall we renounce it. On the contrary, we shall firmly embrace it."[251]

In 1143, the fourteenth year of the pontificate of Innocent II, some citizens of Tripoli, on the African coast, promised to surrender that city to his sovereignty if he sent people to reside there. This the king confirmed by an oath.

Taking the envoys at their word, Roger sent three hundred knights with horses and provisions. George, who was leading the force, went to lay siege to three sides of the city.[252] In the event, he could not occupy it because the men who had promised to surrender the city behaved deceitfully and reneged on their promise.

In the same year, Pope Innocent, who was gravely ill, encouraged the cardinals to avoid another schism by electing his successor from among a list of five men whose names he advanced to be father of all the world. The pontiff asked them to consider this in view of how many people had been killed in the wake of dissension in the past. He immediately showed them forty thousand marks that he commanded be used to defend the faith. Having done this, he went to the Lord on the twenty-fourth of September. He had been Pope for thirteen years, seven months and eight days.

Succeeding him was Guy of Castello, with the name Celestine [II], whose pontificate was destined to last for five months and fifteen days.[253]

Apogee

King Roger wished to be confirmed in his sovereign rights, which had been recognized by Celestine's predecessor. This Roger undertook not by prevailing upon Papal will through bland requests, but forcibly, motivated by necessity. He would make use of any means, even using the Beneventans.

What else can be said? The king abolished those exemptions that he had conceded the Beneventans in the days of Anacletus and Innocent from taxes on services and transport which had been imposed ever since the advent of Norman rule. Moreover, the barons who held lands around the city occupied Beneventan territory.

These measures greatly harmed the Beneventans, who sent ambassadors to exhort the king to reinstate the tax exemptions they had formerly enjoyed by royal favour. In response, Roger sent his chancellor, Robert, to examine the charter of privileges claimed by the Beneventans.[254] Having read the charter, Robert kept it until he was able to copy it for the king's review. Then he left Benevento with the original charter without announcing his departure.

Being harassed and feeling tormented, the Beneventans were afraid to leave their city. Having left the city to go see the Pope, the archbishop was arrested along the way by Thomas of Fenucolo. However, the suffering that daily afflicted and tormented the Beneventans was eventually brought to the attention of the Pope.

In 1144, the first year of Celestine's pontificate, Cardinal Ottaviano and the Roman consul Cencio Frangipane were sent by the Pope to treat with King Roger II. In Palermo, before they could begin negotiations the king received a letter telling him of the time and day of the death of Pope Celestine, and that Cardinal Gerard[255] had succeeded him as Pope Lucius [II].

The king was delighted to learn of this. He summoned the ambassadors Cardinal Ottaviano and Consul Cencio to his presence and said, "Tell me why you have come here and what you wish to request." They replied by presenting their credentials and explaining their reason for coming to Palermo.

After listening attentively, the king told them that Pope Celestine had died on the eighth of March, and that he was succeeded by Gerard, formerly chancellor, who had taken the name Lucius.[256]

The ambassadors were sad and amazed at this news. The king then sent them back to Rome with a letter for Pope Lucius stating that he was very pleased to hear of his election and very much wished to meet with him.

This designated meeting took place in Ceprano[257] at the church of Saint Paternian on the fourth day of the following June [1144]. The king and his sons, the duke and prince, fell prostrate on the ground before the pontiff, kissing his feet. They were then permitted the kiss of peace on the face and professed themselves the Pope's servants. Following the celebration of the holy liturgy, the king presented to the Pope a coronet made of gold. His sons gave the pontiff a golden vase and two silken palliums beautifully embellished with gold thread.

Following the benediction and a banquet, there were talks about the necessity for peace. Lucius advanced Papal claims to the Principality of Capua. The king and his sons, in reply, stated their wish to keep these lands. The matter was discussed from noon to dusk without a peace treaty being negotiated. In fact, these discussions put further distance between the papal and royal parties.

What words can be added? For nearly a fortnight the royal army remained there, its ranks augmented by more troops arriving every day. In the end, both parties left in disagreement. Pope   Lucius went back to Rome and King Roger made his way to Sicily.

Following these developments, the king's sons laid siege to Veroli [a Papal town], destroying its vines and other crops. In their zeal they conquered some fortified towns in Campania.

The king returned with a fleet that transported an army. He besieged Terracina but could not subdue it. His sons, meanwhile, took Marsia, Amiterno and all the territory up to Rieti. Robert [of Selby], the king's chancellor, then razed Rieti by fire.

Roger, Duke of Apulia, and Alfonso, Prince of Capua, were both destined to die during the lifetime of their father, whose later years bore the sign of great agony.[258]

The king wed the sister of Count Hugh of Molise, who bore him a son named Simon who the sovereign made Prince of Capua.[259]

Wishing to use his resources to conquer the African kingdom and Tripoli, the king negotiated and concluded the truce proposed by Lucius that he had rejected while his sons were still alive. With this, he confirmed that he would not harass the Beneventans or infringe on Papal territory.

The king sent to Africa twenty thousand men with a hundred ships, capturing many lands whilst plundering some cities and fortresses. Roger's army conquered Tripoli and its islands.

Roger also captured some fortresses along the Balkan coast.[260]

VII
FLUIT SANGUIS PER QUEDAM LOCA

Whilst blood flows in some places, the waters off Gaeta are calm from dawn to dusk. In 1145, Pope Lucius [II] died. He was succeeded by Eugene [III], whose pontificate lasted eight years and four months.[261]

Men of Faith

Pope Eugene had been vicedominus[262] of the Pisan archdiocese and then a monk at the Cistercian abbey of Clairvaux. During the pontificate of Innocent II, he was sent by Bernard of Clairvaux to the church of Saint Anastasius the Martyr at Aquas Salvias near the city of Rome as the abbot of its new community. Living honestly and religiously as a cardinal, he was elected Pope. On that occasion, Bernard of Clairvaux wrote him a letter, titled *De Consideratione,* a treatise of extraordinary interest.[263]

In a profound examination, the work treats topics involving the Papacy and themes deriving from it, including its complexities. It concerns the nature of the divine, postulating that humility and piety form the path to a person's ascent into the splendor of heaven.

Eugene was educated with such doctrines. Following the Council of Rheims [of 1148] he visited Clairvaux humbly, showing its poor monks the true glory of the Papacy. All were amazed that his humility and virtue were so profound despite his being Pope.

The coarse woolen robe he wore was part of his being. Day and night he wore the scapular. Externally he was a pontiff but internally he was a monk. In itself, this was difficult, linking two opposing traits in one man.

He was accommodated on plush cushions of purple. His bed was covered by blankets and enclosed in a pavilion of purple silk, but if one removed the coverings he would find straw beneath woolen canvas. Man looks at superficial appearances, God looks into the heart.

He spoke to his brothers tearfully, exhorting and consoling them with his passionate discourse, expressing his heart with every breath as a brother and friend, not as a lord and master. Because his large retinue did not wish that he remain at the abbey too long, he took leave of his brother monks and set out for Italy, to a place near Rome where he died.[264]

In 1147 the Holy Roman Emperor Conrad[265] and the King of France Louis [VII] went to Jerusalem [on the Second Crusade]. In 1148, Africa was conquered by King Roger, whilst many Greek islands were attacked and plundered.[266]

In 1149 [as mentioned above], the city of Rieti was set afire by Robert [of Selby], chancellor of the King of Sicily.

In the year 1153 Pope Eugene [III] was succeeded by Anastasius [IV], whose pontificate lasted one year and three months.

On August twentieth of the same year Saint Bernard, Abbot of Clairvaux, died at the age of sixty-three during the reign of the illustrious Frederick[267] in the Holy Roman Empire whilst the King of the Franks was the most pious Louis [VII], the son of Louis [VI].

The great abbot wrote the following works: The Twelve Steps of Humility and Pride, The Annunciation and the Blessed Virgin's Consent, On Loving God, On Precept and Dispensation, In Praise of the New Knighthood, On Grace and Free Choice, Life of Saint Malachy of Armagh, Sermons on the Song of Songs.[268]

Long Live the King

In the year 1154, Roger [II], King of Sicily, Apulia and Terra di Lavoro died. He reigned for twenty-four years.[269] He was the first to unite the Duchy of Apulia and the Principality of Capua to the Kingdom of Sicily to constitute one realm, something which had never been done previously.

Although in past times he was ferocious, cruel and greedy in his conquests, he later became peaceful and kind, moral and just, bringing to his kingdom a tranquility so great that nobody in it dared raise his sword against another. As he neared the end of his life, Roger was quite devoted to the Roman Church, even sending to Rome timber beams from the forest at Castro Cerreto[270] for the church dedicated to Saint Paul the Apostle.

He was succeeded by his son, William [I], who reigned for twelve years.

In youth, William was so strong that he could bend a pair of horseshoes, one placed atop the other, with his bare hands. Once a horse loaded with baggage was trapped in a hole on a bridge. Others tried to pull the equine free but failed. Finally William pulled the horse free with his own strength, unassisted by the others. For this his father nicknamed him "Strong Arm."[271] In the struggle against the lands that resisted royal rule, he was the first among the knights to charge. He once flung a golden staff that was later found on the ground. He wore an unkempt black beard, and his ferocity and appearance made him hated and feared by many people.

Therefore, during the first year of his reign, Robert the former Prince of Capua and Robert of Loritello the king's kinsman, along with Ranulf's nephew, Andrew [of Rupecanina], and other exiles, raised an army with some Byzantines. They entered and captured Apulia and Terra di Lavoro.

But during the second year of his reign, King William undertook a campaign against the Byzantines. He destroyed the city of Bari, where he punished and hanged many citizens.

Robert of Capua tried to flee but was captured at the Garigliano River by Count Richard of Aquila. With many others, he was imprisoned on the king's orders. Robert was blinded with boiling oil.[272]

Permitted safe conduct out of the kingdom, some of the defeated men took refuge at Benevento. The king subsequently reached an accord[273] with the Pope confirming royal authority over the lands of the realm. With this, William formally exiled many great nobles from the kingdom for their disloyalty.

Whilst he lived in complete safety within the walls of his palace, this king placed many disloyal men in chains. He made Maio, a man from Bari, his amiratus.[274] This man deceived the king, who thought him the most loyal of all. Therefore, William believed nobody who spoke against Maio, nor did he bother to travel much around the kingdom. Not being loyal to the king, Maio began to plot his death, hoping to take the throne for himself.[275]

For this reason, he secretly tried to bring people to his side with promises of freedom [the return of exiles] or land. In that regard, some barons, having inferred his disloyalty, wanted to warn the king of it, but Maio prevented them from getting close to the sovereign.

A few barons made a strict pact to accuse Maio of his disloyalty openly. The king responded by saying that the traitors were those who sought to discredit such a trusted counsellor.

This led to the kingdom being disrupted, with some people

saying the king was dead, others saying he was a simpleton, and still others believing him to be gravely incurably ill.

A certain faction, in fact, united itself with the king's opponents. They called upon Robert of Loritello and the brave knight Count Andrew [of Rupecanina], along with other exiles and enemies, to return to the kingdom on the pretext of the king being dead. Returning in the fourth year of the king's reign, these men occupied a good part of Apulia and Terra di Lavoro.

In those times the Arabs came to occupy Africa[276] and the island of Tripoli because of the ineptitude of the amiratus. In truth, the king was preoccupied with leisure and the construction of a splendid palace in his gardens.[277] When asked by the king about the situation in Africa, Tripoli and Apulia, the amiratus, fearing that his lord would be irritated to learn the truth, replied, "All is well and peaceful."[278]

The king, being a candid and honest man, believed the words of the amiratus, whose deceit would be his undoing.

Returning from some baths, he was attacked and killed by Matthew [Bonello], his son-in-law, who was a kinsman of the king (sic).[279]

The king, with incredulity at the accusations made against his amiratus, took a public position against Matthew and all who implied that Maio of Bari was corrupt.

This led to open rebellion. Prisoners freed from the palace dungeon moved to assassinate the king. The palace was invaded by a mob of subjects once they heard the king was dead, even though the freed prisoners refuted this. Even so, the Palermitans crowned his young son, Roger [William being imprisoned].

After King William was released, along with Richard of Mandra, who later became a count and constable, and three others, he addressed the crowd from a window. An arrow loosed by somebody in the crowd hit and killed young Roger, who was standing at the window next to his father.

The rebels had completely plundered the royal treasure. While imprisoned, King William had promised safe conduct for the rebels if they released him. With these men he exiled his half-brother, Simon, and his nephew, Tancred [of Lecce].[280]

Learning that Matthew of Bonello [who fled Palermo] was at Taverna, the king gathered an army and burned the town.[281] Then he commanded that Matthew be blinded.[282]

The king then imposed a heavy tax [redemption money] on the towns that had given hospitality to those who planned and executed the revolt with Bonello.

Before these events, in September 1159, when Pope Adrian [IV] died at the end of a pontificate lasting four years and nine months, Roland [Bandinelli] was elected as Alexander III.

When Alexander considered renouncing this honour out of humility, a minority of cardinals exploited the occasion to elect the cardinal Octavian of Monticelli.[283] As the majority of cardinals did not wish to submit to the minority, Alexander acceded to accept, and was crowned Pope.

Octavian [Victor IV] did not wish to relinquish the pontificate, so he went to Liguria to enlist the support of Emperor Frederick [Barbarossa]. It is said that Frederick swore to honour Octavian so long as the [anti]Pope obeyed him. Receiving Victor with every honour, Frederick commanded his subjects to obey him as the Catholic Pope.

Some German prelates, favoring their heavenly king over their earthly one, abandoned their bishoprics, leaving the German lands and finding refuge with Pope Alexander. Understanding the problems with the emperor resulting from the controversy, the Pope went to France. Octavian returned to Rome accompanied by some of the cardinals who supported him.

In this way, both men claimed the apostolic dignity, but the greater number of prelates and monarchs supported Alexander.

A monastery was consecrated at Gualdo [by John of Tufara] on the twenty-fifth of July in 1161. The same year, a multitude of locusts invaded Apulia, covering and destroying fields and trees. It was not possible to kill so many insects with clubs and sticks in one day because just as many would appear the following day. This infestation occurred during two consecutive summers around Venafro and Isernia.

In 1162 King William imposed a burdensome tax throughout the kingdom. The following year, Emperor Frederick destroyed the city of Milan, which he had attempted to subdue for seven years.[284]

The antipope Victor IV [Octavian] died in 1164. The cardinals he created elected another antipope [Paschal III], who the more senior cardinals abandoned, passing to the side of Pope Alexander.

In 1165 Pope Alexander III visited Sicily. He then returned to Rome.[285]

William, King of Sicily, died on the fifteenth day of May in the year 1166.[286] He had reigned for twelve years. He was succeeded by his son, William [II], who revoked certain taxes in the kingdom and, after three years, permitted exiles to return.[287]

VIII

IMPERATOR FREDERICUS VOLENS CAPERE

In 1167 Emperor Frederick, wishing to take Pope Alexander prisoner, besieged Rome and damaged part of the Basilica of Saint Peter. The Pope and a few cardinals left the city secretly and went to Benevento. Having lost many knights and troops [to disease], he withdrew, leaving at Tusculum his chancellor Christian [Archbishop of Mainz] and his ally Rainald [Archbishop of Cologne].

Vicissitudes

The same year, Christian arrived with the exiled Count Andrew of Rupecanina, killing around seven thousand Romans at Tusculum, and taking many prisoners.[288]

In the year 1168, the Spaniard (sic) Stephen [of Perche] was appointed chancellor and master of the Kingdom of Sicily by the queen [Margaret], the mother of William [II] who was still a minor.[289] Using deceit, Stephen sought to usurp control of the kingdom. He wanted to kill the king and his younger brother.[290]

To achieve this, Stephen used deception to justify arresting Count Richard of Mandra and some chamberlains who wished to oppose him. Some imprisoned and others were blinded. Miraculously, Richard was freed, and thus spared such a fate. He killed the man who had wished to blind him, and returned to the palace to liberate the young king. He then expelled Stephen from the kingdom.[291]

In 1169, those who had been exiled returned after making peace with the king. In the same year (sic), Emperor Frederick lifted his siege of Rome.[292] The Lombard League, not tolerating German hegemony regarding rights and laws, united and courageously defended itself against the emperor, who wished to subject the region arbitrarily to his will.

To that end, some Lombards founded a city called Alessandria, known to others as the "City of the Pallium."[293] So well was it protected by rivers that the emperor dared not even think of attacking it. Indeed, this city, and all the cities of Lombardy, defeated the imperial forces in a series of battles. The emperor could obtain nothing from them even if, based on law, they were obligated to pay him taxes.

In March of the year 1170 Pope Alexander left Benevento for Veroli. During the same year Saint John of Tufara[294] died at Gualdo, and Count Richard of Mandra died.[295]

In 1174, King William [II] sent a fleet to Alexandria, where many men were captured by the Muslims.[296]

In 1176, Pope Alexander returned to Benevento. Near Cella the chancellor Christian [Archbishop of Mainz] of Emperor Frederick captured Richard of Sangro and many others of the Kingdom of Sicily.[297]

The following year, a peace treaty was concluded at Venice between the Pope, the Holy Roman Emperor Frederick I, and the Byzantine Emperor Manuel I Comnenus, and other Christian monarchs.[298] The King of Sicily wed the daughter of [Henry II] the King of England.[299]

In March of 1178 Pope Alexander returned to reside in Rome.

The next year, the pontiff held a general council in the Lateran, promulgating many canons.[300] There was a red moon on the nineteenth of August.

Pope Alexander III died [in 1182] following a pontificate lasting two days short of twenty-two years. During this time we saw the return of honour for the clergy, the defense of the weak, and the limitation of the power of the strong.

Whilst in France during the time of his troubles with Frederick I, Alexander met the exiled Thomas Becket, Archbishop of Canterbury.[301] Becket resisted the nastiness of the King of England [Henry II], who sought, inappropriately, to force the clergy, like all his other subjects, to submit to royal civil authority. Refusing to comply, Saint Thomas fled England and found refuge in the dominion of the French king [Louis VII], to whom the Pope commended him. The English king, despite frequent entreaties to the Pope, failed to convince the Archbishop of Canterbury to submit. Yet Henry feigned a truce. The saintly man paid the price of justice with his own martyrdom.

The year 1183 (sic) saw the death of Andronikos [I], the Byzantine Emperor, a cruel man related by blood to an earlier emperor.[302] Having marched on Constantinople with a Muslim army provided by [Kilij Arslan II] the Sultan of Konya, he killed [Maria "Porphyrogenita"] the firstborn daughter of Manuel Comnenus. He massacred many Latins and forced others into exile.[303]

But vengeance did not long nourish his reign. Because he practiced the art of divination, Andronikos understood from a spirit that he was destined to lose his realm through assassination to a man named Isaac.[304] Andronikos ordered his accomplices to kill Isaac, but Isaac prevailed, killing the men sent to murder him.

After blinding and killing Andronikos, Isaac had himself crowned. He was later blinded and deposed by his elder brother, Alexios.[305]

In 1184 (sic), William II of Sicily sent a fleet to attack the Byzantine Empire. There they captured Thessalonika and many other cities.[306]

On the twenty-third of November of that year, William, the Abbot of Fossanova and some monks visited Santa Maria della Ferraria.

In 1186 (sic), Pope Lucius [III] died.[307] He had been Pope for four years, two months and eighteen days. In the same year (sic), Jerusalem was captured by the Muslims led by Saladin.[308]

Transition

In 1188 (sic) Pope Urban [III] died.[309] His pontificate lasted a year. Pope Gregory VIII died in 1888 (sic). He was Pope for one year and eighteen days.[310]

King William II of Sicily died on the eighteenth day of November in 1189. He was pious, just, pacific, attractive and generous.

He peacefully ruled the Kingdom of Sicily, with Apulia and Terra di Lavoro. He protected the rights of all his subjects. He was loved by the church, to which he conceded freedom and made many donations. He took as his consort the daughter of the King of England. He betrothed Constance, his patrilineal aunt, to Henry, King of Germany, son of the Emperor Frederick [Barbarossa].[311]

This path was chosen because William, for the fact of his personal sins, died without heirs.[312]

William was at peace with most of the Christian princes. The lone exception was the Byzantine Emperor, who had betrothed his daughter [Maria "Porphyrogenita" Comnenus] to William but reneged on this promise.[313] For this reason, William launched campaigns against the Byzantines.

The peace and justice that dwelled in the kingdom during William's time was greater than what existed in the reigns before or after his.[314] King William reigned for twenty-four years.

IX

TANCREDUS PATRUUS EIUSDEM COMES LICIE

In 1190, on the eighth of December (sic), Tancred of Lecce was crowned in Palermo as King of Sicily.[315]

Empire

On the orders of Henry [VI] of Germany, the Archbishop of Mainz and Henry of Kalden marched into Italy with a large army but their first campaigns met with little success.[316]

Philip [II] of France and Richard [I] of England stopped in Messina for more than a month on their way to Jerusalem, receiving from King Tancred many gifts.[317]

In 1191 Pope Clement [III] died. His pontificate had lasted three years.

Richard of England and Philip of France took the city of Acre[318] from the Muslims. The island of Cyprus[319] was captured by the King of England and Ascalon[320] was taken.

In the same year, Henry, King of Germany, was crowned Holy Roman Emperor at Rome by Pope Celestine.[321] Then, against Papal will, he entered the Kingdom of Sicily, besieging Naples, attacking it with siege engines from the first of June until the fifth of September, when the city surrendered. But in view of a grave pestilence, he withdrew.[322]

In 1192, Count Berthold, who was sent by Emperor Henry, entered the kingdom.[323] He conquered the County of Molise and, with Margrave Conrad [Muscaincervello], devastated many lands.

The abbot William of Ferraria died on Saint Benedict's Day, succeeded by Nicholas.

In 1193, Tancred arrived and captured back all the lands that Henry had taken except for Rocca d'Arce.[324] The same year, Tancred's son, Roger, wed Irene [Angelina], daughter of Isaac [II], the Byzantine Emperor, who died on the first of March the same year, having reigned for four years (sic).[325]

Emperor Henry returned in 1194, entering the kingdom. He captured Salerno and destroyed it.[326] Then he burned the suburb of the town of Presenzano and occupied its castle. Following this, he went to Palermo, thus subduing the entire kingdom.[327]

In 1195, Henry and Constance celebrated Easter in Bari.[328] They ordered the city's walls destroyed. Henry then returned to Germany and Constance went to Palermo.

Returning in 1196, Henry ordered the destruction of the walls of Naples and other cities. He ordered Richard of Acerra hanged in the month of December.[329]

In 1197, the emperor subjected the entire kingdom to increased taxes. Many of those [barons] he mistreated and oppressed went into exile.

Henry ordered the burning of the head cantor of the church of Palermo. He commanded that a deacon be drowned in the sea with some nobles. It is said that, when the queen reproved him for this, the emperor angrily threatened her at sword-point and would have killed her were it not for the intervention of Markward [of Anweiler].[330]

Hearing of these incidents, the Sicilians, Latins and Greeks as well as Arabs, rebelled against the emperor. But when leaders of the army they gathered learned the queen was safe, the people were placated and submitted to the emperor.

The emperor betrothed Irene [Angelina], the widow of Roger, son of Tancred, to Philip, his brother.[331] Irene was living in the royal palace of Palermo when Henry arrived. Hearing of this marriage, the Byzantine Emperor rejoiced and recognized the event by sending ambassadors seeking friendship.

Thinking he might bring many lands under his control, Henry sent ambassadors to Saladin at Damascus to encourage him to leave Jerusalem, which he had recently captured.[332]

Henry sent ambassadors to the Byzantine Emperor in Constantinople and to al Mansur[333] in Ifriqiya.

But the brother of the Byzantine Emperor, learning of this friendship with the Latins, led an army of Greeks against Isaac. He blinded him and deposed him.[334] Then, shamefully, he expelled the German ambassadors the Holy Roman Emperor and King of Sicily, Henry, had sent to Constantinople.

Inheritance

Henry, Holy Roman Emperor, fell ill and died on the twenty-fifth day of August (sic).[335] He was entombed in Sicily in the city of Palermo.

He left the Kingdom of Sicily to Constance, his wife, establishing that young Frederick would succeed, to the Empire as well as the Kingdom, upon reaching the age of majority. That same year [1197] the empress fell ill.

Celestine [III] died on the eighth day of January, his pontificate lasting six years and eight months. Succeeding him was Innocent [III], who was elected the same day. He was crowned in the month of March. He was young in age but mature in his sensibilities and habits, highly literate and intelligent.

There was a lunar eclipse on the fifth of March[336] in the

beginning of the evening. The moon took on various colors and shapes, first black, then red, then becoming ever smaller until light became darkness.

Empress Constance died in Sicily in the month of November in 1198. She reigned for one year, having in April founded the monastery of Saint Fortunato.

In 1199, Markward, Margrave of Ancona, Molise and Romagna, imperial seneschal, aspiring to become regent, gathered a great number of knights. The previous year, he was outside the realm on a mission. Returning, he devastated and pillaged the lands around Cassino and many others before going to Sicily.[337]

Markward now committed acts even more vile than these on the pretext that the emperor had made him regent of the kingdom.[338] Opposing this, the Pope responded [following Constance's death] by claiming authority over the Kingdom of Sicily based on the will of the late Queen of Sicily, to whom, in any case, the realm appertained by hereditary right more so than to the late Henry.[339] In this conflict, the kingdom was at risk for massacres, famines, the sword (duels), pestilence and sundry hangings.

One night during the month of March in 1200, Count Dipold [of Acerra] attacked San Germano, which he plundered almost to the point of starvation.[340]

In the month of August, the abbot Robert left the abbey of Ferraria, succeeded by Thaddeus[341] as prior in January of the following year.

In the month of June of 1201, Walter [III] of Brienne, who had wed [Elvira] the daughter of the late King Tancred, came from Burgundy at the invitation of the Pope.[342] He had sworn to harbour no grievance against Frederick II, who in those times was a boy under the Pope's protection. Walter had nothing against the Latins [Normans] but he rather resented the Germans, who he chased out of the Kingdom of Sicily so far as he could. In fact, they did not wish to obey the Pope, to whom the regency belonged.

Upon entering the realm, he was victorious in his first battle, defeating Dipold near Capua.[343] Then, at a battle near Bari, he so weakened the German knights that they were reluctant to fight him.[344]

This encouraged the Latins of the realm to vehemently oppose the Germans. In this way Peter of Celano[345] obtained the County of Molise and burned the city of Venafro, where he had earlier been defeated by Dipold, who captured his eldest son [Bernard].

The Fourth Crusade

In 1202, a great number of Franks[346] and men from beyond the mountains who took up the cross together with the Count [Baldwin] of Flanders and the Doge [Henry Dandolo] of Venice, reached Constantinople, bringing with them [Alexios IV Angelus] the son of the Byzantine Emperor [Isaac II Angelus Comnenus] who had been disinherited by his uncle, Alexios [III].[347]

The crusaders and pilgrims were promised commensurate compensation and passage to Jerusalem, which had been occupied by the Muslims, if they first captured the city of Constantinople. In 1203, the Latins conquered Constantinople and restored it to Alexios, son of Isaac.[348]

The [Byzantine] Greeks did not wish to pay the passage costs promised by Alexios, who was made emperor. Alexios himself then refused to reimburse the costs the Latins had incurred.[349] With this, the Greeks deposed and imprisoned Alexios, replacing him with a certain Mourtzouphlos [Alexios Doukas], who the emperor released from prison.[350]

This man was elected prince of the city. Having contact with the Latins, he tried to bring them to his side to assist him, hoping to be enthroned. He promised to honour the accord [for payment] that had been stipulated by young Alexios. But the Latins, inferring that this man had shown disloyalty to his own lord and liberator, did not fall prey to his deception. Rather, they encouraged him to free Alexios. Mourtzouphlos, instead, went to the prison and killed Alexios by strangulation.[351]

Following the burial, Mourtzouphlos crowned himself and began a campaign against the Latins, Christ's own crusaders. Although they understood themselves to be in a difficult situation, the Latins, despite the setbacks caused by these machinations, took up the sword and began to defend themselves as if the Greeks were the enemies of Christ.

During the first attack they defeated Mourtzouphlos, confiscating the imperial banner and an icon of the Mother of God embellished with gold and gems.[352] Commissioned by Saint Helen, this sacred icon, consecrated with sacred relics, had been borne without dignity by one such as Mourtzouphlos.[353] Much other booty was also taken.

Even though Mourtzouphlos closed himself within the walled city, fortified with towers and catapults, the crusaders prevailed during a second attack.

A siege of three days on the imperial palace, called the *Blachernae,* gave the crusaders time to rest before a third assault. With this, they entered the palace, which the Greeks abandoned.

Here they found a great quantity of gold and silver, precious stones and royal robes. It was said that there was more wealth gathered in this place than in the entire Latin world.

Subsequently, Mourtzouphlos, who had tried to ascend the throne through treason and murder, was killed.[354]

God's vengeance was thus wreaked upon the Greeks, who, not wishing to submit themselves to the Prince of the Apostles and the Roman Empire, had separated from the unity of the

Catholic Church. They instead were abetted by the enemies of Jesus Christ, who offered them arms and other means to oppose the pilgrims who had taken up the cross in exalting the tradition of God.

Because, as the scriptures say, "every kingdom divided against itself will be ruined," the Greeks were so divided that, in the space of one year, four emperors were eliminated, unceremoniously deposed from the imperial dignity, with the exception of Alexios, the brother of Isaac, who fled.[355]

Later, Alexios [III Angelus] was captured, along with his wife and children, by [Boniface] the Marquis of Monferrat and taken to Italy (sic) as a prisoner.[356]

The Latins elected as their Emperor of Constantinople the very noble Baldwin, Count of Flanders. The ambassadors they sent to Pope Innocent III returned with the pontiff's permission to elect a patriarch. They thus elected a wise Venetian man[357] to be approved and consecrated by the same Supreme Pontiff.

In the year 1205 Pope Innocent III consecrated the bishops of Ostia and Tusculum and many others, among whom the patriarch chosen in March by the Latins at Constantinople. Alexios, the former Emperor of Constantinople, was taken as a prisoner in Lombardy.[358]

Walter, Count of Brienne, was taken prisoner by Count Dipold and died in captivity.[359]

In 1206, Walter Palear, chancellor of the Kingdom of Sicily, took young Frederick, who was twelve years old, from the power of the Germans.[360]

The abbot of Ferraria attended a chapter for the second time.

In February of the year 1207, Pope Innocent III removed his luxurious clothes, casting these aside along with his precious vestments, which is to say those of scarlet color, and palliums of Armenian gold. He renounced golden cups and goblets, and belts and bridles of gold and silver. He donned simple clothing, which is to say a white tunic of woven wool and a coat of lamb's fleece. He established precise stipends for notaries and for the scribes of the curia, and a legal limit to the fees that they could charge for their services.[361]

He established at Rome a universal nunnery where all nuns [regardless of their order] could meet but were obligated to stay. He ordered construction of a hospice for foreigners visiting Rome with the purpose of accommodating pilgrims, to whom he generously granted many gifts.

In July of the year 1208, Pope Innocent III held a meeting of the curia at San Germano near Cassino.[362] Here he made Count Peter of Celano, Count Richard of Aquila [Fondi] and many other counts and barons, and also rectors of cities, swear to respect in a scrupulous manner his mandate to keep peace in the Kingdom of Sicily and to help the cause of King Frederick, their lord, who was still in his minority. He appointed the aforesaid counts Peter and Richard[363] as justiciars of the kingdom for Apulia and Terra di Lavoro.

On the twenty-ninth of July of the same year there was a lunar eclipse.[364] Gradually the moon was obscured until, around midnight, nothing was visible. The stars were visible, but the moon became visible again just before dawn. Specifically, the upper and lower parts of the orb were visible, while the rest of it was invisible throughout the day.

In the same year [1208] Philip of Germany was assassinated.[365]

Construction of the chapter house was begun in the Lucida Valley.

Frederick

In September of the year 1209, Frederick, son of the late Emperor Henry, illustrious King of Sicily, wed [Constance] the daughter of the King of Aragon.[366]

In the same year, Otto [IV] of Brunswick, the King of Germany, was crowned Holy Roman Emperor[367] by Pope Innocent on the occasion of the dedication of Saint Michael Archangel.

The next month, at dusk, there appeared in the west a globe brighter than all the stars, which for almost half an hour traced a path towards the west with a long, luminous tail. Then, transforming itself into the form of a coil, was visible for another hour.

The same year, there were great earthquakes in many provinces. In the province of Valvina and Teatina large towers and edifices collapsed. In this year Count Peter of Celano betrothed his daughter, Stephanie, to the son of Count Dipold. In this way they formed an alliance, having been enemies.

In 1210, Peter and Dipold accompanied Otto [IV] into the Kingdom of Sicily. They reached Capua, where they remained from November until the following April. During the same year, Emperor Otto created Dipold Duke of Spoleto. To Peter he gave the March of Ancona.[368]

In 1211, Emperor Otto gathered an army of counts of the Kingdom of Sicily. He marched into Apulia as far as Bitonto, and then into Calabria, establishing order in the realm.

Once he was back in Germany, Otto learned that the princes there were beginning to rebel in view of his excommunication[369] and because he had invaded the Kingdom of Sicily contrary to his oath.

In 1212, when Otto had returned to Germany, King Frederick [II] arrived at Rome with three galleys.[370] There he was received with great honour by the Romans and by Pope Innocent. From Rome, Frederick traveled toward Germany through Genoa, Pavia, Cremona and Verona.[371]

The Pope promised to crown Frederick as King of Germany if the German princes consented to it. Having set aside Otto, Innocent was now willing to crown Frederick Holy Roman Emperor.[372]

With this, he excommunicated all of those who still supported Otto. This was followed by widespread sedition in the German lands. Whilst some supported Otto, others supported Frederick. Otto realized that his horns were unhoned and he had lost his ears, like the stupid donkey of fable.

Spanish Crusade

On the twenty-sixth (sic) day of July in 1212, before the feast of Saint Mary Major [5 August], the King of Castile [Alfonso VIII], the King of Navarre [Sancho VII], and the King of Aragon [Pedro II] led an army of Christian crusaders against Miramamolín [Muhammad al Nasir], King of the Moors, and other Muslims.[373]

In that year, this Muhammad al Nasir had sent arrogant letters to the Christian kings of Spain. With the help of Christ, they defeated and killed more than forty thousand Moors in a place in Spain called Navas. In truth, there were fewer than forty (sic) martyrs among the Christians.[374]

They reconquered the fortified town of Calatrava and a Cistercian monastic village that the Moors had occupied. The Christians, chasing the Muslims for some miles, reached their camp, where they found cases full of crossbows and arrows. According to some, it would have taken forty thousand mules to transport all these weapons. In the same place the Christians found lances, staffs and long arrows made of enough wood to feed fires to cook meals for the entire army for two days.

Forcing the Moors into retreat, the Christians took two

cities, Ubeda and Goliza, which they razed to the ground, killing all the Muslims present. They killed no fewer than they had killed in the previous battle.[375]

Albigensian Crusade

Arnald [Amalric], the Bishop of Narbonne, who the Pope had recruited from his place as Abbot of Cîteaux, led a Christian army to subdue the errors of the Cathars in Spain (sic). So persuasive was this sect that its proponents convinced the Count of Saint Gilles [Raymond VI of Toulouse] to renounce his strict faith.[376] They attacked Catholics.

Priests the Cathars found celebrating the sacred mysteries were mutilated, blinded and killed.

Learning of this, Nicholas of Aversa, the devout abbot of Fossanova, with the abbot Thaddeus of Ferraria, wished to record these facts. Whilst they were visiting the abbey at Cîteaux, the monks explained that some Cathars tore out the tongue of a prelate the heretics found in Provence chanting the mass with two priests. They blinded and castrated one of the priests, gravely wounding the other and leaving both to die.[377]

Another priest, whose tongue was removed when he was imprisoned for more than a year at Montpellier, whilst later listening to the gospel on the night of the Epiphany, could only grunt as he heard the words "When all the people were being baptized Jesus was baptized too" [Luke 3:21], unable to utter the verse as he wished. At that moment a great light like a ray of the sun appeared above him, and a thunderous voice from above roared, "You will have your tongue again, that you may praise the Lord!"

This priest is alive and well and can speak. He become a monk at the monastery of Saint Peter at Cluny. Those who saw him without a tongue, as well as others, showed the visitors that the man's tongue was indeed restored by God.

So, during the last three years, the bishop [Arnald] was sent to weed out the Cathar heretics whereas, until then, he was a Cistercian abbot in the Lord's service. With God's help, he was so successful in rooting out these Albigensian heretics that not one remains in the province of Albi.[378]

XI

ALIO ANNO REX FREDERICUS

In the course of 1213, the second year of his travels, King Frederick, being well-received by the Germans, besieged Emperor Otto at Brunswick.[379]

Wars and Crusades

In 1214, King Philip [II] of France and his son, Louis [VIII], fought a war against Otto of Brunswick and in Britain against King John of England. The English were defeated by the French.[380] It is said that eleven thousand men-at-arms were lost in that war.

In the same year, [Aldobrandino] the Marquis of Este took back the March of Ancona, of which Emperor Otto had deprived him, together with the County of Loreto.[381]

In 1215, Innocent III ordered the collection of a tax throughout Italy, in France and in Germany for the reconquest of Jerusalem.

During January of the same year, Father Thaddeus, Abbot of Ferraria, named Father Walter as the first abbot of the Church of the Holy Spirit at Gulfincori (sic).[382]

In March there was an eclipse of the moon.[383]

Thaddeus deposed Abbot Walter, who had fallen into the sin of simony. At a chapter at Cîteaux, he was authorized to replace Walter with a man named Baldo.

In July of the same year, on the feast of Saint James, Frederick was crowned at Aachen by the princes of Germany, where many others took a vow to go on crusade beyond the sea to reconquer Jerusalem.[384]

The same year, in the month of November, during the eighteenth year of the pontificate of Innocent III, the third year of the reign of Frederick in Germany and his eighteenth in Sicily, a general synod was convened at the Lateran in Rome.[385] It saw the participation of nine hundred bishops, four hundred archbishops, and two patriarchs, namely those of Jerusalem and Constantinople.

The Patriarch of Antioch, who was ill and therefore could not attend, sent his vicar. The Patriarch of Alexandria was represented by his brother. At this council and the meetings about the various disciplines following it were constituted many canons.[386]

Pope Innocent III died on the sixteenth day of July in the year 1216. He was interred at the city of Perugia in Tuscany.

It is said that at his tomb the blind, the insane, and those affected by other infirmities were cured with the help of God. He was Pope for eighteen years and five months. At Rome he ordered construction of a hospice for the poor in honour of the Holy Spirit. He pronounced great discourses. He subdued kings, kingdoms and empires. He fought and crushed arrogant heretics. He encouraged Catholics and forced out heretics. Sending forth an army of crusaders, he fought and forced to flight the king of the Moors who in Spain had risen against Christians and, with his people, blasphemed the name of Christ. He restored to obedience to Rome the Church of Constantinople and its empire, long separated by arrogance. Through the work of Cistercian abbots, he brought to Christianity the pagans of northern Europe.

In the same year, Cencio [Savelli], the cardinal-priest of the basilica of the martyred saints John and Paul, who had recently rebuilt the Casamari[387] church, was elected Pope with the name of Honorius [III] three days after the death of his predecessor.

In April 1217, Peter [II], Count of Courtenay, kinsman of Philip, King of France, was crowned Emperor of Constantinople by Pope Honorius at the monastery of Saint Lawrence outside the Walls in Rome.

Peter crossed the Adriatic accompanied by the Pope's envoy Cardinal John Colonna. With a great number of Franks, they were captured and imprisoned by the Byzantine Greeks through trickery. He was taken to a Greek prison, where he remained for longer than a year.[388] The cardinal, however, was set free in a year.

In the same year (sic) John, King of England, died. He left his son [Henry III] and his realm under the protection of the Roman Church. Consequently, Pope Honorius excommunicated Louis, the son of Philip, King of France, who had invaded England.[389] This ecclesiastical censure brought father and son [Philip and Louis] to peace with the young son of King John.

In the month of June (sic) in 1218, Otto, who was once Holy Roman Emperor, died near Brunswick.[390]

The same year, a great number of Romans, Italians and men from beyond the Alps departed on a crusade to Jerusalem.

In 1219 the city of Damietta, which is also called Memphis (sic), in Egypt, was liberated by the Christian crusaders following a siege of two years. This was achieved more through divine help than human effort.[391] It was conquered by the Christians, who entered at night, during November on the feast of Saint Leonard.[392]

There many thousands of Muslims were killed. No Chris-

163

tians were killed and only one was wounded. In the city was found a great quantity of gold and silver, and clothes of silk. Much grain was stored there.

Cardinal Pelagio [Galvani], the Papal legate, was the first to attack, leading his own army alongside the Templar grand master. John of Brienne, King of Jerusalem, was also present, along with the Knights Hospitallers and other crusaders.[393] In the same year, following the conquest of Damietta, the crusaders occupied the city of Tanis, where they killed many Muslims and erected a bishopric. Bishops and archbishops were also installed at Damietta.

In May of the year 1220, wishing to receive the imperial crown and to cross the sea to reconquer Jerusalem and defeat the Muslims, Frederick, King of Sicily and Germany, with the assent of most of the princes and dukes, crowned his son, Henry, as King of Germany.

In the same year, Abbot Thaddeus of Ferraria, on the orders of Pope Honorius, visited the monastery of Saint Mary at Monte Vergine.[394] There he deposed the abbot, the prior and the chief cellarer and all the officials. The only exceptions were the deacon, the sacristan and the hospitaller, who were faithful witnesses.

These measures were taken in the month of May of the eighth indiction. During the following month the same pontiff sent the same abbot, with the prior John and cellarer Simon of Ferraria, to the monastery of Saint John at Gualdo. There it was necessary to reform the regular observance, which had fallen into poor practice. During the same year [1220], the Pope sent to the abbot of Ferraria a letter expressed in the following tone.

"The honourable bishop, servant of the servants of God, sends greetings and an apostolic blessing to the worthy abbot of Ferraria of the Cistercian Order. The sons, prior and community of Saint Mary in the Lucida Valley, in the diocese of

Acerra, humbly ask us you and your successors to visit their monastery once every year to ensure that it models its charity according to the rule of the Cistercian Order. Sensitive to their request, we authorize you to do so, as visiting inspector, reforming and correcting deficiencies as you see fit. Do so in a fraternal spirit, in conformity to the manner that the community of Ferraria is administered. Given in the fourth year of our pontificate."

Power

In November of 1220, on the feast of Saint Cecelia on the Sunday of the Holy Trinity, Frederick, son of Emperor Henry and Empress Constance, being King of Sicily and King of Germany, was crowned Roman Emperor with his consort, Constance, by Pope Honorius.[395]

Frederick was acclaimed by a great crowd of archbishops, bishops, abbots, counts, barons and other nobles, Italian as well as German, in a glory greater than the Romans, Germans and magnates of the Kingdom of Sicily had ever seen on the occasion of the coronation of any other Roman Emperor.

Because it was considered right that this emperor should go to help the crusaders who conquered Damietta in Egypt, many dukes, counts and barons took up the cross.

Whilst in the city, Emperor Frederick issued laws regarding the freedom of churches, clergy, refugees and other classes.[396]

At Capua, he convened the famous conference at which he abolished the privileges that he and his father had conceded regarding the governance of the kingdom. He ordered that those feudal laws and obligations, and ecclesiastical rights, that had existed since the death of King William II be abrogated. This was very damaging to the church. He eliminated tithing for the laity and the half-tithing for the clergy, with the exception of the Knights Hospitaller, the Knights Templar, and estates belonging to the Cistercians.[397]

Then he sent a fleet against the Muslims at Alexandria and Damietta.[398]

On the thirty-first day of August in 1221 the Christians in Damietta relinquished that city and its environs to Saphadin [al Adil I], Sultan of Damascus, from whom that part of Egypt had been taken. Impeded and trapped by the overflowing waters of the Nile, the troops led by the Papal legate Cardinal Pelagio and King John of Jerusalem were tormented by hunger on their way to besiege the fortress of Cairo where they had decided to attack the Muslims.

But God opposed the Muslims, who brashly trusted in their own strength. In fact, Saphadin himself, though a Muslim, provided food and water to the same Christians he might have been expected to kill by the sword and with starvation. Instead, he escorted them to the Christian city of Acri, where he freed twenty thousand crusaders he had taken prisoner.

XII
DIE SABBATI TERTIO IDUS FEBRUARII

On Saturday, the eleventh day of February in 1223, Emperor Frederick, coming from Teano, visited the abbey of Ferraria on his way [to Ferentino] to meet Pope Honorius III.[399] Owing to the unsuitability of other lodging in the area, Frederick dined in the chapter house of the abbey with King John of Jerusalem, Archbishop Nicholas of Taranto and others of the court.[400]

Jews

The same year [1223], some pilgrims from beyond the Alps, passing through the area near Ferraria, stopped to visit the abbey. They recounted to the abbot and the brothers that in Armenia[401] they had met a certain Jew who had been present at the Passion of Christ.

The Jew, it was said, cried out as Jesus was being taken to be tortured, "Go, seducer, to get what you deserve!"

"I will go and you shall wait until my return," Jesus responded.

The Jew had lived for hundreds and hundreds of years, becoming old but never physically ageing beyond thirty years. He cannot die until the Lord returns.[402]

Muslims

In 1224, Emperor Frederick ordered that more than fifteen thousand Muslims be transferred to Apulia from the mountains of Sicily, where they had erected fortifications for three years that the king besieged for three years.

Hunger forced these Muslim men down from the mountains, along with women and children. The emperor forced these families to take up residence at Lucera in Apulia.[403]

Destiny

During the same time, Frederick, acting on the advice of the Papal curia, recruited serfs from the fiefs of Cistercian abbeys in Sicily, Apulia and Terra di Lavoro, where they worked as cowherds, shepherds and farmers, to construct castles and houses in the kingdom's cities lacking their own hospices.[404]

With this project in mind, Frederick imposed taxes upon the population generally, with the exception of clerics and knights lacking land and serfs.[405]

Furthermore, he decreed that nobody could sell victuals, even those he raised himself, outside the kingdom. For this reason, livestock and food found a good market that could not be obtained otherwise.

Only Caesar could buy at a good price and sell, to whom he wished, at a high price.[406] In the times of Frederick's adversary, Otto of Brunswick, the counts and barons rebelled against their sovereign, disowning him and expelling him from the kingdom, giving him six times the evil he deserved.

On the advice of Pope Honorius and the curia, Frederick wed [Yolanda] the only daughter of King John of Jerusalem, heiress of his kingdom.

Because Frederick did not wish that Acre and other cities

of the Kingdom of Jerusalem might fall into John's hands, the amity between the men became enmity. The two remained separate from each other even at meetings and banquets. John went to France, where he wed [Berengaria of León] the daughter of the King of Castile [Alfonso IX].

In March of the year 1228 (sic) Pope Honorius died in Rome.[407] He was entombed at the basilica of Saint Mary Major. His pontificate had lasted four months short of eleven years. He erected the abbey at Casamari at his own expense; he was a patron of the Cistercian Order, granting it many indulgences. He led Christendom in great peace. Through his great friendship with Frederick II he obtained freedom for all his churches and for the clergy.

For this reason, during his pontificate the clergy were not subjected to secular justice and many clerics no longer feared committing illicit acts and violence. One night, in the city of Isernia, some of them destroyed houses, mills and gardens, cutting vines and stealing livestock belonging to the monastery of Ferraria in that locality. Elsewhere in the kingdom incidents such as these and others occurred, in violation of every law.

Ugolino, the Bishop of Ostia, succeeded to the See of Rome as Gregory IX. He was an eloquent man of letters who showed an alert intellect. This Pope exhorted Frederick, repeatedly insisting that he cross the sea to reconquer Jerusalem, which the Muslims had taken from the Christians, occupying it for more than forty years. He placed at Frederick's disposition a multitude of crusaders.

Suffering a seriously illness, Frederick passed much of the next year in the kingdom while others, including many German princes led by Thomas, Count of Acerra, departed for the crusade.[408] Having crossed the sea, they waited uselessly for Frederick's arrival.

Some of these men, having achieved nothing, returned to Europe, muttering curses upon Frederick and Gregory. In fact, having become an object of derision for the Muslims, many deserted. These men affirmed that, having made a great effort for such an important enterprise, henceforth they would not even minimally consider advice and exhortations to participate in this kind of mission.

Learning of these facts, the Pope excommunicated Frederick for having failed to keep his word to embark on the crusade.[409] News of the excommunication was diffused throughout Christendom.

The emperor, for his part, made it known to his fellow sovereigns that it was only a serious illness that delayed his departure.[410]

In the next year, whilst preparing to depart, Frederick refused to set out on the crusade unless his excommunication was lifted. Nevertheless, he set sail [in June 1228] not with a great multitude of men-at-arms from throughout Europe but with a lesser number from his own kingdom. During his voyage, he captured the island of Cyprus and the principalities of Antioch and Armenia.[411]

EPILOGUE

By September of 1228 Frederick II was in Acre. At Jerusalem in February of the following year he concluded a ten-year peace with Kamil that would keep the city, if not the entire crusader kingdom, in Christian hands for a while.

The Templars and Hospitallers were irritated by this but the Teutonic Knights supported Frederick. In the end, the Sixth Crusade was a pacific one.

In March, Frederick was acclaimed King of Jerusalem. This ceremony was boycotted by Gerald of Lausanne, the city's Catholic patriarch, but the act itself was recognized by most of the people.[412] Frederick's wife, Yolanda, through whom he claimed Jerusalem, had died shortly after giving birth to a son, Conrad, in 1228. By any reasoning, this boy was the heir to the crown Frederick now claimed.[413]

In June 1229, Frederick returned to Italy to find his father-in-law, John of Brienne, ravaging his lands in southern Italy with the approval of Pope Gregory. It didn't take long for Frederick's army to restore order, and the next year he made a tenuous peace with Gregory.

In 1231, Frederick issued his Constitutions of Melfi, a remarkable legal code for the Kingdom of Sicily.[414] A few laws stand out.

Like England's Magna Carta, the Constitutions of Melfi made a speedy judgment the right of civil litigants and even criminal defendants. Juridical procedures are clearly established, while practices such as trial by combat (knights duelling to win a legal dispute) are essentially abolished. The idea that justiciars (district judges) could not hear cases in lands where they held feudal estates was a prescient idea, similar to modern statutes proscribing conflicts of interest which might require a judge's recusal from a case. Jews, but not Christians, could practice usury, though Judaic law formally discourages this. A man of the kingdom could divorce his wife if adultery were proven; the same practice among Muslims presumably already existed and may have been an influence here. The law on divorce, though clearly weighted in favor of the husband, was innovative for its era. In fact, divorce had existed, in one form or another, among Christians since the faith's earliest days. The sale of toxic foods and potions was outlawed, and the burning or disposal of certain toxic substances was prohibited; flax and hemp couldn't be soaked in water near towns and yew (which can emit toxins) could not be disposed of in rivers.

Theft, trade and even the comportment of physicians are considered at length. So is cattle rustling, coin shaving and the forgery of documents, for which the punishment is severe.

Extensive legislation is devoted to women's rights, and to those of children. The statute defining penalties for mothers who prostitute their daughters implies that this occurred, but there are equally severe penalties for rape, and violence against prostitutes.

In a precedent which paralleled developments elsewhere, daughters were allowed to succeed to feudal property and titles of nobility in the absence of male heirs, a practice which survived into the nineteenth century as the "Sicilian Succession."

A few laws seem less enlightened. Adultery itself is a crime, but a husband might not be punished if he kills his adulterous wife and her lover immediately upon catching them in the sexual act *in flagrante delicto*. A peasant who strikes a knight or noble might have the offending hand chopped off unless he can prove that he acted in self defense.

A curious section – to the modern mind – is the proscription on the use of paper for legal documents, with requirement of the use of parchment or vellum for this purpose. Parchment was, of course, more durable, less susceptible than paper to damage from moisture, folding or even ink. Frederick's kingdom was ahead of most of Europe in the use of paper, a Chinese invention introduced in the Aghlabids' Sicilian emirate during the ninth century.

Many challenges (and further excommunication) confronted Frederick during the next two decades. Endless trials and tribulations awaited him, especially in Germany and northern Italy. In the Italian communes raged a chronic conflict between the *Ghibellines* who supported the Holy Roman Emperor and the *Guelphs* who championed the cause of the Pope.

Fortune spared Frederick the defense of the Holy Roman Empire against a formidable Mongol-Tatar army, the emergent "Golden Horde," that made its way westward in 1241 after having sacked Kiev. In response to the invader's letter demanding homage, Frederick said that he might consider such a proposition, but only if he could be Batu Khan's falconer. Frederick's lengthy treatise on falconry and the care of birds was a scientific landmark and the lengthiest intellectual tome authored by a medieval European monarch.

A patron of the arts and sciences, Frederick encouraged the use of a vernacular language at court, fostering development of the Sicilian School of poetry expressed eloquently by Ciullo of Alcamo and others. He established a university at Naples.

At his death in Apulia of natural causes in 1250, Frederick was accorded the singular epithet *Stupor Mundi,* "Wonder of the World."[415]

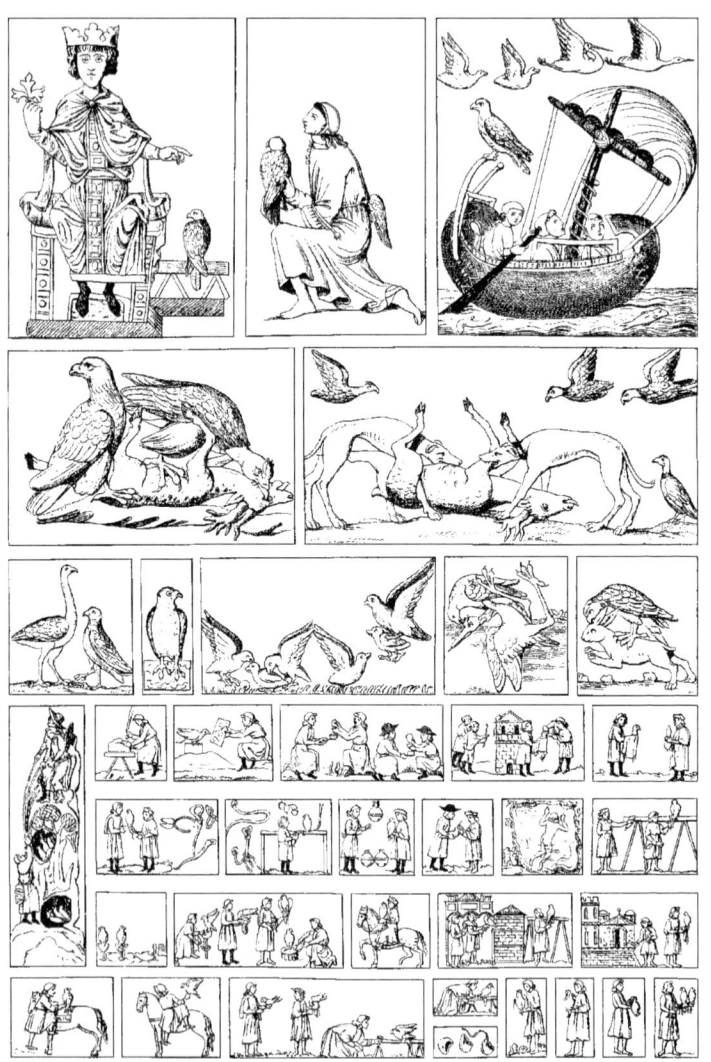

This engraving shows illuminations from the falconry treatise of Frederick II. The upper-left image appears on this book's cover.

GENEALOGICAL
TABLES

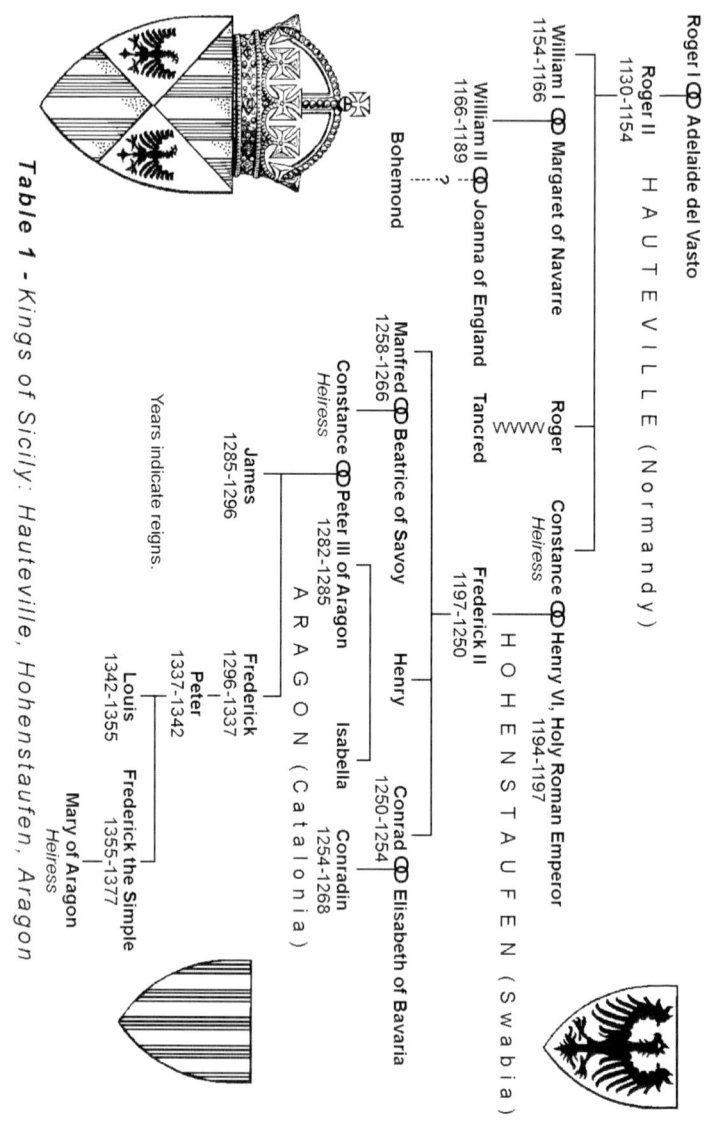

Table 1 - Kings of Sicily: Hauteville, Hohenstaufen, Aragon

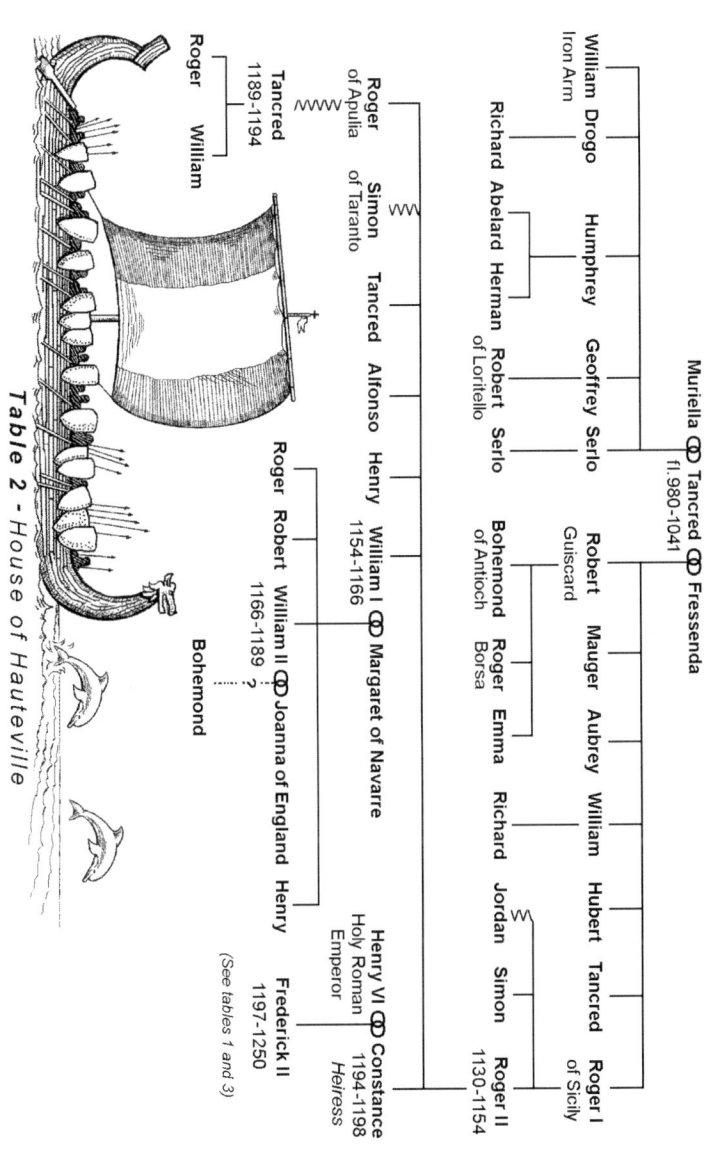

Table 2 - House of Hauteville

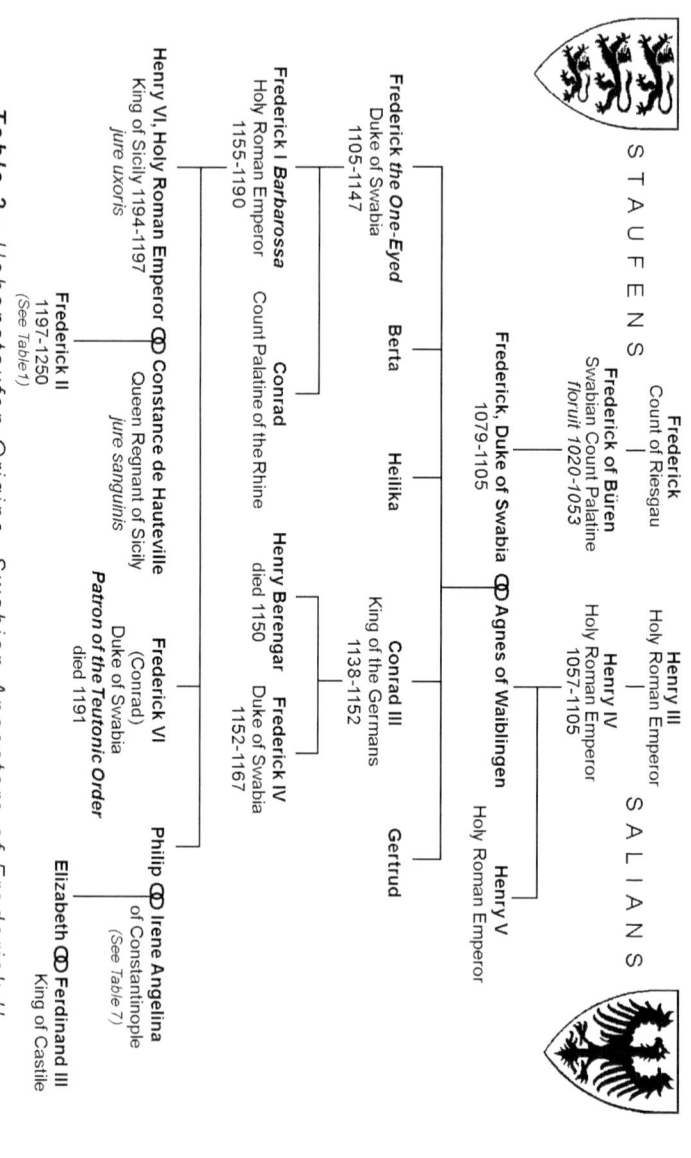

Table 3 - *Hohenstaufen Origins: Swabian Ancestors of Frederick II*

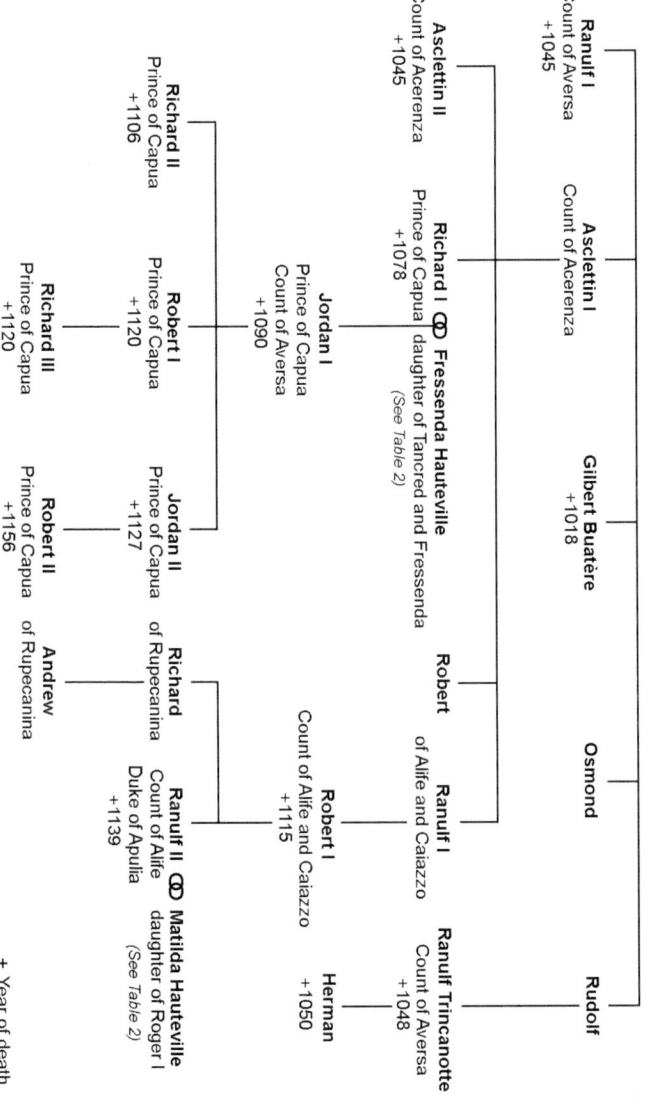

Table 4 - *Drengot Dynasty of Capua and Aversa*

+ Year of death

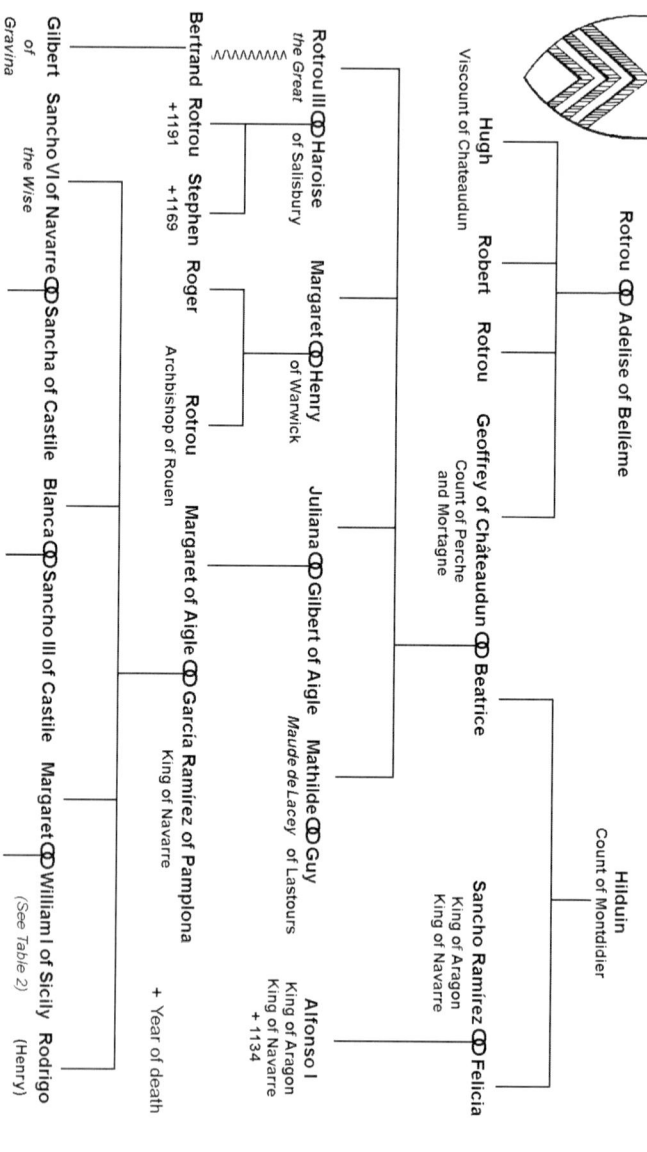

Table 5 - *Perche Family of Normandy and France*

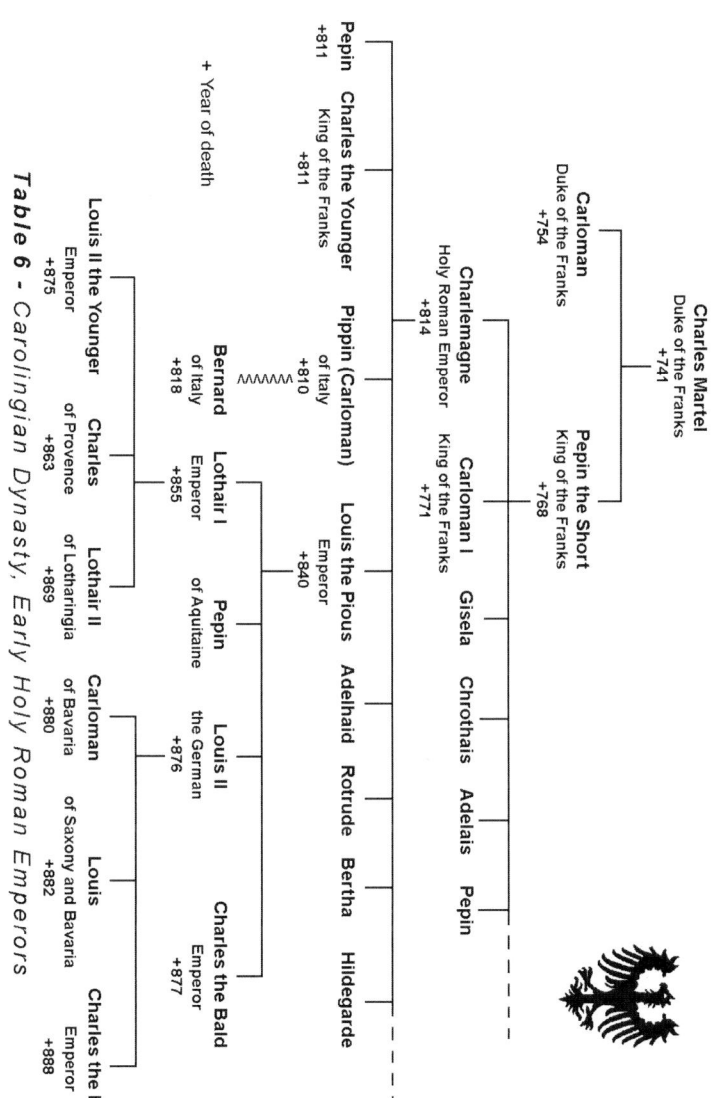

Table 6 - Carolingian Dynasty, Early Holy Roman Emperors

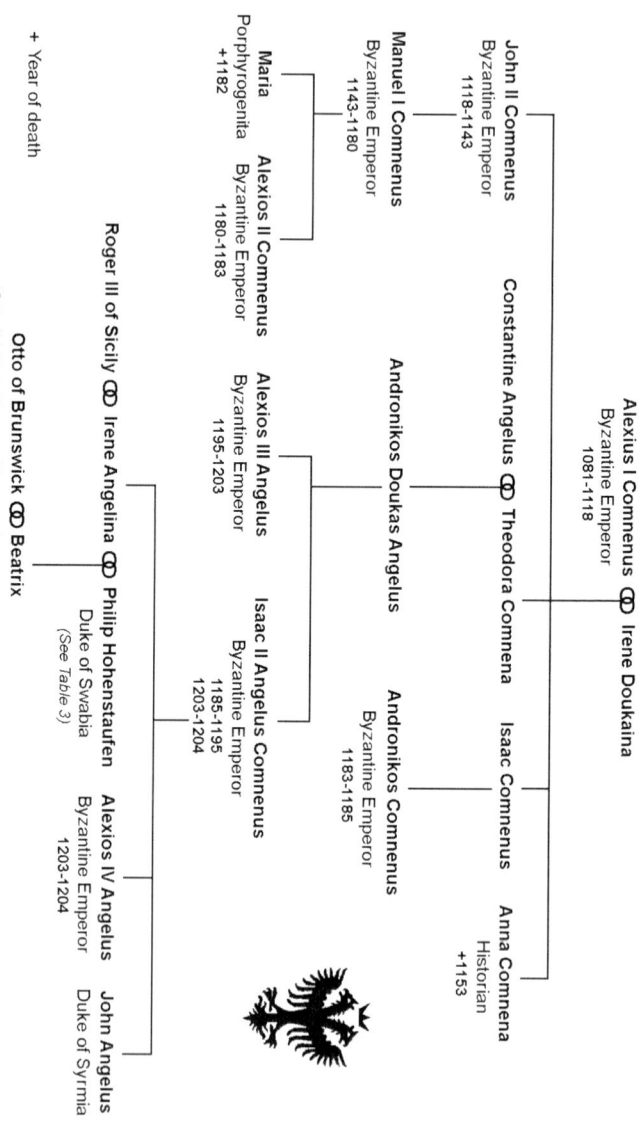

Table 7 - Commnenus Dynasty of Constantinople

+ Year of death

Alexius I Comnenus
Byzantine Emperor
1081-1118
⚭ Irene Doukaina

John II Comnenus
Byzantine Emperor
1118-1143

Constantine Angelus ⚭ Theodora Comnena

Isaac Comnenus

Anna Comnena
Historian
+1153

Manuel I Comnenus
Byzantine Emperor
1143-1180

Andronikos Doukas Angelus

Andronikos Comnenus
Byzantine Emperor
1183-1185

Maria
Porphyrogenita
+1182

Alexios II Comnenus
Byzantine Emperor
1180-1183

Alexios III Angelus
Byzantine Emperor
1195-1203

Isaac II Angelus Comnenus
Byzantine Emperor
1185-1195
1203-1204

Roger III of Sicily ⚭ Irene Angelina ⚭ Philip Hohenstaufen
Duke of Swabia
(See Table 3)

Alexios IV Angelus
Byzantine Emperor
1203-1204

John Angelus
Duke of Syrmia

Otto of Brunswick ⚭ Beatrix
(Otto IV, Holy Roman Emperor)

APPENDIX 1

Personages

These notes are intended as very concise introductions to some key figures. Except for a few persons of an earlier time (like Charlemagne) who are mentioned in the chronicle, they lived after 1050. Minor figures not profiled here are described in the end notes, for example Henry of Kalden in notes 316 and 365. Chroniclers are mentioned in Appendix 4. These listings are alphabetical but based on traditional English nomenclature for Arabic names such as Saladin, Jubayr, Idrisi and Kamil. Note *Yolanda* for Isabella of Jerusalem and *Isabella* for Elizabeth of England (consorts of Frederick II).

Adelaide del Vasto. In widowhood, the third wife of Roger I acted as regent of Sicily and some peninsular Italian lands until her son, the future Roger II, reached the age of majority. Her unique regency is largely ignored by historians, but Adelaide managed to unite a multiethnic, multi-faith dominion. In 1112, she entered into an ill-fated marriage to King Baldwin I of Jerusalem.

Alexander III. Roland Bandinelli of Siena succeeded Adrian IV, the Englishman Nicholas Breakspear, in 1159. Lasting until

1181, his pontificate extended through much of the reigns of King William I and his son King William II, with good relations reflected in the Treaty of Benevento concluded with the Kingdom of Sicily in 1156. Alexander took what, in retrospect, was a moderate stand regarding the rights of the church in England and Thomas Becket. He recognized Portugal as a kingdom.

Anacletus II. The pontificate of Peter Pierleone (Pierleoni), a Roman nobleman, began in 1130, when he was elected by a majority of cardinals on the same day Pope Innocent II was nominated by eight electors chosen by the dying Honorius II. This provoked a Papal schism, with Innocent supported by Bernard of Clairvaux and others outside Italy. In Italy, the cause of Anacletus was championed by Roger II, who he recognized as the first King of Sicily. Following his death in 1138, Anacletus II came to be regarded as an antipope.

Anna (Constance) Hohenstaufen. Born *Constance* in 1230, this daughter of Frederick II and Bianca Lancia was the sister of Manfred and, from 1244, the wife of John III, Emperor of Nicaea, who was a pretender to the Byzantine throne. Her marriage was part of a dynastic alliance; the Emperors of Nicaea reigned over an exiled court, Constantinople being occupied by "Franks" from 1204 until 1261.

Benjamin ben Jonah of Tudela. This Navarrese rabbi and merchant visited the Sicilian court, probably in the summer of 1171 near the end of the regency of Queen Margaret. His diary lends us an insightful account of his travels in the eastern Mediterranean. Benjamin recorded much about the Jewish communities he encountered.

Bernard of Clairvaux. Though known as the first great reformer of the Cistercian Order, this French abbot was involved in a number of important political events during the twelfth century. Instrumental in ending a wicked Papal schism, Bernard attended the Second Lateran Council and advocated the Second Crusade. His writings are many. He died in 1153.

Bianca Lancia of Agliano. Born into a feudal family in Piedmont after 1200, Bianca (sometimes Beatrice) became Frederick's mistress and later his wife, and for some time seems to have lived in eastern Sicily. The chronicler Salimbene di Adam reports that Frederick II wed her soon before she died, but historians debate her year of death (though generally favoring 1242-1244). After the death of Frederick's wife Isabella of England in 1241, Bianca lived with her children in the castle at Mount Sant'Angelo, traditional residence and dower of the Queen Consorts of Sicily.

Charlemagne. Charles "the Great," the eldest son of Pepin the Short, King of the Franks, enlarged his dominions to include what are now Germany, France, Austria, Switzerland, the Netherlands and Belgium, along with the northern third of Italy and a piece of northeastern Spain. By the time he died in 812, he had been crowned Holy Roman Emperor and united much of western Europe for the first time since the fall of the first Roman Empire. The state he guaranteed the popes in central Italy existed until 1870. Not for nothing has Charlemagne been called the "Father of Europe."

Conrad I of Sicily. Also known as *Conrad IV of Germany,* he was born in Andria (in Apulia) in 1228 to Frederick II and his consort Yolanda (Isabella) of Brienne, who died soon thereafter. He wed Elisabeth Wittelsbach of Bavaria, who in 1252 gave birth to a son, also Conrad (Conradin), who he never saw. Conrad I died of illness (probably malaria) at Lavello in May

1254. Though recognized as King of Sicily and King of Germany, he was never crowned Holy Roman Emperor and he was King of Jerusalem only as pretender.

Conradin. "Conrad the Younger" was *Conrad II of Sicily,* the son of Conrad I (see above) and Elisabeth Wittelsbach of Bavaria. Conradin succeeded his father in 1254 as King of Sicily, Duke of Swabia and (by pretension) King of Jerusalem. Raised in Germany, he was never King of Germany ("King of the Romans") or Holy Roman Emperor. He was executed in 1268 following his defeat at the Battle of Tagliacozzo. This was the end of the Hohenstaufen dynasty.

Constance of Aragon. This was the first wife of Frederick II. By then she was already the widow of King Emerich of Hungary, by whom she bore a child who died very young. Constance herself died in 1222. Henry, her son by Frederick II, was born in 1211 and died in 1242.

Constance of Hauteville. This posthumous daughter of Roger II became queen regnant in 1194, the same year she gave birth to a son and heir, Frederick II, by the Holy Roman Emperor Henry VI. She was crowned the following year but died in 1198. Constance was the last monarch of her dynasty to rule the Kingdom of Sicily.

Dipold von Schweinspünt. This Bavarian baron, sometimes *Dietpold,* went to southern Italy with the first expedition of Henry VI. He immediately became infamous for his raids on feudal and monastic estates. Following Henry's death, Dipold supported the ambitions of Markward of Anweiler, and then Otto of Brunswick.

Elisabeth Wittelsbach of Bavaria. Born around 1227, Elisabeth, the eldest daughter of Otto II Wittelsbach, wed Conrad (see above), a son of Frederick II, in 1246. In 1252, she bore him a son and heir, Conradin. Five years after Conrad's death, the widowed Elisabeth married Count Meinhard II of Gorizia, who held extensive lands in Tyrol, by whom she bore six children. Through her mother, Elisabeth was descended from the Hohenstaufens.

Francis Bernardone of Assisi. Although he is not mentioned explicitly in the *Ferraris Chronicle,* Francis was present with the crusaders at Damietta during the ill-fated Fifth Crusade, when he famously met Sultan al Kamil. Their conversations, about which little is known, have been much romanticized. Francis, who died in 1226 and was canonized two years later, was survived by his Order of Friars Minor (Franciscans). He is the patron of animals and environmentalists (ecologists).

Frederick I. The Hohenstaufen monarch known as "Barbarossa" (for his red beard) was crowned Holy Roman Emperor in 1155 and he is a central figure in the second half of Europe's eventful twelfth century. Although, by the end of his reign, he managed to enlarge his empire and force the northern Italian communes to submit to his authority, his attempts to invade the Kingdom of Sicily failed. His relationship with Rome was complex, often stormy. Frederick I died in 1190 on his way to the Third Crusade while crossing the Saleph River.

Frederick II. Holy Roman Emperor, King of Germany, King of Sicily, King of Jerusalem. Reigning until death in 1250, Frederick Roger Hohenstaufen was one of the most remarkable monarchs of the thirteenth century, so noted for his intellect that he was nicknamed *Stupor Mundi,* "wonder of the world."

Frederick Hohenstaufen of Antioch. This son of Frederick II was born outside marriage around 1223, later acting as Imperial Vicar in the March of Ancona and then much of Tuscany from around 1244 until his father's death. His mother was a certain Matilda "d'Antioco" from southern Italy. Frederick of Antioch proved himself an able administrator and military commander. He died in 1256.

George of Antioch. To the Arabs and Greeks he was (respectively) *emir of emirs* and *archon of archons,* and the most trusted official at the court of Roger II. He captured parts of what are now Tunisia and Libya. George, who predeceased Roger, is depicted in a mosaic in the Martorana, a church he founded in Palermo.

Gregory IX. Zealous Ugolino di Conti di Segni, a cousin of Pope Innocent III, became Pope in 1227, succeeding Honorius III. Gregory supported the suppression of the Jews in central and western Europe and the military campaigns (the Baltic Crusades) against the Orthodox Christians in Poland and Lithuania. He was a sworn enemy of Frederick II, who he excommunicated and whose lands in Italy he tried to invade. He died in 1241.

Guaimar III. Succeeding his father, John II, this Lombard was Prince of Salerno from the last decade of the tenth century until his death in 1027, and the first to have contact with the Normans if there is any truth to the story of these visitors expelling the Arab pirates around 999. He brought Gaeta, Sorrento and Amalfi under his influence, also annexing parts of Calabria and Apulia to his dominion.

Mohammed ibn Hawqal. Raised in Baghdad, though he may

have been born elsewhere, this traveling merchant described Sicily as it existed in 972 (361 AH). He died a few years later.

Henry "the Younger" Hohenstaufen. Born in 1238, this son of Frederick II and Isabella of England (see below) was called "the Younger" because his elder half-brother, also Henry, firstborn son of Frederick II by Constance of Aragon (see above), had died in 1242. Henry the Younger, who was briefly the governor of Sicily, died in 1254.

Henry VI. Son of Frederick I "Barbarossa" Hohenstaufen of Swabia, Henry became King of Germany in 1190 and Holy Roman Emperor the next year. By right of his wife, Constance Hauteville (see above), he became King of Sicily in 1194. He died in 1197, succeeded by his young son, Frederick II.

Honorius III. Succeeding Innocent IV, Cencio Savelli was elected to the See of Peter in 1216. The Franciscan and Dominican orders were approved during his pontificate. He died in 1227.

Abdullah al Idrisi (Edrisi). Born into a distinguished mercantile family with ties to Morocco, the court geographer of Roger II left us the *Book of Roger,* a fine description of the topography and agriculture of Sicily. His long-lost silver planisphere depicted a spherical earth. He mentioned the making of spaghetti at Trabia east of Palermo.

Innocent II. Gregory Papareschi, a diplomat, became Pope in a controversial election in 1130 (see Anacletus II) which found him exiled from Rome for part of his pontificate. Nevertheless, he convened the Second Lateran Council. The Papal schism ended with the death of Anacletus, now considered an antipope, in 1138. Innocent died five years later.

Innocent III. Born around 1161, Lothar di Conti di Segni became Pope in 1198. Young Frederick II was placed under his protection, and Innocent brokered his marriage to Constance of Aragon. Innocent III claimed supremacy over all European monarchs, making frequent use of interdict and excommunication. He incited the infamous Fourth Crusade which led to the sack of Constantinople and establishment of the "Latin Empire." Innocent advocated the ruthless suppression of the Albigensians (Cathars). He died in 1216.

Innocent IV. Sinibaldo Fieschi, a Ligurian, was elected Pope in 1243. Although his father was a count in a mercantile family of Genoa, Sinibaldo detested compromise. Innocent is often credited with inventing the European concept of legal incorporation in the *persona ficta*, but he also introduced the torture of "heretics" as a formal practice with the bull *Ad Extirpanda*. He died at Naples in 1254.

Irene "Angelina" Comnenus. The daughter of Isaac II Angelus Comnenus of Constantinople, Byzantine Emperor, wed Roger, the eldest son of King Tancred, as part of a peace agreement in 1193. Unfortunately, Roger died later that year and Tancred died early in 1194. After Henry VI and his consort, Constance Hauteville, were crowned as Sicilian sovereigns, Irene was betrothed to Henry's brother, Philip of Swabia, who became King of Germany in 1198. She died a widow a decade later, having given birth to six children.

Isabella of England. "Elizabeth," daughter of King John of England, married Frederick II in 1235 in a political union advocated by Pope Gregory IX. Born in Gloucester in 1214, she bore at least four children before her untimely death at Foggia in 1241. Among them was Henry "the Younger" (see above) who died in 1254. Isabella was the sister of Henry III of England. She is buried at Andria Cathedral.

Joanna (Joan) of England. This daughter of Henry II "Plantagenet" of England and Eleanor of Aquitaine wed King William II in Palermo in 1177. As a widow, she went on the Third Crusade with her brother, Richard Lionheart, in 1191. In Palestine, Richard tried to marry her off to Saladin's brother as a peace offering. Returning to Europe, Joanna wed Raymond VI of Toulouse as his third wife. She died following childbirth in 1199.

John of Brienne. This King of Jerusalem betrothed his daughter, Yolanda (see below), to Frederick II, who claimed that kingdom through her. Following the failed Fifth Crusade, and with Jerusalem in Muslim hands, he went to Italy to seek help from the Pope. John infamously seized some of Frederick's Apulian lands whilst the latter was away on the Sixth Crusade. In 1229 he became the (Latin) Emperor of Constantinople, dying in that city in 1237.

John of Procida. Born in Salerno around 1210, this brilliant physician served as chancellor to Frederick II and as young Manfred's tutor. He later enjoyed a distinguished diplomatic career under the Aragonese, though by his death in 1298 he reputedly entertained Angevin sympathies.

Abu Hussain Mohammed bin Jubayr. Born in Valencia around 1145, this traveler became high secretary of the Emir of Granada before embarking on a voyage eastward across the Mediterranean to Mecca. Returning to Spain in 1184, he visited Sicily. Jubayr died in Egypt in 1217.

al Kamil. This Ayyubid sultan was the son of Saladin's

brother, Saphadin (see below). He ruled much of Egypt and other areas, including Damietta, which was occupied by Europeans during the Fifth Crusade. He negotiated a peace with Frederick II during the Sixth Crusade which placed Jerusalem under Christian administration for a time. He died in 1238.

Lothair III. Lothair of Supplinburg (also known as Lothair II) was elected King of the Germans in 1125. He was Holy Roman Emperor from 1133 until his death in 1137. Lothair's imperial reign was challenged by the Hohenstaufens.

Louis IX of France. Canonized in 1297, the ever-crusading Louis of France reigned from 1226 until his death during the Tunisian Crusade in 1270. Preserved in an urn at Monreale Abbey, outside Palermo, his heart is the chief bodily relic of him that survives (except for a finger his corpse at Saint-Denis was removed by revolutionaries in 1793).

Maio of Bari. As *amiratus,* this royal counsellor was the highest court officer, effectively the head of day-to-day government, until his death in late 1160, when his assassination by Matthew Bonello set off a bloody revolt. He founded the church of San Cataldo in Palermo, probably as the chapel of his residence nearby.

Manfred Hohenstaufen. Son of Frederick II and his mistress Bianca Lancia, Manfred, born at Venosa in 1232, was Conradin's regent and was crowned in Palermo in 1258 based on widespread but unfounded rumors of the young monarch's death. He ruled the Kingdom of Sicily until 1266, when he was killed at the Battle of Benevento.

Margaret Hohenstaufen. Born in 1230, King Manfred's sister was married to Thomas II of Aquino, Count of Acerra.

She should not be confused with her namesake Margaret, her half-sister born in 1241, who was Frederick's daughter by Isabella of England and who wed Albert of Thuringia.

Margaret of Navarre. Born in northern Spain in 1135, she wed William I, future King of Sicily, in 1149. Upon his death, she became the regent for their son, William II. Ruling in the young monarch's name, she was the most powerful woman in Europe and the Mediterranean for five years.

Markward of Anweiler. As a *ministerialis,* Markward was only a minor baron. He rose to serve as the seneschal of Henry VI and briefly the *de facto* regent of the Kingdom of Sicily during the minority of Frederick II. Markward died in 1202 after having created much unrest in the peninsular part of the kingdom.

Matthew of Aiello. This notary became a royal counsellor, and eventually vice chancellor, during the reign of William II, who he outlived. With Archbishop Walter, Matthew supported the election of Tancred (over Constance) as sovereign. He founded Palermo's Magione church where King Tancred was entombed.

Matthew Bonello. This troublesome baron, who held Caccamo and other lands, is infamous in history as one of the chief leaders of a revolt against William I. It is perhaps ironic that such a traitor is commemorated by the name of a street next to Palermo's cathedral.

Melus of Bari. Supported by Guaimar III (see above), this Lombard rebel, who seems to have been born in Bari, took control of that Byzantine city, which he then lost. In 1016 he recruited some Norman mercenaries to challenge the Byzantines, only to be defeated by a force sent from Constantinople that included the Varangian Guard.

Michael Scot. This gifted scholar from southern Scotland or northern England was a mathematician, science advisor and astrologer at the court of Frederick II. Several of his works survive. He died around 1232.

Nilos Doxopatrios. Whilst in Sicily at the court of Roger II, this cleric who once served the Patriarch of Constantinople wrote a treatise around 1143 defending the theological and ecclesiastical position of the Orthodox Church in the wake of the Great Schism of 1054. He worshipped at the Martorana church.

Otto of Brunswick. Crowned Holy Roman Emperor in 1209 as Otto IV, this prince of the Welf dynasty was the son of Henry the Lion, Duke of Bavaria, and Matilda (sometimes Maud), a daughter of Henry II of England and Eleanor of Aquitaine, and therefore a nephew of King John of England. His power waned as Frederick II brought Germany under his influence. Otto died in 1218.

Ranulf of Alife. This member of the Drengot dynasty (see Table 4) was a cousin of Robert of Capua, who he supported against Roger II. Ranulf II was count of Alife, Caiazzo and other towns, and briefly (if illegally) Duke of Apulia. He was married to Matilda, daughter of Roger I and sister of Roger II. Ranulf died in 1139.

Richard Palmer. Hailing from England, Richard was a bishop, first of Syracuse and then Messina. He was also a royal counsellor and sometime diplomat. He died shortly after 1190.

Robert "Guiscard" Hauteville. This elder brother of Roger I obtained most of the Lombard lands in southern peninsular Italy by conquest and a few through marriage to Sichelgaita, the daughter of Guaimar IV of Salerno (and sister of Gisulf II). He led the conquest of Sicily, finally brought Bari under Norman control, and occupied parts of the Byzantine Empire. In 1084 he forced the retreat from Rome of Henry IV, the Holy Roman Emperor, a feat that served as a signal of Norman strength to the whole of Europe. Robert Guiscard (whose nickname means "crafty") died in 1085.

Robert of Capua. The House of Drengot (see Table 4) was a rival to the Hautevilles in the northwestern region of the peninsular part of the kingdom of Sicily. Robert II of Capua, who died dispossessed of his lands in 1156, was the last of his dynasty to rule with anything like sovereign authority.

Robert of Selby. Mentioned in the chronicle because he set fire to the town of Rieti, this Englishman was probably from the town in Yorkshire whose name he bore. He was a friend of Thomas Brun (see below). Robert became the chancellor of King Roger II in 1131. As governor of Campania, he surrendered Salerno to Robert of Capua in 1137, but he marched on Benevento in 1143. Robert of Selby died in 1152.

Roger I. Arriving in Sicily with his brother, Robert "Guiscard" of Hauteville, in 1061, Roger became the island's ruler as its "great count," retaining many Arab and Byzantine institutions whilst introducing Norman feudalism. He died in 1101, succeeded by his young sons, Simon and then Roger II.

Roger II. The son of Roger I succeeded his father (and elder brother) and was crowned King of Sicily in 1130. Recognized as one of the greatest, most enlightened leaders of his era, he ruled a polyglot kingdom that encompassed Sicily, Malta, peninsular Italy south of Rome, and part of Tunisia. Upon his death in 1154, he was succeeded by William, his last surviving son.

Saladin. This Sunni sultan, fully An Nasir Salah al Din Yusuf ibn Ayyub, ruled Egypt and Syria as the founder of the Kurdish Ayyubid dynasty from 1174 until 1193 after succeeding the Fatimids. Praised for his pragmatism and courage, he famously took control of Jerusalem in 1187.

Saphadin. The Ayyubid sultan al Malik al Adil ad Din Abu-Bakr Ahmed ibn Najm ad-Din Ayyub ruled Egypt and Syria, as Al Adil I, until 1218. He was a brother of Saladin (see above) and the father of al Kamil (see above).

Sibylla of Acerra. The widow of King Tancred was granted "safe conduct" to Germany by Henry VI and Constance but her young son, William (who had been crowned as William III), was probably killed in captivity. Her brother, Richard of Acerra, was executed in 1196. Sibylla herself ended up in France and her daughter, Elvira, wed Walter III of Brienne, who fought against the Germans in Italy.

Stephen of Perche. This French-born cousin of Margaret of Navarre was briefly chancellor of the realm during her regency. His effort to curtail corruption made him unpopular with the baronage, prompting his dismissal. In the *Ferraris Chronicle* he is misidentified as being "Spanish."

Tancred. This was the illegitimate son of Roger of Apulia, the elder brother of William I. In youth, Tancred, who (as an inheritance from his mother) held Lecce in Apulia, was involved in plots against his uncle, William I, but in 1189 he succeeded William II as king. He died in 1194, and was probably interred in Palermo's Magione, a church he endowed. He was succeeded by Constance, the daughter of Roger II.

Thomas Becket. The martyred Archbishop of Canterbury, known to history for his dogmatic defense of ecclesiastical authority in England, studied in Italy but never set foot in Sicily. He corresponded with Margaret of Navarre, who gave refuge to his kin during Becket's exile in France resulting from the archbishop's conflict with Henry II.

Thomas Brun. Arriving in Sicily before 1137, probably with Robert of Selby (see above), Thomas "Brown" was for some years the master of the royal *diwan,* or treasury. Following the death of Roger II, he returned to England, where he became the almoner of Henry II and advocated the wider use of Hindu-Arabic numerals.

Urban II. Born in France as Odo of Châtillon, Urban, who spent much of his pontificate outside Rome, is remembered as something of an enforcer of canon law, taking a stand against such practices as simony. He preached the First Crusade. In his long conflict with Constantinople he was supported by the Normans, and he gave Roger I "legatine" authority to approve episcopal appointments in Sicily.

Walter, Archbishop of Palermo. Ambitious, French-born Walter was the royal tutor before becoming the kingdom's highest-ranking prelate and a royal counsellor, or *familiare.* He lived into the reign of Tancred, whose claim to the crown he adamantly supported over that of Constance, the daughter of Roger II.

William I. William "the Bad" was the fourth-born son of

Roger II by Elvira of Castile, ruling from 1154 until 1166. His reign was plagued by intrigues and baronial revolts, and the loss of territories in Africa. He wed Margaret of Navarre, who served as regent until their son, also William, reached the age of majority.

William II. William "the Good" succeeded his father in 1166 under the regency of Margaret, his mother, reaching the age of majority late in 1171. He wed Joanna of England in 1177 but seems not to have fathered any children. He reigned during a prosperous era, hence his favorable epithet. Upon his death in 1189, the crown was disputed by Tancred and Constance (both mentioned above).

William "Iron Arm" Hauteville. With Drogo, William was one of the first of the Hauteville brothers to arrive in Italy, where he supported Ranulf Drengot, the lord of Aversa. In 1038, William and other Normans, along with a contingent of Lombards, served the Byzantines in the failed effort of George Maniakes to occupy Sicily. There he earned his nickname by slaying the emir of Syracuse with one stroke in single combat. William eventually received Melfi from Guaimar IV, the Lombard Prince of Salerno, but he also gained some Calabrian lands before his death in 1046.

Yolanda of Brienne. Yolanda, or Isabella, Brienne of Jerusalem was the daughter and universal heiress of John of Brienne, King of Jerusalem. She wed Frederick II, as his second wife, in 1225. Her father lost Jerusalem but Frederick claimed it by right of young Yolanda. She died in 1228 from complications in giving birth to Conrad, who succeeded Frederick in 1250.

APPENDIX 2

Timeline

999 - Normans defend Salerno against Arabs. Approximate period of Norse landings at L'Anse aux Meadows in Newfoundland; *Groenlendinga Saga* (the Greenlanders' Saga) and *Eiriks Saga* (Erik's Story) mention such sea travels.

1004 - Fatimids establish large library and *dar al-hikma* (house of wisdom) in Egypt.

1008 - Fatimids re-establish diplomatic relations with China.

1016 - Norman knights first participate in major battles in southern Italy. First Turkish raids in Armenia.

1018 - Bulgarian lands conquered by Byzantines, who also defeat Lombards at Battle of Cannae, in Apulia, where many Norman knights are felled.

1019-1037 - Rule of Ahmed al-Akhal in Sicily.

1037-1040 - Rule by usurper Abdallah Abu Hafs in Sicily.

1038-1042 - Byzantine forces of George Maniakes briefly occupy parts of eastern Sicily; army includes Greeks, Normans, Lombards and Norse Varangian Guard under Harald Hardrada.

1040 - Hasan as-Samsam begins his rule of Sicily; deposed in 1044.

1044 - Sicily divided into four qadits; rivalry among emirs worsens. Peninsular southern Italy divided among Lombards, Normans and Byzantine Greeks.

1045 - Zirids of Tunisia rebel against Fatimids to unite with Abbasids of Baghdad. Cathedral of Gerace (Calabria) consecrated.

1053 - With extinction of Kalbid dynasty, three important emirs divide control of Sicily.

1054 - Great Schism between eastern and western Christianity. Christians of Apulia, Calabria and Sicily initially remain "eastern" (Orthodox) under the ecclesial jurisdiction of the Patriarch of Constantinople rather than "western" (Catholic) under the Pope in Rome.

1055 - Seljuk Turks occupy Baghdad.

1056 - Agnes of Aquitaine regent of Holy Roman Empire until 1061. Arab poet ibn Hamdis born in Sicily; departs in 1078.

1059 - Melfi becomes capital of Normans' Duchy of Apulia.

1060 - Unsuccessful Norman attack on Messina.

1061 - Battle of Messina. City and parts of Nebrodian and Peloritan region occupied; permanent Norman presence.

1066 - Battle of Hastings leads to complete Norman conquest of Saxon England. Battle of Messina forms partial pattern of this invasion of an island from a continent; some Norman knights fight at both battles.

1071 - Normans attack Palermo; Norman invaders are led by Robert de Hauteville, Arab defenders by Ayub ibn Temim. Byzantines lose Battle of Manzikert to Seljuk Turks.

1072 - Siege of Palermo ends in January with Norman occupation under Roger and Robert Hauteville. Greek Orthodox Bishop Nicodemus removed from authority over Christian community.

1075 - Investiture Controversy begins as conflict between Papacy and Holy Roman Emperors.

1077 - Robert Guiscard seizes Salerno from his brother-in-law, Gisulf II, effectively eliminating Lombard influence in southern Italy. Excommunicated Henry IV, Holy Roman Emperor, does penance at Canossa.

1081 - Suppression of revolt led by renegade "emir" Bernavert (Bin al Wardi) at Catania; another of his revolts is suppressed at Syracuse in 1085.

1083 - Roger I appoints Latin (rather than Orthodox) Bishop of Palermo and Gallican Rite is introduced in new churches.

1084 - Bruno founds Carthusian Order in Germany.

1087 - Ibn Hammud, Emir of Kasr'Janni (Enna), last major Arab stronghold, surrenders to Normans in 1087; Noto falls in 1091. Dozens of fortified Arab-founded (or repopulated) towns dot the island: Calascibetta, Caltanissetta, Caltagirone, Mussomeli, Marsala (Mars'Allah), Misilmeri, Cammarata, others.

1095 - Roger II, future King of Sicily, is born at Mileto. Pope Urban II preaches First Crusade.

1096 - First Crusade begins; some Norman knights participate under Bohemond Hauteville (later Prince of Antioch).

1097 - Odo of Bayeux, Earl of Kent, younger brother of William the Conqueror, King of England, dies in Palermo *en route* to the Crusade while visiting Roger I.

1098 - Roger I, as Great Count of Sicily, becomes Papal Apostolic Legate, with right to approve island's Catholic bishops. Cistercian Order founded at Cîteaux (Cisteaux) in France.

1099 - Crusaders conquer Jerusalem.

1101 - Roger I dies, succeeded by Simon, his eldest living, legitimate son, who is still a minor. Roger's widow, Adelaide del Vasto of Savona, is regent.

1105 - Young Simon dies, succeeded by his brother, Roger, as ruler of Sicily under Adelaide's regency.

1108 - Bohemond of Antioch becomes vassal of Byzantine Emperor.

1109 - Bertrand of Toulouse occupies Tripoli (Lebanon).

1112 - Young Roger II reaches the age of majority.

1113 - Order of Saint John (Knights Hospitaller) based in Palestine chartered by Pope Paschal II. Establish commanderies in Italy and later.

1119 - Knights Templar founded in Palestine. (Preceptories in Sicily later confiscated by Frederick II.)

1120 - Council of Nablus establishes legal code for Kingdom of Jerusalem.

1122 - Concordat of Worms between Papacy and Holy Roman Empire.

1123 - First Lateran Council forbids Roman Catholic clerics wives or concubines; until now Catholic priests were permitted to marry before ordination.

1125 - Christian army defeats Seljuk Turks at Battle of Azaz.

1130 - Roger (henceforth as "Roger II") crowned first King of Sicily.

1131 - Cathedral of Cefalù erected.

1135 - Beginning of "Anarchy," a civil war over royal succession, in England.

1136 - Construction of Saint-Denis near Paris; Gothic movement begins.

1138 - Death of Anacletus II ends Papal schism (which began in 1130); Innocent II universally recognized as Pope. Major earthquake around Aleppo.

1139 - Second Lateran Council makes celibacy mandatory for Roman Catholic priests, reiterating a canon established in 1123 but not widely enforced.

1140 - Roger II introduces ducat. Assizes of Ariano, important legal code asserting royal authority, traditionally dated to this year.

1143 - Nilos Doxopatrios authors theological treatise supporting the Eastern Church. Martorana church (Palermo) built in Norman-Arab style for Greek Orthodox community by George of Antioch.

1145-1148 - Second Crusade; participation by Sicilian knights is limited.

1146 - Legal principles expressed in Assizes of Ariano are in force by this time.

1147 - Second Crusade begins but participation by Sicilian knights is limited. Almohads displace Almoravids in northwestern Africa and southern Spain.

1149 - William, future King of Sicily, weds Margaret of Navarre.

1154 - *Book of Roger* completed by court geographer Abdullah al Idrisi. Roger II dies and reign of King William I "the Bad" begins. Constance, daughter of Roger II, born after his death.

1155 - Frederick Barbarossa crowned Holy Roman Emperor.

1156 - Treaty of Benevento between Papacy and Kingdom of Sicily.

1158 - Qaïd al Brun (Thomas Brown), treasurer at William's court, returns to England to reform exchequer of Henry II, thus influencing European accounting principles. He uses Hindu-Arabic numerals, later popularized in Christian Europe by Leonardo Fibonacci of Pisa (briefly a guest of young Frederick II in Sicily) in 1202.

1160 - Mahdia, last Norman stronghold in North Africa, is lost.

1161 - Matthew Bonello leads revolt of Norman barons, resulting in death of Roger, firstborn son of Margaret and William. Rhum Sultanate makes peace with Byzantine Empire.

1166 - Reign of young King William II "the Good" begins under his mother's regency. Queen Margaret gives hospitality to exiled kin of Thomas Becket. Gradual latinization of Sicilian language continues; Latin (Roman Catholic) influence predominates among Christians.

1169 - Major earthquake in Catania and southeast.

1170 - Thomas Becket murdered in Canterbury Cathedral. Peter Waldo establishes evangelical Waldensian church, precursor of Reform (Protestant) movement.

1171 - Estate near Volturno River ceded to John of Ferraris, a Cistercian monk from the abbey at Fossanova. King William II reaches age of majority. Benjamin of Tudela visits Sicily. Saladin deposes Fatimids, establishes Ayyubid rule.

1174 - Sicilian fleet led by Tancred of Lecce attacks Alexandria. Work begins on Monreale Abbey. Style of this cathedral is Norman-Arab on Romanesque plan with Byzantine mosaic icons, including earliest public holy image of Thomas Becket (canonized in 1173).

1175 - William II signs treaty with Venetians. Henry II of England signs treaty with Irish.

1176 - Betrothal of William II to Joanna of England. Byzantines lose much of Anatolia to Seljuk Turks.

1177 - Wedding of William II and Joanna of England. Treaty of Venice between Pope and Holy Roman Emperor.

1178 - Sicilian treaty with Holy Roman Empire. Romuald Guarna of Salerno leaves Sicily.

1179 - Third Lateran Council convened by Pope Alexander III. Abbey of Santa Maria della Ferraria consecrated as first Cistercian foundation in Kingdom of Sicily; its church is the first true Gothic structure in southern Italy.

1181 - Sicilian treaty with Tunisia. Pope Alexander III dies.

1182 - Massacre of the Latins in Constantinople.

1183 - Death of Queen Margaret of Sicily. Monreale becomes archdiocese.

1184 - Major earthquake in Calabria. Bin Jubayr visits Sicily and records his impressions.

1184 - Construction of Palermo's new cathedral.

1185 - William II invades Byzantine lands.

1186 - Constance, daughter of Roger II, weds Henry VI, future Holy Roman Emperor.

1187 - Saladin captures Jerusalem. William II sends fleet to Palestine.

1189 - Death of William II. Succeeded by Tancred of Lecce.

1190 - Richard Lionheart, brother of Queen Joan of Sicily, occupies Messina with Philip II of France for several months *en route* to Third Crusade. Death of Frederick I "Barbarossa," Holy Roman Emperor; succeeded by Henry VI.

1193 - Death of Saladin.

1194 - Death of King Tancred, the last male of the Hauteville dynasty to rule as King of Sicily. Holy Roman Emperor Henry VI of Hohenstaufen arrives and rules by right of his wife, Constance Hauteville.

1195 - Constance crowned Queen of Sicily.

1196 - Joanna, widow of William II, weds Raymond VI of Toulouse.

1198 - Death of Queen Constance; she is succeeded by her son, Frederick II, who weds Constance of Aragon.

1199 - Death of Queen Joanna at Rouen.

1204 - Latins ("Franks") sack Constantinople during Fourth Crusade, establishing "Latin Empire." By this time most of Italy's Christians are "western" (Roman Catholic).

1206 - Mongols unite under Genghis Khan (Temujin), who conquers large parts of Eurasia.

1210 - Francis of Assisi meets Pope Innocent III; founds Order of Friars Minor (Franciscans). Albigensian Crusades begin. Birth of John of Procida. Otto IV invades Italy.

1212 - Frederick II reaches age of majority.

1215 - Magna Carta in England. Dominic of Osma (of Caleruega, Spain) founds Order of Preachers (Dominicans or "Blackfriars"), confirmed by Papacy in 1216.

1217 - Cleric and scientist Michael Scot (born 1175) translates *On the Sphere* by the Arab astronomer Al-Bitruji (or Alpetragius, who died circa 1204). Fifth Crusade begins.

1220 - Frederick issues Assizes of Capua.

1221 - Frederick issues Assizes of Messina.

1223 - Frederick visits Santa Maria della Ferraria. Following execution of Arab rebel leader Morabit in Sicily (in 1222), thousands of Muslims from Iato area, who had revolted with their leader Ibn Abbad (or Benaveth), are deported to Lucera and other towns in Apulia. Many Muslims have already converted to Catholicism. Jews from occupied Jerba (in Tunisia) invited to Sicily. Transfers of Muslims to mainland Italy continue until around 1246.

1224 - University of Naples founded by Frederick II.

1226 - Frederick II summons Imperial Diet of Cremona.

1228 - End of *Ferraris Chronicle*.

1229 - Frederick II, accompanied by Saracen guards and Italian and German knights, goes on Sixth Crusade as King of Jerusalem. Signs peace with Ayyubids without war.

1230 - Upon his return from Jerusalem Frederick suppresses Templar preceptories in Sicily and defeats John of Brienne in Apulia.

1231 - Constitutions of Melfi become legal code for Kingdom of Sicily under Frederick II.

1233 - Cathars of France persecuted as heretics by first Inquisition.

1240 - Ciullo of Alcamo composes poetry in Sicilian language. First of a series of major revolts by Sicilian Arabs, including some Christian converts, but Frederick retains trusted Saracen guards and court officers.

1241 - Mongol-Tatar army of Batu Khan arrives in central Europe after having sacked Kiev. Leads to foundation of "Golden Horde."

1244 - Fall of Jerusalem to Khwarazmian forces.

1245 - First General Council of Lyon convoked by Pope Innocent IV.

1248 - Crusade to Egypt by Louis IX of France.

1250 - Death of Frederick II, succession of his son Conrad.

1252 - Papal bull *Ad Extirpanda* institutes use of torture on heretics in Inquisition.

1254 - Death of Conrad IV Hohenstaufen (Conrad I of Sicily); Manfred, natural but legitimized son of Frederick, becomes regent for Conrad's young son (Conradin). Death of Pope Innocent IV.

1255 - Manfred is excommunicated by Pope Alexander IV but reclaims much of southern Italy from Papal control.

1258 - Manfred crowned King of Sicily. Baghdad falls to Mongols.

1261 - Byzantine Empire restored when Constantinople falls to Greek control.

1266 - Charles of Anjou (brother of Louis IX of France) becomes king of Naples and Sicily following defeat of Manfred at Battle of Benevento.

1268 - Young Conradin, a (legitimate) grandson of Frederick II and last Swabian claimant, is executed in 1268 following defeat at Battle of Tagliacozzo. Hohenstaufen dynasty now extinct.

APPENDIX 3

Popes

Sisinnius 708
Constantine 708-715
Gregory II 715-731
Gregory III 731-741
Zachary 741-752
Stephen II (III) 752-757
Paul I 757-767
Stephen III (IV) 767-772
Adrian I 772-795
Leo III 795-816
Stephen IV (V) 816-817
Paschal I 817-824
Eugene II 824-827
Valentine 827
Gregory IV 827-844
Sergius II 844-847
Leo IV 847-855
Benedict III 855-858
Nicholas I 858-867
Adrian II 867-872
John VIII 872-882

Marinus I 882-884
Adrian III 884-885
Stephen V (VI) 885-891
Formosus 891-896
Boniface VI 896
Stephen VI (VII) 896-897
Romanus 897
Theodore II 897
John IX 898-900
Benedict IV 900-903
Leo V 903
Sergius III 904-911
Anastasius III 911-913
Lando 913-914
John X 914-928
Leo VI 928
Stephen VII (VIII) 929-931
John XI 931-935
Leo VII 936-939
Stephen IX 939-942
Marinus II 942-946

Agapetus II 946-955
John XII 955-963
Leo VIII 963-964
Benedict V 964
John XIII 965-972
Benedict VI 973-974
Benedict VII 974-983
John XIV 983-984
John XV 985-996
Gregory V 996-999
Sylvester II 999-1003
John XVII 1003
John XVIII 1003-1009
Sergius IV 1009-1012
Benedict VIII 1012-1024
John XIX 1024-1032
Benedict IX 1032-1045
Sylvester III 1045
Benedict IX 1045 (restored)
Gregory VI 1045-1046
Clement II 1046-1047
Benedict IX 1047-1048 (restored)
Damasus II 1048
Leo IX 1049-1054
Victor II 1055-1057
Stephen IX 1057-1058
Nicholas II 1058-1061
Alexander II 1061-1073
Honorius II 1061-1072 (antipope)
Gregory VII 1073-1085
Victor III 1086-1087
Urban II 1088-1099

Paschal II 1099-1118
Gelasius II 1118-1119
Callixtus II 1119-1124
Honorius II 1124-1130
Innocent II 1130-1143
Anacletus II 1130-1138 (antipope)
Celestine II 1143-1144
Lucius II 1144-1145
Eugene III 1145-1153
Anastasius IV 1153-1154
Adrian IV 1154-1159
Alexander III 1159-1181
Lucius III 1181-1185
Urban III 1185-1187
Gregory VIII 1187
Clement III 1187-1191
Celestine III 1191-1198
Innocent III 1198-1216
Honorius III 1216-1227
Gregory IX 1227-1241

APPENDIX 4

Chroniclers

The *Ferraris Chronicle* boasts features typical of both chronicles and annals. Clearly, its author had access to a number of sources of recorded information. Philological studies, as well as simple comparisons, show that in some instances he drew from these directly, paraphrasing short passages, and that elsewhere he summarized what he read. Direct, verbatim copying occurs rather rarely.[416]

Some original material is present. Apart from a few details regarding the Norman era which are not reported elsewhere, original information is found in the narrative spanning the reign of Frederick II, who the chronicler almost certainly met in 1223 when the emperor visited Santa Maria della Ferraria and dined with the monks. Acting out of humility, or perhaps fearing his abbot's censure, the monk who wrote *Ferraris* does not explicitly mention himself meeting Frederick.

Not every chronicler is nearly so humble. Sometimes, being a participant in an event described, a chronicler cannot resist the temptation to mention himself by name, using the third-person point of view. An example is this passage from Romuald of Salerno regarding the successful negotiation of a treaty between Emperor Frederick I "Barbarossa" and Pope Alexander III:

"The Emperor Frederick, being in Venice with Romuald, Archbishop of Salerno, and Roger, Count of Andria, sent his ambassadors, namely Hugh of Boncompagno and Rudolph, his great chamberlain, to King William to exchange oaths confirming the peace."[417]

It is true enough that Romuald was one of the negotiators of the Treaty of Venice in 1177, yet he seems to have been given to what we Italians call *protagonismo,* the desire to place oneself, as if a "protagonist," at the center of attention. Most chroniclers eschew this approach.

In fact, the identities of most annalists, and some chroniclers, are unknown. We do not know who wrote *Ferraris,* and the identity of Hugh Falcandus remains a point of contention among scholars.

Annals are essentially "diaries" that record a sequence or simple chronology (timeline) of events as they occur, organized as succinct entries according to year. Chronicles are "narratives" which typically lend more background, detail and insight (commentary) to the events they recount.

In many cases, however, the difference between the annal and the chronicle is rather subtle. By definition, both are contemporaneous (or nearly so) to the events they describe, and one imagines their writers recording notes before composing "finished" entries in an annal or narratives in a chronicle. There exist several genres of chronicle. The typical chronicle has a single author whereas, over time, an annal is likely to be written by numerous authors.

Writing in 1867, William Stubbs drew the distinction between chronicles and annals thus:

"The difference between chronicles and annals was not, as it has been sometimes stated, that the former belong to universal, the latter to national or particular history, but that the former have a continuity of subject and style, whilst the latter contain the mere jottings down of unconnected events. The annals are the ore, the chronicles are the purified metal out of which the historian elaborates his perfect jewel."[418]

He went on to define the chronicle by paraphrasing Gervase of Tilbury (who was briefly present at the court of William II of Sicily), saying that, "a contemporary chronicle is a record of acts and events which the actors and eyewitnesses thought worthy to be remembered."

For our purposes, such definitions will suffice. Among the other medieval literary prose genres we find histories (Anna Comnena), travel diaries (Benjamin of Tudela) and, arguably, eloquent letters (Thomas Becket). There are also the words of churchmen like Bernard of Clairvaux and Francis of Assisi.

Chroniclers like the monk at Ferraria were the journalists of the Middle Ages, offering us details and perspectives we could not likely find elsewhere. Our knowledge of past events would be much the lesser without them. This volume's Introduction explains the difference between "live" and "dead" chronicles, and how *Ferraris* is both.

The study of medieval chronicles and annals is a vast field unto itself. Herewith a few works are very concisely described for their influence upon *Ferraris* or for their use in confirming the facts presented by the Cistercian monk.

Falco of Benevento

As his name implies, Falco was born in the Papal city of Benevento, where he seems to have lived for most of his life. He began his career as a scribe and notary in the Papal palace and later became a judge. In addition to his chronicle, which covers the years from 1102 to 1139 (probably 1099-1146 if some text in *Ferraris* is indeed his), a number of charters bearing his name are known to us.

His family was of the minor Lombard nobility, a fact that fostered in Falco a certain resentment of the Normans reflected in his *Chronicon Beneventanum*. As befits a papal retainer, he openly supported Pope Innocent II against Anacletus II, the antipope who crowned Roger II in 1130; this led to Falco's brief exile from Benevento.

Of the chronicles that most influenced the author of *Ferraris*, Falco's work is the most evident and perhaps the most opinionated.

Hugh Falcandus

Several theories have been advanced about his identity.[419] Whoever "Hugh Falcandus" was, it is clear that he had close, if not privileged, access to the royal court in Palermo. The tone of his writing is often cynical, even sardonic, and historians have long questioned his objectivity. Yet his chronicle has been seriously studied for centuries, and one of the surviving codices bears annotations attributed to Petrarch and Boccaccio.

His chronicle was the first written during Italy's Norman era to find its way into print. Martin Gervais de Tournay published it in Paris in 1550 as *Historia Hvgonis Falcandi Sicvli de Rebus Gestis in Siciliae Regno*. This was a source consulted by Thomas Fazello, whose history of Sicily, *De Rebus Siculus,* was published eight yeas later.

To Falcandus is also attributed the *Epistola ad Petrum Panormitane Ecclesie Thesaurarium de Calamitate Sicilie.*

It is generally accepted that the essential details cited by Falcandus are accurate, and indeed some are readily corroborated by contemporaneous sources. The challenge for the modern scholar lies in discerning what is most likely factual from what probably is not. For the most part, Falcandus is blatant enough in his character assassinations for us to distinguish fact from subjectivity. Indeed, a few of his descriptions of personalities may be quite precise.

The evidence suggests that Falcandus disliked Romuald Guarna of Salerno, who he almost certainly knew personally.

Romuald of Salerno

Archbishop of the prosperous diocese of Salerno from 1154 until his death in 1181, Romuald Guarna of Salerno was born into the nobility that held estates in parts of southern Italy. His *Chronicon sive Annales* covers part of the middle of the twelfth century, complementing other works such as those of Falcandus.

The Guarna were a family of clerics and jurists. At Salerno's medical school, Romuald studied other subjects as well as medicine. These included law, history and theology. He reputedly knew a young Gilles of Corbeil. Romuald served Pope Paschal II as a diplomat.

Delegating some of his episcopal duties to underlings, he became an effective diplomat for King William I and then for William II. Accompanied by Bishop Hugh of Palermo, in 1156 he negotiated the Treaty of Benevento with Pope Adrian IV. Two decades later, he concluded the Treaty of Venice.

He was Archbishop of Palermo from 1161 to 1166.

Romuald's self-serving chronicle, but not his ambitious career, ended by 1179, the same year that saw him participating in a church council condemning the Albigensians (Cathars) as heretics.

Archbishop Romuald was one of the *familiares* (royal counsellors) appointed to assist Queen Margaret in governing the Kingdom of Sicily. By the time Romuald died in 1181, he may have been seventy.

A few passages from his *Chronicon* are presented in the following appendix.

Amatus, Godfrey and William

Apart from the three chroniclers already profiled, whose work was almost certainly known to the *Ferraris* author, there are three others whose labors, completed by 1100, may well have been known to him.

Amatus of Montecassino was a Benedictine monk of Cassino who died in 1090. The earliest surviving copy of his *History of the Normans* exists only in French translation as *L'Ystoire de li Normant.* It is an informative account of the Normans' conquests in Italy.

Godfrey (Geoffrey) of Malaterra was likewise a Benedictine monk, and quite possibly Norman. After spending some years in Apulia, he settled in Sicily. His *De Rebus Gestis Rogerii Calabriae et Siciliae Comitis et Roberti Guiscardi Ducis Fratis Eius* takes us to 1099.

William of Apulia wrote the *Gesta Roberti Wiscardi,* an epic poem completed around 1098 in praise of the deeds of Robert "Guiscard" Hauteville. William seems to have been part of the court of Guiscard's son, Roger Borsa, to whom the work is dedicated.

Paul the Deacon.

Written late in the eighth century, Paul's *Historia Langobardorum* may be the source of some information in the *Ferraris Chronicle,* most obviously the sections addressing the Longobard era.

Alexander of Telese

This abbot at a Benedictine monastery not far from Benevento wrote the *Ystoria Rogerii Regis Sicilie Calabrie atque Apulie,* which covers the rise of Roger II and his reign until 1136. Undertaken at the request of Matilda, the sister of Roger II, the work reflects her view, being a singular example of a chronicle of medieval Sicily that incorporates a woman's perspective into its pages.

Richard of San Germano

As his chronicle was completed after *Ferraris,* Richard cannot be said with certainty to be an influence on the monk of Santa Maria della Ferraria, though it is quite possible that the two men knew each other. Richard began his career at Cassino and later became a chamberlain of Frederick II. Spanning the years from 1189 to 1243, the *Chronica Regni Siciliae* is an important source for Frederick's reign. Initially, Richard intended his work to be a continuation of the annals for which his monastery is known, the *Annales Casinenses* (see below). His chronicle provides us a good basis for confirming the accuracy of many details mentioned in *Ferraris* during the reign of Frederick II because Richard was actually present at many of the events he wrote about. Significantly, Richard's lengthy *Chronica Regni Siciliae* is the only chronicle besides *Ferraris* that was written about Frederick in the Kingdom of Sicily (albeit not far from Papal lands) during his reign rather than after his death.

Peter of Eboli

The focus of the illuminated *Liber ad Honorem Augusti sive de Rebus Siculus,* a work in verse sponsored by Queen Constance and completed in 1196, is the brief reign of Henry VI as King of Sicily. Although it is a classic example of an effort by the victor (Henry) to glorify himself whilst disparaging the vanquished (Tancred), it contains much useful information about the period it covers. However, the work of Peter of Eboli does not seem to be an influence on *Ferraris,* whose author may not have even known of it.

Annals of Cassino

The *Annales Casinenses* seems to be the chief work of its kind consulted in the writing of the *Ferraris Chronicle.* It begins with the year 1000, its very first entry referring to the expulsion of the Muslims from Salerno by the Normans. The part relevant to the period covered by *Ferraris* ends with the year 1212. This is, in fact, one of the principal sources of basic information for this period.

It should not be confused with the *Monte Cassino Chronicle,* the *Chronica Monasterii Casinensis,* written by Leo of Ostia and Peter the Deacon.

Other Annals and Chronicles

There are several other works with which the monk at Santa Maria della Ferraria seems to have been familiar, and perhaps borrowed from. One of these is the *Chronicon Vulturnense,* written by a monk named John and completed in 1130 at the monastery of Saint Vincent, up the Volturno River from Santa Maria della Ferraria.

The lengthy *Annales Cavenses* compiled at the monastery of Cava, near Salerno, covers much of the Middle Ages, with entries to 1318.

The *Annales Ceccanenses,* or *Chronicon Fossae Novae,* was written early in the thirteenth century by a monk at Fossanova Abbey near Ceccano, a Cistercian monastery associated with Santa Maria della Ferraria.

The *Chronicon Salernitanum* (Salerno Chronicle) was completed in 974 and covers the history of the Longobards in the southern part of Italy up to that time.

The *Annales Beneventani* were compiled at the Saint Sophia Monastery in Benevento early in the twelfth century, being an invaluable record of the papal city, a surviving codex ending in 1128. A related work is the *Chronicon Beneventani Monasterii Sanctae Sophiae* (Chronicle of Saint Sophia of Benevento), which ends in 1119 and includes a chartulary.

The *Chronicon Ducum et Principum Beneventi, Salerni et Capua et Ducum Neapolis* was likely compiled at the San Severino monastery in Naples during the middle of the tenth century.

The *Cronica* of the Franciscan friar Salimbene di Adam was written beginning around 1282, the year of the War of the Sicilian Vespers. Born in 1221, a young Salimbene knew Frederick II as the emperor was nearing the end of his reign; in that way he differs from Saba Malaspina and Bartholomew of Nicastro, who wrote during the same period.

Beyond Italy

Copies of certain chronicles written in France, Normandy, England, the German lands and the eastern Mediterranean may well have made their way to the monk of Ferraria, offering details about such news as the martyrdom of Thomas Becket, the Anglo-French War or the crusades, but most of the accounts of events that occurred in Italy are doubtless drawn from the various sources mentioned above, as well as (for the three decades immediately prior to 1228) the monk's direct knowledge.

Oderic Vitalis, like Robert of Torigni (see note 312), lived in Normandy, yet some parts of his *Historia Ecclesiastica* offer details about events in Apulia and Calabria up to 1142. This information was probably provided by Siculo-Norman knights who visited his abbey, Saint-Evroult, and from writings Oderic was supplied by chroniclers at other monasteries. Oderic's history, like some of the other works mentioned here, is useful for concordance.

The *Ferraris* account of the First Crusade is not drawn exclusively from a single source. Chronicles dealing with the First

Crusade were written by Fulcher of Chartres, Albert of Aachen, Raymond of Aguilers and Baldric of Dol. The *Gesta Francorum* was written around 1101 by an author whose identity is unknown to us.

An interesting work relevant to Hauteville participation in the First Crusade, something mentioned in *Ferraris,* is the *Gesta Tancredi* in praise of Tancredi of Galilee and Bohemond of Antioch (see note 138). This was written by Ralph of Caen.

Anna Comnena's *Alexiad* was written before 1153, with a focus on the Byzantine Empire. A few decades later, William of Tyre wrote his *Historia.*

Geoffrey of Villehardouin wrote a chronicle about the infamous Fourth Crusade, *De la Conquête de Constantinople.* This complements an account by Nicetas Choniates, whose history of the Byzantine Empire concludes with the year 1207.

Otto of Freising, a Cistercian, wrote what many consider to be the definitive chronicle of the reign of Frederick I "Barbarossa." Otto died in 1158.

Rigord, who died in 1207, wrote about Philip II of France, according him the title *Augustus.*

Several contemporary chronicles consider the life and martyrdom of Thomas Becket. The *Ferraris* account of Becket's death is too sparse to reveal a specific influence.

The *Chronica Majora* of Matthew Paris gives us a number of references to Frederick II, most significantly his letters to King Henry III of England (Frederick's brother-in-law from 1235 to 1241), but that work begins with the year 1235, effectively continuing the earlier *Flores Historiarum* of Roger of Wendover. Obviously enough, Matthew was writing *after* the period covered by the monk of Santa Maria della Ferraria.

Chronicles in Arabic are not to be overlooked, but there is no evidence to suggest that the monk who wrote *Ferraris* read that language or consulted such sources. He certainly entertained very little sympathy for Cathars, Greek (Orthodox)

Christians or Muslims. His orientation was Latin in every sense.

The prolific writings of Bernard of Clairvaux were widely known among his brother Cistercians.

Canonical Translations

Many of the Norman-Swabian chronicles of Italy were published by Lodovico Muratori in the *Rerum Italicarum Scriptores* series in the eighteenth century. Most of these were republished, with notes, during the next century in *Cronisti e Scrittori Sincroni Napoletani* by Giuseppe Del Re. Some annals, as well as the chronicle of Salimbene di Adam, were published by Georg Pertz as part of the *Monumenta Germaniae Historica* series. (For these publications see this volume's Sources.)

Scholars tend to regard the first translation of a historical text into a particular modern language as the "canonical" edition in that tongue, and in some cases these are now part of the public domain. For some chronicles first translated centuries ago we now see the publication of "modern" or "updated" editions.

This is especially true of much-studied medieval literary works such as those of Dante, of which numerous translations have been published.

One may well question whether these various "updated" translations are truly necessary, but the trend toward publishing them may be fading if only because, in the twenty-first century, access to instant digital downloads and print-on-demand reprints of older publications would seem to obviate much of the perceived need for new editions. Works such as the *Rerum Italicarum Scriptores* are no longer the exclusive province of a few public or university libraries.

APPENDIX 5

Chronicon

These translations of a few passages from the *Chronicon* of Romuald of Salerno appeared in the author's *Margaret, Queen of Sicily* in 2016. Those beginning with the murder of Thomas Becket were the first translations from the *Chronicon* published in English, while the others were effected without reference to any existing (published) translation. For ready identification, the initial sentence of each section appears in the original Latin. The text is presented in the same sequence as it is by Romuald rather than strictly chronologically.

Construction of the Zisa Palace

Eo tempore Rex Guilielmus palatium quoddam altum satis et miro artificio laboratum prope Panormum aedificari fecit, quod Zisam appellavit, et ipsum pulchris pomiferis et amoenis viridariis circumdedit, et diversis aquarum conductibuset piscariis satis delectabile reddidit.

At that time [1165] King William ordered to be erected near Palermo a rather high palace, built with admirable technical competence, which he called the Zisa, surrounded by fruit trees and splendid gardens, rendering it pleasurable with numerous fountains and lakelets.

Accession of King William I

Defuncto autem Rege Rogerio, Guilielmus filius ejus, qui cum patre duobus annis et mensibus decem regnaverat, illi in regni administratione successit.

With the death of King Roger [February 1154], his son, William, who had reigned alongside his father for two years and ten months, succeeded to the throne. Following the death of his father, and in the presence of the realm's great nobles, William was solemnly crowned on Easter, which was very near [4 April]. Among those in attendance was Robert of Bassonville, Count of Conversano and matrilineal cousin of the King.

Marriage of William I

Rex autem Guilielmus, adhuc vivente patre cum esset princeps capuanorum, Margaritam filiam Garsie Regis Navarre duxit uxorem, de qua plures liberos habuit: Rogerium quem ducem apulie constituit, Robertum quem capuanorum principem ordinauit, Willelmum et Henricum.

When his father was still alive, William, whilst Prince of Capua, wed Margaret, daughter of García, King of Navarre [in 1149], who bore him several sons, namely: Roger, who he created Duke of Apulia, Robert, who he invested as Prince of Capua, and William and Henry.

Frederick I [Barbarossa] was very annoyed to learn of the pact between the King of Sicily and Pope Adrian IV, as well as the Papal recognition of the investiture (sic) of young William with the Kingdom of Sicily [crowned as *rex filius* in 1151] and the Duchy of Apulia.

Queen Margaret Named Regent

Rex autem Guilielmus circa Quadragesimam fluxu ventris et molestia coepit affligi.

During the beginning of Lent [March 1166], William was struck by a bout of dysentery. For a time the condition subsided, but by the middle of Lent it worsened, and the King believed himself at the gate of death. He repented and confessed himself, freed some prisoners, forgave a redemption tax he had imposed in Apulia, and made his last testament. In this will he named his elder surviving son, William, as his heir, and confirmed the younger, Henry, as Prince of Capua, as he had already designated.

The King left much money to be spent [for the poor and to glorify God] for the salvation of his soul, and decreed Queen Margaret, his wife, to be keeper and governor of all the realm and of his sons. Finally, he appointed as royal counsellors [familiares] Richard, Bishop-Elect of Syracuse, and Matthew, his High Notary, both being wise, prudent men who were proven experts in law and known to his wife and sons.

Death of King William I

Sed quum praedicta passio ingravesceret, rex Guilielmus Romualdum salernitanum archiepiscopum, qui in arte erat medicinae valde peritus, ad se vocari praecepit.

As the illness became grave, King William called to his presence Romuald, Archbishop of Salerno, who was learned in the art of medicine. Arriving around Easter [24 April], the prelate was received with honour and he prescribed a number of remedies. However, trusting in the authority of his own counsel, the monarch used only the cures he thought most beneficial. And so, the Saturday following Easter, the fever rose and the dysentery worsened.

The King died, aged forty-six, during the afternoon of the seventh day of May, of the fourteenth indiction, around the ninth hour of daylight [3 PM], having reigned alongside his father and then alone for fifteen years and ten months. He was entombed in the chapel of Saint Peter [the Palatine Chapel] in the royal palace.

He was tall, robust and attractive, proud, desirous of prestige, victorious in naval and land battles. He was despised in his realm, where he was feared more than loved. He was greedy in obtaining money for himself and not very generous in spending it on others.

In bestowing honour and wealth he edified those loyal to him. He prosecuted traitors, condemning some to penury and others to exile.

Frequently did he attend liturgy, and he showed great respect for the clergy. He had the Palatine Chapel decorated with marvelous images in mosaic, enhanced by precious stones, its walls covered in various types of marble. He had it appointed in gold and silver, with lush tapestries. The chapel was served by numerous clerics, endowed by as many ecclesiastical benefices. The monarch ensured every reverence toward God in the divine office celebrated there.

Accession of King William II

Quo defuncto, Guilielmus, filius ejus maior, natus annos duodecim, illi in regno successit.

The deceased sovereign was succeeded by William, his eldest son, who was aged twelve years. On the Queen's command, and on the advice of the archbishops, barons and people, he was proclaimed King two days following his father's death.

Indeed, on that day of his coronation, he arrived at the Church of Saint Mary [the cathedral] in Palermo escorted in pomp by a royal cortege that bestowed great glory upon him. He was anointed and crowned by Romuald, Archbishop of Salerno, in the presence of numerous archbishops, bishops and barons. In great honour, and to the joy of the people, he processed to the palace with the crown on his head.

Queen Margaret's First Acts as Regent

Regina vero, utpote mulier sapiens et discreta, manifeste cognoscens animos populi sui, propter molestias quas a rege Guilielmo passi fuerant, plurimum esse turbatos, illos ad amorem et fidelitatem filii sui beneficiis credidit provocandos.

The Queen, being a wise and prudent woman, and knowing well the spirit of the populace, which was very disturbed for the mistreatment the subjects had endured under the late William I, undertook through many concessions to instill their love and fealty toward her son. Acting on sage counsel, she opened the jails and released many prisoners, restoring their lands and forgiving their debts.

She allowed counts and barons who had left the realm to return, restoring to them the estates that had been confiscated. By royal grace, she very generously granted many lands to churches, counts, barons and knights.

Through these and many other acts the fealty and spirit of affinity of the people for her son increased greatly, to the point that those who were already loyal became even more ardently loyal and those who were devoted became further devoted to him.

In those times Qaïd Peter, a eunuch who was master chamberlain of the palace, fled with some others to the court of the King of Morocco, taking with him much money.

Manuel [Comnenus], Emperor of Constantinople, learning of the death of King William I, sent ambassadors to his young successor in Sicily to convey the message that he wished to establish, of his own volition, peace with him, William II. He proposed to William the betrothal of his only daughter, universal heiress to his [Byzantine] Empire, along with the right of succession.

The Queen Regent and the King convoked a council to consider this proposal, sending and receiving many ambassadors. They renewed the traditional peace, but the negotiation of the betrothal remained open for the numerous details that had to be stipulated.

For the many concessions made to their subjects, King William and his mother soon earned their esteem, governing the Kingdom in peace and tranquility.

Henry, Margaret's natural [illegitimate] brother, arrived at the court in Sicily. The King granted him the County of Montescaglioso and betrothed to him a daughter of King Roger.

In those same days [in 1166] Stephen, son of the Count of Perche, also arrived in Sicily. This cleric was kin to Queen Margaret, who named him Grand Chancellor and then arranged for him to be consecrated Archbishop of Palermo.

Before long, Stephen was governing the entire realm as he saw fit, having become very familiar with the King and the Queen Regent.

Murder of Thomas Becket Reported

Illis autem diebus Thomas Cantuariensis archiepiscopus, vir religiosus ed Deum metuens, dum pro libertate ed ecclesiarum justitiis Henrico regi angliae viriliter repugnaret, de Anglia exire compulsus ad regem Lodovicum venit in Franciam, qui eum ob suae religionis reverentiam satis officiose recepit, et per aliquos annos in terra sua honeste detinuit, et quae erant illi necessaria, liberalitate regia ministravit.

In those times, Thomas, Archbishop of Canterbury, a devout and god-fearing man, strove to preserve the rights and freedoms of the church which King Henry II of England tried to usurp. This forced Thomas into exile in France at the court of King Louis VII, who accorded the cleric every courtesy and for some years granted him hospitality in his realm, providing him with every necessity.

Finally, at the request of Pope Alexander III and King Louis, Thomas, Archbishop of Canterbury, made peace with the King of England, who permitted him to return to his church. Over time, King Henry, acting on the counsel of malicious men, began to provoke the clergy and deprive the church of her rights.

Coming to learn of this, Archbishop Thomas, defying all fear and never deviating from the path of justice, defended the church's freedom through words and deeds as a good shepherd protects his flock.

Since the discord increased day by day, with words and actions annoying the monarch ever more, some English knights decided to act in a manner that would please their sovereign. To that end, Hugh de Morville, William de Tracy, Reginald FitzUrse, Richard le Breton and Robert de Broc (sic) ignored the reverence due the priesthood and the fear to be shown in the face of God. On the day following the Feast of the Innocents [29 December 1170], they killed Thomas by striking his head with a sword while he prayed before the altar of the cathedral. They immediately fled, pursued by nobody, keeping their remorse to themselves.

The bells of the city and the abbey rang out to announce news of the evil act. Monks, priests and laity entered the cathedral to find, unspeakably, the body of their pastor who had been cruelly killed next to the altar. Tearfully, between heartfelt groans and sighs, they buried him in honour in his own church during a Pontifical [solemn] liturgy to the sound of hymns.

The just and merciful Lord, who looks upon his own not only in the future but the present, permitted Archbishop Thomas to be venerated as a martyr, as much for the pain he suffered as for the cause he defended. His murder, for having upheld truth, made Thomas famous and celebrated in all the world through many supernatural manifestations and recent miraculous events.

When the Pope [Alexander III] heard of the certainty and veracity of those miracles, the decision was announced to his fellow prelates of the canonization of Thomas as a martyr, his name to be inscribed in the catalogue of martyrs. It was ordered that his martyrdom be celebrated every year on the anniversary of his death.

The King of England heard that public opinion was against him, implying that he had prior knowledge of the crime perpetrated against the Archbishop, and these voices persecuted he who was not to blame. Confident in the purity of his innocence, Henry sent some of his bishops and clerics to Anagni to see Pope Alexander.

Before the Pope and his cardinals, Henry's emissaries publicly swore on the Holy Gospels that their King was innocent of having spilled the blood of that just man, and that he had no part in the crime that was committed. His knights, who did not fear assaulting the Archbishop, had given thought to their deed, recognizing their crime and their dishonesty. They now submitted themselves humbly at the Pope's feet, publicly proclaiming their guilt and their sacrilege, imploring that he permit them to make penance for the crime they had committed.

The Pontiff condemned the guilty knights in the strongest terms for their evil, affirming that the judgement of God would be visited upon them if they did not atone for their sin with a suitable penance.

He ordered them to go on pilgrimage to Jerusalem, barefoot and clad in cilices [hairshirts], visiting the holy places in pain and piety. He ordered them to go thenceforth to Black Mountain, which is near the city of Antioch. There, only by fasting, meditating, praying and grieving for the rest of their lives, ever asking for divine mercy, might they repent of so vile a crime.

Maria "Porphyrogenita" Comnenus Fails to Arrive

Eo tempore quum Emmanuel imperator Constantinopolitanus frequentibus nuntiis delegatis filiam suam Zura Mariam Guilielmo regi Siciliae in uxorem tradere promisisset, tandem ex conventione ultriusque partis factum est, quod imperator, praesentibus legatis ejusdem regis, in anima sua jurare fecit, et juramentum suum magnatum suorum jurejurando firmari, quod in termino et loco ab utraque parte praefixo filiam suam regi pro uxore transmitteret.

At that time [1171] Manuel, Emperor of Constantinople, in the frequent messages borne by his ambassadors, had promised the betrothal of his daughter, Maria, to King William of Sicily. At the end of these negotiations, both parties were agreed that the Emperor, in the presence of William's representatives [as witnesses], would swear on his very soul to send his daughter to the King to a place that was mutually agreed upon.

The terms of the betrothal were confirmed by an oath sworn collectively by the Imperial nobles. In the same manner, the King and those near him [the Queen and court] swore to welcome the daughter of the Emperor.

Having done so, William, being a just and god-fearing man, and seeking to honour his oath, went to Taranto with his younger brother Henry, Prince of Capua, and waited there for a time for the arrival of Maria, who was to be accompanied by Manuel's emissaries.

Then the devout prince went to the shrine of Saint Michael

on Mount Gargano to pray before going to Barletta, where he stayed for several days.

But the Emperor, abandoning his oath and his promise, failed to send his daughter to meet the King of Sicily at the time and place agreed upon.

Death of Prince Henry of Capua

Quo rex cognito per terram beneventanam transiens, Henricum ca-puanorum principem fratrem suum, quia infirmus erat.

Knowing this [that Maria Comnenus had not arrived at Taranto], William, while passing through the Benevento region, sent his brother, Henry, who had fallen ill, ahead to Salerno. Meanwhile, William visited Capua and then made his way to Salerno.

Henry boarded a galley for Palermo. There the illness worsened, and he died in the middle of June in the year of Our Lord 1172, of the fifth indiction, aged thirteen. He was interred with honour next to the tomb of Roger II, his grandfather, in the Church of Saint Mary in Palermo.

Having remained in Salerno for a few days, William boarded a galley with Walter, the venerable Archbishop of Palermo, and Matthew [of Aiello] the Vice Chancellor, and returned to Palermo, where, according to proper usage, he immediately learned of the death of his brother. At first William suffered terribly, both mentally and physically, but he eventually accepted the wise counsel of those loyal to him, finding consolation for his pain through his faith in the Lord.

Proposed Betrothal of Beatrice Hohenstaufen

Interea praedictus cancellarius ex mandato imperatoris nunctios ad Guilielmum Siciliae regem transmisit, suadens et postulans, ut ipse, im-

peratoris filia in uxorem accepta, cum eo pacem perpetuam faceret et ipsi se amicabiliter couniret.

The chancellor of the Holy Roman Emperor [Frederick I "Barbarossa"], acting on his lord's orders, sent ambassadors to William, King of Sicily, asking him, and prevailing upon him, to stipulate a perpetual peace. To seal this accord, the Emperor asked William to accept his daughter [Beatrice] as his bride.

But King William, being a devoutly religious, Christian ruler, knew that this marriage would not please Pope Alexander III. Indeed, it would have brought with it great damage to the Church of Rome.

Out of reverence for God and respect for Pope Alexander, he chose not to accept a union with the daughter of the Emperor, nor the peace accord presented. For his part, Frederick was greatly offended at this rebuke and did not forget it. His daughter died shortly afterward.

Joanna "Plantagenet" of England

Interea rex Guilielmus consilio Papae Alexandri, Heliam Trojanum electum et Arnulfum caputaquensem episcopum et Florium de Camerota regium justitiarium ad regem Henricum in Angliam misit, ut ei Joannam minorem filiam suam in uxorem daret.

In those times [1176] King William II, acting on the advice of Pope Alexander III, sent to King Henry II in England as his emissaries Elias, Bishop Elect of Troia, Arnolf, Bishop of Capaccio, and Florio of Camerota, royal justiciar, to ask for the hand of Joanna, his young daughter.

Henry, accepting the counsel of Pope Alexander and his princes, happily consented to the request of the [Sicilian] sovereign. He sent his daughter as far as the port of Saint-Gilles in the company of the royal emissaries and some of his own nobles.

Knowing this, King William sent Alfano, Archbishop of Capua, Richard, Bishop of Syracuse, and Robert, Count of Caserta with twenty-five galleys to meet Joanna there. From Saint-Gilles, the three prelates escorted Joanna aboard a galley and set out for Naples. Unaccustomed to sea travel, the girl suffered a bout of sea sickness.

They stopped at Naples to celebrate Christmas. Then they travelled by land via Salerno and Calabria to Sicily. At Palermo, Joanna was met by King William and his great nobles, and received with the great honour due her.

Then King William summoned the most distinguished noblemen of Sicily, and a great multitude of the populace, for his solemn nuptials with the daughter of the King of England in the Palatine Chapel, where the betrothed were married and crowned in the Year of Our Lord 1177 in the month of February of the tenth indiction [on Sunday the thirteenth].

CHRONICON
ROMUALDI II.
ARCHIEPISCOPI SALERNITANI.
In Chrifti nomine incipit Chronica.

DE ÆTATIBUS.

Rima mundi ætas eft ab Adam ufque ad diluvium, côtinens annos, juxta Hebraicam veritatem mille fexcentos quinquaginta fex, juxta feptuaginta verò Interpretes duo millia ducentos quadraginta duos ; generationes verò juxta utramque editionem numero decem, quæ univerfali eft deleta diluvio, ficut primam cujufque hominis oblivio demergere confuevit ætatem. Fuerunt Noë filii tres, ex quibus ita. funt ortæ gentes. De Japhet quindecim. De Cham triginta. De Sem XXVII. Sem annos duos poft diluvium genuit Salem : à quo Samaritæ & Indi. Sale genuit Heber : à quo Hebræi. Heber genuit Falech, cujus tempore turris ædificatur, & linguarum divifio fit. In folo Heber prifca remanfit lingua, quia in ea confpiratione non fuit. Turris verò duo millia CLXXIV. dicitur pafsuum. Hanc Nembroth gigas conftruxit. Hac ætate Scitharum regnum oritur, ubi primus regnavit Ihannus. Tunc & regnum Ægyptiorum ubi primus regnavit Thoës. Dehinc regnum Affiriorum, ubi primus regnavit Belus, quem dicunt Saturnum quidam : deinde Ninus, qui condidit

A | Ninivem. Hoc tempore Abraham nafcitur : & poft mortem Nini à Semiramide Regina reædificata eft Babylonia, ubi regnavit annos quadraginta.

Secunda ætas à Noë ufque ad Abraham generationes juxta Hebraicam veritatem complexa decem, annos autem ducentos nonaginta duos ; porrò juxta feptuaginta Interpretes anni MLXXII. Generationes verò XI. hæc verò quafi pueritia fuit generationis populi Dei, & ideo in lingua inventa eft Hebræa, à pueritia namque homo incipit nofcere loqui, quæ idcirco appellata eft, quòd fari non poteft. Ab Adam itaque ufque ad Abraham juxta Hebraicam veritatem computantur anni mille

B | nongenti quadraginta octo, fecundùm feptuaginta Interpretes fiunt anni tria millia trecenti quatuordecim.

Tertia ab Abraham ufque ad David generationes juxta utramque auctoritatem XIV. annos verò, fecundùm Hebræorum auctoritatem nongentos quadraginta duos complectens; juxta feptuaginta verò Interpretes anni tria millia CXXXVII. hæc velut quædam adolefcentia fuit populi Dei, à qua ætate incipit homo poffe generare, propterea Matthæus Evangelifta generationum ab Abraham fumpfit exordium, qui etiam pater multarum

C | gentium conftitutus eft, quando mutatum nomen accepit. Ab Adam verò juxta Hebræorum auctoritatem ufque ad David fiunt anni duo millia octingenti nonaginta, fecundùm feptuaginta Interpretes tria millia CV. Cur autem annorum hæc diverfitas fit, in fequentibus oftendetur.

Quarta à David ufque ad tranfmigrationem

B₂

Romuald's chronicle in Rerum Italicarum Scriptores *(1725)*

NOTES

1. See *Friderici II Diplomata* (in Sources), book 14, part 1, pages 103-105.

2. See Schmeidler, op. cit. (in Sources), which offers direct comparisons between *Ferraris* and the texts of several chronicles and annals, providing a keen analysis of the phraseology and content. See also Loud, Graham, "The Genesis and Context of the Chronicle of Falco of Benevento," *Anglo-Norman Studies IV: Proceedings of the Battle Conference 1992* (1993), pages 177-198.

3. "Without hesitation, King Peter summoned his admiral, Lord Roger of Lauria, ordering him to undertake this mission. Arriving in the waters around Messina, the Aragonese fleet began to seize or destroy every Angevin cargo ship it encountered." See Mendola, Louis, op. cit. (in Sources), pages 131, 208.

4. This observation about spelling refers specifically to the *Spinelli Codex,* in Palermo, the oldest known manuscript, dating from around 1330, and the only copy to preserve the original Sicilian. The chronicle itself was written between 1288 and 1295 as the memoir of John of Procida.

5. See Kehr, Karl, "Ergänzungen zu Falco von Benevent" (in Sources).

6. As recently as 1992, one of the leading scholars in the field overlooked *Ferraris* while identifying the chronicle of Richard of San Germano as the only one written in the Kingdom of Sicily during the long reign of Frederick II. See Matthew, Donald, op.cit. (in Sources), page 336.

7. Gaudenzi believed there to be, in effect, two works. See *Monumenti Storici* (in Sources), pages 2-3.

8. See Loud, Graham, *Roger II and the Creation of the Kingdom of Sicily* (in Sources), pages 130, 247-249.

9. A decisive factor in Byzantine military campaigns at this time had little to do with strategy itself. For a generation or two, the problem was raising troops. An epidemic of bubonic plague in 541 decimated the population of the Byzantine Empire, rendering a reconquest of Italy all but impossible.

10. For such descriptions we look to Mohammed ibn Hawqal in the tenth century and Abu Hussain Mohammed bin Ahmad bin Jubayr in the twelfth.

11. See Makdisi, John, op cit. (in Sources).

12. Over the years, these two accounts of the Normans' arrival in southern Italy have given rise to two schools of thought, each supporting one "theory" (tradition) or the other. It is the author's conviction that they are not mutually exclusive. In their general outlines, both descriptions mention Norman knights being in Italy for pilgrimages. Neither tradition seems slavishly faithful to fact, but neither does one contradict the substance of the other. Indeed, there may have been other bands of Norman knights errant present in Italy besides those mentioned. For more on the "Gargano" and "Salerno" traditions see Joranson, op.cit. (in Sources).

13. One may very loosely describe the minor emirates that existed by 1060 as *taifas,* though they were not identical to what existed in Spain. At times the city of Bal'harm (Palermo) was, in effect, a semi-autonomous emirate. There was not much open warfare among the numerous Sicilian emirs, who all owed allegiance to the Fatimids, but neither was there much unity.

14. Gérard de Bourgogne (of Burgundy), whose pontificate ended with his death in July 1061, is known to posterity for reforming the procedure for Papal elections to ensure that assembled cardinals, not Roman aristocrats, selected the pontiff.

15. This Carloman (who died as a monk in 754) was the eldest son of Charles Martel, and therefore the elder brother of Pepin the Short. The

text states *Karolomagnum fratem Pipini regem francorum,* "Carloman, brother of Pepin, King of the Franks." He should not be confused with Carloman I (who died in 771), the second surviving son of Pepin the Short and younger brother of Charlemagne. See Table 6.

16. In the translation, *Longobard* refers to the population that conquered a large part of Italy in the seventh century. The term *Lombard* refers to their descendants amalgamated with the Italian population after *circa* 900; by 1060 some peoples, such as the Sicilians, generically referred to most feudal lords of peninsular Italy who were not Byzantine Greek or Norman as "Lombards." Latin texts rarely make such distinctions.

17. Constantine's pontificate actually lasted from 708 to 715.

18. More precisely, Adrian was involved in two synods. He confirmed the Second Council of Nicaea that began in 787, which approved the veneration of icons whilst excommunicating iconoclasts, thus mending a conflict with the churches of the east, and sent delegates to Frankfurt in 794 to respond to demands by Charlemagne (who had received a poor Latin translation of the decision taken at Nicaea) that this policy be nullified.

19. There is more to this episode than the chronicler reveals. Following the death of Carloman I (see note 15), upon which Charlemagne confiscated his brother's property, Gerberga, the deceased brother's widow (Charlemagne's sister-in-law), fled with her two sons, obtaining refuge at the Longobard court in Pavia. Charlemagne conquered this and much other territory in northern Italy, a region ruled by subsequent Holy Roman Emperors, including Frederick II.

20. The Longobard invasion, which was effectively a mass migration, arrived in Italy in 568. In mentioning the Pope, the chronicler refers, more specifically, to the Longobards' siege of Rome a few years later. The pontificate of Benedict I lasted from June 575 until his death in July 579. Justin II, Eastern Roman Emperor, ruled from 565 to 574.

21. Pannonia straddled parts of what are now Austria, Croatia, Hungary, Slovenia and Slovakia.

22. A Lombard duchy was smaller than a principality.

23. Note that the lengths of many of these reigns as stated by the chronicler are imprecise. He begins with the Gausian dynasty. Like some other Germanic peoples (notably the Goths and Vandals), the Longobards first accepted Arianism before embracing doctrines espoused at the Council of Nicaea (in 325). This was true of the only Gausian king, Alboin, and his immediate successors.

24. Alboin reigned from 565 to 572. The chronicler seems to have inverted years and months.

25. Cleph's actual rule began in 572 and lasted until his assassination in 574.

26. Authari, sometimes Agilolf, reigned from 584 (following an interregnum) until his death in 590. He is known for extending Longobard influence southward, where he tried (but failed) to conquer Calabria.

27. Agilulf "the Thuringian," a cousin of Authari, ruled from 590 to 616. His truce with Pope Gregory I brought an end to three decades of open conflict with the Papacy. In 603, at his wife's urging, Agilulf renounced Arianism. He erected the cathedral of Monza and extended his realm southward into Umbria.

28. This is the abbey at Monte Cassino, destroyed not by Agilulf but by his nominal vassal, zealous Zotto of Benevento, in 577.

29. This is correct. Adaloald, who reigned from 616 to 626, was the son of Agilulf.

30. Arioald, who actually ruled from 626 to 636, owed his position to his

father-in-law, being married to Gundegerga, the daughter of King Agilulf. Arioald repelled an incursion by the Avars into what is now northeastern Italy. He accepted Arianism.

31. The ancient Roman settlement of *Forum Iulii* is now Cividale del Friuli in northeastern Italy. This position facilitated a good defense against tribes like the Avars that were likely to invade from the east.

32. Here time is abbreviated, for Gisulf I held Benevento from 689 until his death in 706.

33. It should be noted that at this early date the Latin *dux* usually referred to a *leader* generically, rather than to a duke (see also note 50).

34. This probably refers anachronistically to the attack of 860 (see note 88). Muslim invaders (encouraged by wicked Athanasius of Naples) again destroyed the abbey of Saint Vincent in 881 and Monte Cassino two years later. The reconstruction of Saint Vincent was undertaken in 904. Paldo, Taso and Tato may be apocryphal figures but the *Volturno Chronicle* mentions them "founding" the abbey in 731.

35. Rothari, of the Harodingian dynasty (formerly lords of Brescia), was elected king in 636, succeeding Arioald. He held all of northern Italy except Venice and Ravenna, which remained Byzantine. He is known for his legal code, the Edict of Rothari. This monarch died in 652.

36. In fact, the reign of Rodoald, son of Rothari, was rather brief, probably lasting for months rather than years, and ending in 653. Here the monk's source seems to be the *Historia Langobardorum* of Paul the Deacon.

37. Aripert I was the son of Gundoald, from Bavaria, who ruled Asti. Aripert was King of the Lombards from 653 to 661.

38. Grimoald I had ruled Benevento (647-662) before becoming King of

the Lombards from 662 until 671. This followed a brief reign by Aripert's sons, Perctarit (Berthari) and Godepert (Gothbert). See also note 58.

39. This was the son of Aripert I (see note 38). Perctarit's second reign was from 671 until 688.

40. Cunipert, the son of Perctarit, ruled from 688 to 700.

41. Liutpert, the son of Cunipert reigned from 700 to 702, when he was deposed by Raginpert, son of Godepert (see note 38).

42. Aripert II, son of Raginpert (see note 41), ruled from 701 to 712. He was the last of the line of the Bavarian dynasty that began with Aripert I in 653 (see note 37).

43. This probably refers to its expansion but see Paldo, Taso and Tato in note 34.

44. Ansprand ruled in the spring of 712, succeeded by his son, Liutprand.

45. Liutprand's reign lasted from 712 to 744. He is remembered for his Donation of Sutri (in 728), which granted strategic lands to the Pope; this was the first expansion of Papal territory beyond the environs of Rome and a cornerstone of what later became the Papal State.

46. Hildeprand "the Useless," nephew of Liutprand (see note 45), reigned briefly in 744 until he was overthrown by Ratchis, the ruler of Friuli.

47. Ratchis, who overthrew Hildeprand (see note 46), ruled from 744 to 749.

48. Aistulf was the brother of Ratchis, who he succeeded. He ruled as King of the Lombards from 749 until his death in 756.

49. Desiderius, who was mentioned at the beginning of this chapter, ruled

from 756 to 774. His daughter wed Charlemagne, who conquered the Italian kingdom.

50. As per note 33, the Latin *dux* did not initially denote *duke* as we understand that title. There is no precise year when it came into use as an actual title signifying hereditary royalty (and eventually nobility). Here it is used according to customary practice, with Zotto considered the first Duke of Benevento. In the Beneventan context, dukes were vassals of the Longobard kings, but (beginning in 774) princes exercised sovereign authority.

51. Zotto ruled from 571 until 591.

52. In fact, Arechis I ruled from 591 to 641. Aside from the length of the reign, there seems to be confusion between Arechis I and Arechis II (see note 53), the latter being referred to in the next paragraph.

53. Here the reference seems to be to a later Arechis, namely Arechis II, who founded Saint Sophia in Benevento around 760. Arechis II was Duke of Benevento from 758 to 774, and then Prince of Benevento until 787.

54. There were twelve Dukes of Benevento between Arechis I (duke until 641) and Arechis II (duke from 758). The ordinal numeration in these notes takes them into account, but that of the chronicler does not.

55. Grimoald III, son of Arechis II, ruled from 788 until his death in 806. In 792, he was forced by Charlemagne's sons (Pepin and Charles) to submit to Frankish authority.

56. This was probably Grimoald IV, who was not the son of Grimoald III. He ruled from 806 to 817.

57. This may have transcended ordinary astrology.

58. This episode actually relates to the Siege of Benevento by Constans II

(who then ruled from Syracuse in Sicily) in 663 against the authority of an earlier Grimoald, namely Grimoald I, who was Duke of Benevento from 647 to 662 and King of the Longobards from 662 to 671 (see notes 38 and 60). The story about astrology may be a metaphor for the fact that Grimoald I was an Arian, and therefore a heretic in the eyes of the church.

59. Barbato was Bishop of Benevento from 664 until his death in 683.

60. This passage merits explanation. The Siege of Benevento was undertaken by Constans II against Romuald, the son of Grimoald (who was absent but came to aid Romuald, relieve the city and defeat Constans). In a conciliatory gesture typical of its era, Romuald offered his sister, Gisa, in marriage to Constans, who, however, was already married to a wife, Fausta, who survived him.

61. Sico I reigned from 817 until his death in 832, succeeding Grimoald IV. He was succeeded by his son, Sicard.

62. Sicard ruled from 832 until his death in 839.

63. Radelchis I ruled from 839 to 851. In 841 he hired Arab mercenaries, who pillaged Capua.

64. Radelgar ruled from 851 to 854.

65. Adelchis reigned from 854 until his assassination in 878.

66. Gaideris, sometimes Waifer, ruled from 878, when his uncle (Adelchis) died, until his own untimely demise in 881.

67. See note 34.

68. Radelchis II ruled from 881 until he was deposed and exiled by his brother (Aiulf I) in 884. He was restored a few years later but again de-

posed, this time by a cousin (Atenulf I of Capua), in 900.

69. Aiulf II ruled from 884 until 890. See note 68.

70. Ursus died in 892, having been deposed, as is described (accurately) in the text. The Byzantines held Benevento until 895.

71. Guy IV, Duke of Spoleto, son of Guy II of Spoleto, was assassinated in 897.

72. That is to say, in the year 901. Radelchis II (see note 68) was restored very briefly, from 897 to 900.

73. Following this initial reign of nine years (901-910) as the surrogate of his father, Atenulf I, Landulf I reigned from 901 to 943, sometimes with his brother, Atenulf II, as co-ruler.

74. This is a slight simplification on the part of the chronicler, for there were still (as we shall see) identifiable Lombard and Byzantine populations in peninsular Italy into the eleventh century.

75. This was Pepin of Herstal, or Pepin II, who consolidated the Frankish lands. He was Duke of the Franks from 687 to 714.

76. Charles Martel, the son of Pepin of Herstal (see note 75), reigned as Duke and Prince of the Franks from 718 to 741. He divided his kingdom between two of his sons, Carloman and Pepin the Short.

77. This was Pepin III "the Short," King of the Franks from 751 until his death in 768.

78. Born in 742, Charlemagne became King of the Franks upon the death of his father, Pepin III, in 768 and (through his Italian conquests) King of the Lombards in 774. He was crowned Emperor of the Romans (Holy

Roman Emperor) in 800.

79. Charles "the Younger," who had been crowned King of the Franks at Rome on Christmas 800 when his father, Charlemagne, was crowned Roman Emperor, predeceased his father in 811. His younger brother, Louis "the Pious" was then crowned co-emperor in 813. See Table 6.

80. Louis the Pious died in 840.

81. Lothair I, the eldest, died in 855. Pepin I of Aquitaine died in 838. Louis "the German" died in 876. Charles "th Bald" lived until 877. The rivalry amongst the three sons of Louis the Pious (see Table 6), each of whom inherited part of the Carolingian realm, has become legendary.

82. Louis II "the Younger" of Italy became Holy Roman Emperor in 844; he died in 875.

83. Named for Lothair II (who died in 869), Lotharingia included the Netherlands, Belgium, Luxembourg, Lorraine and much of Germany.

84. Charles of Provence died in 863.

85. This was not, as the chronicler implies, a recent invasion or even an organized one. For decades, Aghlabids (the chronicler's "Saracens") from Sicily and Tunisia had found work in southern Italy as mercenaries. The civil wars between Lombards, and the Lombard wars against the Byzantine Greeks, sometimes left important port cities like Bari and Taranto poorly defended. Bari was occupied by Aghlabids (though not as part of an actual invasion) around 841. Until 852, the city was held by the "emir" Khalfun, who was succeeded by Mufarrag ibn Sallam. In 857, following his assassination, Mufarrag was succeeded by his brother, Sawdan.

86. This was in 865. Although Louis II "the Younger" did not officially reign over the Lombards of southern Italy (except tenuously as "King of

Italy"), it was feared that the Arabs could invade much of the peninsula if left unchecked. They already controlled most of Sicily, which they could use as a base. Louis was in Apulia by the spring of 867.

87. These localities are spread over a fairly large area far beyond the environs of Benevento itself.

88. Saint Vincent's seems to have been sacked (and burned) in 860. The gold coins were probably similar to the *tarì* circulated in Sicily and Africa. Even a thousand of these would indicate incredible wealth.

89. Louis II died in 875; see note 82 and Table 6.

90. Sicily had already been occupied by the Arabs (see notes 85 and 86), and Louis defeated them at Bari in 871. This passage refers to new waves of mercenaries that began arriving as early as the autumn of 871, not only after 875 as the text suggests.

91. Athanasius (died 898). See also note 34.

92. The Pope referred to was actually John VIII. Sergius II was Duke of Naples from 870 to 877. Athanasius was excommunicated in 879.

93. These were mercenaries acting on the orders of Athanasius (see note 34). A later passage contradicts this number, stating that there were 900 victims.

94. Charles the Bald, Holy Roman Emperor from 875 to 877, was a son of Louis the Pious, and half-brother of Lothair I. For his kinship (as uncle) to his predecessor, Emperor Louis II "the Younger," see Table 6. Despite what the chronicler affirms, the expedition of Charles the Bald to Italy was aborted.

95. The comment about the withdrawal from Italy by Charles the Bald leav-

ing the southern regions open to Arab incursions, though not entirely inaccurate, reflects the chronicler's thirteenth-century view of history (and is noteworthy in that regard).

96. The chronicler's description of Arab activity in peninsular Italy is borne out by the historical record, which mentions such facts as the Arab settlement along the Garigliano River by 900, the Battle of Stilo in Calabria in 982, and the payment of tribute by the Salernitans until 999 (see the Backstory).

97. Robert "Guiscard" of Hauteville became Count of Apulia (also ruling most of Calabria) in 1057 and Duke of Apulia two years later. Terra di Lavoro was an area around Naples (see the first map) within what is now Campania; the greater titles associated with this region in 1059 were the princedoms of Salerno (held by Gisulf II from 1052 to 1077) and Capua (held by Richard Drengot for two decades from 1058).

98. Robert Guiscard did not actually conquer any part of Fatimid Africa. More precisely, his brother, Roger I, maintained a small force in Mahdia in connection with trade. African territory was seized by Roger II in 1135, and Mahdia became a Sicilian protectorate a few years later.

99. This refers to the son of Robert, namely Roger Borsa (who ruled Apulia and Calabria until 1111). However, the island of Sicily was ruled by Roger I, Robert's brother; in that regard the chronicler may be confusing these two Rogers.

100. This refers to William, Duke of Apulia, the son and heir of Roger Borsa. This William succeeded Roger Borsa in 1111, reigning as Duke of Apulia until his own death in 1127. Then, as stated in the next paragraph, the duchy passed to his first cousin once removed, Roger II of Sicily.

101. Amiterno (near the ancient Amiternum) was a city near L'Aquila in Abruzzi. The territory of the Kingdom of Sicily actually extended north-

ward beyond this point.

102. Constance was the aunt of William II, although they were nearly the same age. The Holy Roman Emperor referred to as "Frederick the Great" was Frederick I "Barbarossa."

103. This is slightly simplified by the chronicler. In fact, William II was succeeded, though not without controversy, by Tancred Hauteville (see the second genealogical table). Constance succeeded as queen regnant (the Hauteville dynastic heiress) following Tancred's death. Frederick II did indeed inherit Sicily from his mother and Germany from his father, although he would have to assert his right to be crowned Holy Roman Emperor.

104. The vast Duchy of Benevento became a principality in 774. It was divided into two dominions (Benevento and Salerno) in the ninth century by the Holy Roman Emperor Louis II. However, the chronicler refers to the partition of the territory by Pandulf I "the Ironhead," who became Prince of Salerno in 978; Pandulf divided his large realm between his sons, Landulf IV being given Benevento (and Capua) and Pandulf II getting Salerno.

105. See Appendix 3 for the list of pontificates. It should be reiterated that the durations of the pontificates given in the chronicle are not always accurate.

106. This line, which appears in the chronicle as marginalia, refers to the *filioque* dispute which (among other theological questions) divided the Catholic and Orthodox churches.

107. This attack occurred in 799 but did not result in the loss of Leo's eyes or tongue, although that was its intent. In fact, Pope Leo escaped serious harm and subsequently received the protection of Charlemagne, who he crowned the following year.

108. In fact, Stephen IV was Pope for less than one year, from June 816 to

January 817.

109. Stephen was not yet Pope when Charlemagne died at Aachen in 814.

110. Pope Gregory I died in 604.

111. The pontificate of Paschal I lasted from 817 until his death in 824.

112. Eugene II was Pope from 824 until 827.

113. Louis II was crowned in 844; see note 82.

114. Boniface VI was Pope in April 896. The pontifical chronology of the text omits Marinus I (Martin II) from 882 until 884, Adrian III from 884 to 885, Stephen V from 885 to 891, and Formosus from 891 to 896.

115. This is one of the few pontificates for which the duration given by the chronicler is precise. Theodore II was Pope for just twenty days in December 897.

116. The chronicler refers specifically to the fall of Taormina, the last city conquered by the Aghlabids, in 902. This event marks the complete Arab conquest of the island.

117. Despite the means by which he occupied the Holy See in 903 and 904, Christopher was regarded as a legitimate Pope into the twentieth century. The Catholic Church now lists him as an antipope.

118. The date given in the manuscript is not clear. There were Hungarian incursions into Apulia over the course of several decades, most notably in 922, which may be the event mentioned here. Lando was Pope in 913 and 914.

119. The parentage of young John XI, whose pontificate lasted from 931

until 935, is the subject of scholarly debate.

120. This does not correspond to the precise date of a known incursion. See also note 118.

121. Martin III, Pope from 942 to 946, is also known as Marinus II. See also note 114.

122. Gregory V was Pope from 996 to 999.

123. John XVI has come to be regarded as an antipope. His pseudo-reign lasted from 997 to 998. The chronicler's inclusion of certain antipopes in this list may reflect opinions that prevailed in 1200.

124. Much legend surrounds the life of Sylvester II, Pope from 999 to 1003. The text repeats a fragment of one of the more popular stories.

125. John XVII was Pope from 1003 to 1009.

126. Benedict IX was the young nephew of Pope John XIX. Deposed for corruption, he returned to become Pope on two more occasions. See Appendix 3.

127. Sylvester III was Pope from January to March 1045.

128. Visible in the constellation Leo, this comet may have been considered by some to be a good omen of the Normans' arrival.

129. This refers specifically to the Battle of Civitate in June 1053, a turning point in the Norman conquest of southern Italy. One of the chief sources here is the chronicle of William of Apulia. Pope Leo IX is known for this and for the Great Schism of 1054; he died in Rome in April of that year.

130. Marginalia states the year as 1051, obviously in error, and most sources

give the date of death earlier in the month of April.

131. Rome had been occupied by the forces of the Holy Roman Emperor Henry IV, with whom Gregory had a famously long-running dispute. The Pope was not actually "imprisoned" in Castel Sant'Angelo but took refuge in the fortress. Henry withdrew when faced with the possibility of fighting a pitched battle against Guiscard's seasoned troops.

132. This refers not to Roger Borsa but to his half-brother, Bohemond, who occupied Antioch in 1098 in connection with the First Crusade. Several paragraphs later Bohemond is identified correctly.

133. Peter the Hermit was from Amiens, and *l'Ermite* may have been a familial name rather than a nickname.

134. This passage is slightly misleading. Jerusalem was first occupied by Muslim forces during the reign of the caliph Umar the Great in 637; the chronicler may be alluding to a violent revolt that occurred in 1077. Urban preached the First Crusade at the Council of Clermont (at which Peter the Hermit may have been present) in November 1095 in response to a request for aid by Alexius I Comnenus, the Byzantine Emperor. The chief motive of Alexius was not the reconquest of Jerusalem, though that was a convenient pretext, but the defense of Asia Minor from the Seljuk Turks; he had also been forced to defend his realm against incursions by Robert Guiscard.

135. Here we encounter some political propaganda. In fact, the Church of the Holy Sepulchre was rebuilt in 1048, and (by agreement) permitted to remain open so long as the mosque in Constantinople was kept open. (There is no evidence to support Peter's allegation that the Muslims were using it as a stall.) The style of the existing church resembles the syncretic Norman-Arab style of ecclesial architecture seen in Sicily.

136. This passage reflects the religious zeal that colored European life by

the thirteenth century. There is no conclusive evidence that Peter the Hermit had already set foot in Jerusalem; had he already visited the city he would have found a splendid church.

137. Philip I had been excommunicated; indeed, that was one of the measures Urban reiterated at Clermont (see note 134).

138. Tancred, later Prince of Galilee, was the son of Emma (see the second genealogical table), Bohemond's sister, by a certain Odo the Good; Tancred, who died in 1112, was thus Bohemond's nephew. Here the source may be the *Gesti Tancredi* (see Appendix 4).

139. The last Fatimid emir (actually a vizier) closely associated with Jerusalem before the city fell to the crusaders was al-Afdal Shahanshah (1066-1121). In August 1099, a crusading force led by Godfrey of Bouillon defeated al-Afdal at Ascalon. However, al-Afdal did occasionally attempt to attack the city in the years to come.

140. Paschal II was present at Mileto in July 1101 when he consecrated a church. See *Italia Pontificia,* volume 10 (in Sources), page 145. The Council of Melfi is usually dated to August 1101 (not 1100), when Paschal was returning from Mileto, in Calabria, and going to Canosa, in Apulia; it was at Melfi that he excommunicated the Beneventans.

141. This paragraph is one of the parts of the chronicle attributed to Falco of Benevento.

142. Like the text in the preceding paragraph (see note 141), this passage is usually attributed to Falco of Benevento.

143. Henry IV, Holy Roman Emperor, had abdicated in 1105. He was succeeded by his son, Henry V.

144. The chronicle actually reports this as 1110. Roger Borsa died in Feb-

ruary and Bohemond in March, both in 1111.

145. In the manuscript this passage is earlier in the text, near the beginning of this section, immediately following the first mention of Pope Paschal II. Henry V was crowned in Rome in April 1111. This is confirmed by the entry in the *Annales Casinenses* (see Sources) for that year, on page 306 of the Pertz edition, which also notes that Henry arrived with a large army.

146. Most sources date this to 1112, when Stephen Harding was the third abbot of Cîteaux. Bernard was canonized in 1174.

147. This council, convened in the Lateran in March 1112, justified its action on the basis of Henry having extracted the coronation through coercion (he had taken the Pope prisoner).

148. The structure erected beginning in 1112 no longer exists.

149. This paragraph was extracted almost verbatim from the chronicle of Falco of Benevento.

150. This paragraph is drawn from the chronicle of Falco of Benevento, who, however, describes the events in far greater length and detail. Archbishop Landulf II was removed but reinstalled (he was archbishop until his death in 1119).

151. Jordan II held Ariano from 1102 until his death in 1127. With his brother, Robert I of Capua, he had attacked Benevento in 1114. Their kinsman, Robert of Alife (and Caiazzo), who died in 1115 or 1116, was a also member of the Drengot family (which was either Norman or French) that ruled Capua. For their kinship see the fourth genealogical table.

152. Saint Bruno was Bishop of Segni until his death in 1123; he was canonized in 1181.

153. This passage was extracted almost verbatim from the entry for 1117 in the *Annales Casinenses* (see Sources).

154. Henry's second coronation took place on 25 March 1117. The infamous conflict of Henry V, Holy Roman Emperor, with Pope Paschal II had lasted for many years.

155. A lunar eclipse was visible in Italy on 16 June 1117, not in July as stated in the chronicle. However, a lunar eclipse did indeed occur on 11 December 1117 as the chronicler affirms (see Espenak, *Five Millennium Canon,* in Sources). The "sky afire" on 16 December of that year may be the Aurora Borealis; it is rarely visible in southern Italy but the passage may reflect a report from someplace farther north. Certain atmospheric and celestial phenomena mentioned in the text are difficult to correlate with known events, partly because (apart from occasional use of the "Beneventan calendar" which begins the year in March) the dates given are not always precise, especially for the retrospective parts of the chronicle referring to years before 1195.

156. Maurice Bourdin became antipope, as Gregory VIII, in March 1118.

157. Pope Gelasius II took refuge at Gaeta, where he acted to excommunicate both the Holy Roman Emperor Henry V and the antipope Gregory VIII in April 1118.

158. There is no evidence that Gelasius went to England. He probably sailed directly to France.

159. Guy of Burgundy, Archbishop of Vienne, had initiated the excommunication of Henry V in 1112.

160. Ranulf II of Alife (and Caiazzo and Airola) was the son of Robert (see note 151 and the fourth genealogical table), who he succeeded. Being married to Matilda Hauteville, Ranulf was the brother-in-law of Roger II.

161. Another item (among many) found in the *Annales Casinenses.*

162. The *Annales Casinenses* (the monk's probable source of this information) confirms that this highly-destructive earthquake occurred in 1120.

163. The text gives the saint's name as *Eustasius,* but reference may be to Saint Eutychius, whose feast is observed in May.

164. William, Duke of Apulia, died in 1127. He had succeeded his father, Roger Borsa, in 1111. This is described in a later paragraph.

165. This is one of many details taken from the chronicle of Falco of Benevento, who describes the earthquake in even greater detail.

166. Henry V, Holy Roman Emperor, died in May 1125; here the monk copied Falco's report. Henry was the last monarch of the Salian dynasty.

167. William of Apulia died in July 1127.

168. In the original, *audita morte nepotis sui,* "hearing of the death of his nephew." Here we find an early use of what became, and still is, the Italian practice of referring to an older cousin as an "uncle" or "aunt." As the first cousin of Roger Borsa (William's father), Roger II of Sicily was actually William's first cousin one generation removed, not his uncle. In fact, William and Roger II were about the same age, but the latter was part of the prior generation of the Hauteville family.

169. This included (according to Falco), Romuald, the chronicler and future archbishop, who at this time was probably teaching at Salerno's medical school.

170. This was significant because Amalfi, although controlled by the rulers of Capua and Salerno since the eleventh century, sometimes functioned as an independent maritime republic similar to Genoa, occasionally revolt-

ing against Norman domination.

171. This section, and most of the remainder of this chapter, was freely adapted by the monk from the chronicle of Falco of Benevento, who states that the Pope initially recognized Roger's claims but then (after Roger had returned to Sicily) reneged, thus prompting the siege at Benevento.

172. Robert II of Capua, who also held Aversa, was the only legitimate son (and heir) of Jordan II (see note 151 and the fourth genealogical table), who he had recently succeeded. By 1128, this descendant of the House of Drengot was the only person in southern Italy who might challenge Roger II.

173. For Ranulf of Alife see note 160 and the fourth genealogical table.

174. The army subsequently assembled (with the help of Robert of Capua and Ranulf of Alife) was certainly much larger than this.

175. This may reflect an anti-Norman bias by Falco. It is believed by some scholars that Roger was simply waiting for the poorly-motivated army assembled against him to dissolve.

176. The attack planned for May 1130 never took place.

177. This town is about nine kilometers south of Benevento; its castle is still standing.

178. Here the monk is being economical with the facts. On 14 February 1130, the morning after the death of Honorius II, Gregory Papareschi was hastily nominated by a small faction of cardinals as Innocent II. A separate faction, consisting of those that had not voted in the earlier election, gathered and elected Peter Pierleone, who took the name Anacletus II (and later came to be considered an antipope).

179. In the Latin text this cardinal is simply *Comites,* literally "count." A

Papal diplomat, he later became a supporter of Innocent II.

180. King Louis IV.

181. Falco of Benevento states 150 bishops. This Council of Rheims (Reims) began in October 1131; significantly, Saint Bernard of Clairvaux attended.

182. Amalfi submitted to royal authority in February 1131.

183. The monk mentions this detail about a mistress, whereas Falco of Benevento states only that Matilda had suffered many affronts. Similarly, Alexander of Telese, whose chronicle was written on the initiative of Matilda herself, does not mention Ranulf's marital infidelity specifically. Nevertheless, it is a credible detail. (For Ranulf see also note 160.)

184. This observation about the moon as an omen was taken directly from Falco. The large, full moon is sometimes called a "blood moon." This observed effect was probably atmospheric.

185. These numbers come from Falco. It is interesting that throughout the telling of the episode involving Ranulf the monk's tone is more sympathetic to the king, while Falco (a Beneventan of Lombard origin), whose account is far lengthier, clearly sympathizes with Ranulf. This part of the *Ferraris Chronicle* almost seems like an attempt to "revise" the tone established decades earlier by Falco in order to present a view more favorable to the Normans.

186. This was in July 1132. The Valentine Bridge is an arched Roman span (still standing) across the Calore Irpino River two kilometers east of Benevento; it takes its name from Flavius Valens.

187. The Battle of Nocera is described at greater length by Falco of Benevento and Alexander of Telese. Neither this nor subsequent losses would

prove sufficient to unseat Roger II.

188. The Battle of Nocera was fought on 24 July 1132.

189. Lothair III (sometimes Lothair II) of Supplinburg was Holy Roman Emperor from 1133 until his death in 1137.

190. Lothair was, however, re-crowned Holy Roman Emperor by Innocent II at Rome in June 1133; in Tuscany he held the so-called Matildine Lands of the Papacy as fiefs.

191. Falco states that this was an army consisting largely of Muslims from Sicily. Specifically, these were among the finest longbow archers.

192. This agreement was reached in autumn 1133.

193. Roger II was excommunicated by Innocent II in June 1135 while the pontiff was in Pisa.

194. This attack was doubly convenient. Not only was Amalfi part of the Kingdom of Sicily, as a maritime mercantile city it competed against Pisa for trade.

195. The storm was an early harbinger of autumn, and winter was not usually the preferred time for any kind of campaign. It would take two weeks for a knight to ride from Naples to Palermo, much longer for the part of the army traveling on foot, taking into account such factors as fewer daylight hours by November.

196. According to Falco this was in late 1135.

197. Pescara (in what is now Abruzzi) was not far from the frontier of Apulia; indeed, it was occasionally thought of as part of that region. Frederick II, who was born near Ancona (north of Pescara), was sometimes

referred to as "the boy from Apulia."

198. Marino had been Archbishop of Naples since 1117 or 1118.

199. The Pope was at Viterbo into late April.

200. Henry X, Duke of Bavaria, was married to Lothair's daughter, Gertrude. In the original text the chronicler refers erroneously to *Conrad* [Hohenstaufen], an understandable lapse in view of Conrad (instead of the Welf Henry X) becoming King of Germany in 1138. Falco of Benevento, however, refers to Lothair's son-in-law correctly as *Henry*.

201. Located near Lake Albano, this ancient town is now Albano Laziale.

202. The city itself immediately surrendered but the garrison at the castle did not. This siege of Bari's castle is not mentioned in the surviving codex of Falco's chronicle.

203. This is a slight exaggeration; it is possible that part of northern Calabria submitted to Lothair but probably not Cosenza or any place south of it.

204. This fortified town is located about midway between Melfi and Potenza.

205. The name of this fortress is translated (appropriately) "High Tower," in the original *turris maioris*.

206. The reference to Saint Peter refers not only to the saint himself but, more importantly here, to the authority of the Papacy.

207. Reference to *Florida* is an error copied from Falco's text. The consort of Lothair III was, in fact, Richenza of Northeim, Holy Roman Empress until her husband's death. Falco, of course, describes her visit at far greater

length than the monk does.

208. Gregory was archbishop until 1145.

209. Peregrine di Povo was patriarch (archbishop) until 1161.

210. This was Lothair's exit from the Italian stage; he died in the first days of December in 1137 as he, his wife and his army were crossing the Alps.

211. This is an example of contradictory wording (by Falco of Benevento) that seeks to vilify Roger as a coward. Lothair reached Rome by late October 1137; Roger was already at Benevento during the same month. Considering the time it took to raise an army in Sicily and Calabria, and Roger's arrival in the region at this time, it is not likely that he was deliberately waiting for Lothair to leave the country.

212. This refers to Richard of Rupecanina, Ranulf's brother (see Table 4). However, the town is not specified.

213. This passage reflects the monk's Cistercian bias on the one hand and Falco's sardonic perspective on the other. In fact, Roger II claimed Apulia by dynastic right; the usurper was Ranulf of Alife, lately Duke of Apulia.

214. Falco's account of this battle, though lengthier, gives few details of the actual engagement; for example, archers and foot men are not mentioned.

215. Roger was in Salerno in November.

216. Cardinal Gregory Conti was briefly antipope as Victor IV.

217. The monk quotes (very closely) from a known account. For the words attributed to Bernard see also *Sancti Bernardi* (in Sources), book 2, chapter 7, column 1109, paragraph 43. For a fine Victorian translation into English,

see Morrison, op.cit., pages 211-213.

218. Salerno's medical school was indeed famous. In the twelfth century it was considered one of the finest in Europe.

219. This may be an allegory for recent events related to the Papal schism, such as the role of Bernard, a visitor.

220. Guy of Castello was destined to be elected Pope as Celestine II in 1143.

221. This reckons the beginning of the year from March as per the practice of Falco of Benevento, who, however, gives 25 January 1138 as the date of death.

222. This was the same Cardinal Gregory (see note 216) who had been present at Salerno in November 1137.

223. According to the *Monte Cassino Chronicle* this meeting was in May 1138 and Pope Innocent may have been quite conciliatory to the Pierleone family and the cardinals appointed by Anacletus. See the *Chronica Monasterii Casinensis* (in Sources), book 4, section 130, page 607.

224. The Tre Fontane Abbey is located near Rome at the site where Saint Paul is believed to have been beheaded by the Emperor Nero. Its chief monastic church, dedicated to Saint Vincent and Saint Anastasius, had belonged to the Benedictines.

225. Lothair III actually died in Tyrol in December 1137. See note 210.

226. The original text erroneously refers to Conrad III, crowned as King of Germany in 1138, as Lothair's son-in-law (although that was actually Henry X "the Proud" who as Lothair's heir-designate was expected to become King of Germany). The machinations behind this election led to the

Hohenstaufen dynasty taking power, although Conrad III never became Holy Roman Emperor. For details we look to the chronicle of another Cistercian, Otto of Freising. See also note 200 and the third genealogical chart.

227. Falco describes these attacks in far greater detail, mentioning additional cities. Under the entry for 1138, the *Annales Casinenses* states simply but unequivocally that *Alifas redegit in cinerem,* "Alife was reduced to ashes."

228. Entire volumes have been dedicated to the significance of the Second Lateran Council. Among the most important points were the following: Priests or deacons who have taken wives or concubines are strongly condemned, and constrained to be removed from their ecclesiastical offices. Monks are prohibited from working as lawyers for pay in the civil (secular) sphere. Nuns are forbidden the foundation of convents outside the established religious orders. Use of the crossbow against Christians is prohibited, although it certainly continued. Jousts in tournaments are condemned, yet these continued unabated. Churches are considered a sanctuary for fugitives. Arsonists are denied Christian burial. Children born of incest are banned from inheriting property, while the children and other kin of priests are forbidden the inheritance of church estates. The sons of priests may serve as clergy only in monasteries, not in diocesan churches. The laity has no power over ecclesiastical estates; that is to say, neither a baron nor the son of a priest can claim church land. Bishoprics are not to be left vacant for more than three months; this provides for the speedy election of bishops without inordinate delay.

229. Falco does not mention the volcano by name, stating simply (in a very similar description) that on 29 May the "mountain near Naples" erupted. The *Annales Casinenses* refers explicitly to Mount Vesuvius, not the shallow Solfatara crater at Pozzuoli which was active until 1198.

230. Both the monk and Falco use the phrase *princeps civitatis,* which probably refers generically to the (Greek) "leader" of the citizens, *princeps* in this

case denoting the *first* citizen, Jaquinto. The actual Prince of Bari was Tancred, second son of Roger II, who died around 1138.

231. San Germano, now Cassino, was the town at the base of Mount Cassino. Roger's arrival is mentioned by Falco.

232. The Borrello family, which held important fiefs in Molise into the middle of the thirteenth century, had been present in Italy before the arrival of the Normans. Alexander of Telese (book 2, chapter 69) mentions them paying fealty to King Roger. For more see Ferrari, op.cit. (in Sources).

233. The *Annales Casinenses* mentions the Galluccio incident. The ambush was near Mignano in July 1139.

234. This constituted the Treaty of Mignano.

235. King Roger and Pope Innocent reached Benevento on 1 August 1139.

236. Falco states that Gregory entered the city in September.

237. Rosman (Rosemannus) received an appointment in Sicily under the king's auspices. We find him mentioned as rector of an important church (Saint Lucy of the Sepulchre) at Syracuse in a document regarding land held illegally (by Gaimar, son of Alfano) that was being restored to the Bishop of Cefalù dated 8 September 1141. For an extract see *Documenti Inediti,* pages 41-42.

238. The Assumption is observed on 15 August; Saint Bartholomew's day is 24 August.

239. Through a mistranscription, *Ferraris* reports the Pope's departure from Benevento being on 2 August. Falco states it was 29 September.

240. This was Bishop William III.

241. Falco states that Roger encamped beyond the city walls.

242. This siege in August and September was undertaken by sea as well as land.

243. In connection with this, it should be remembered that many of the Bariots were Greek Orthodox, and perhaps suspicious of Catholic motives.

244. For the "princely" status of Jaquinto see note 230.

245. Falco mentions another detail. A knight freed by the Bariots had been blinded on Jaquinto's orders whilst a prisoner. Learning of this, the king convened a council of judges from Bari, Trani and Troia to decide the fate of Jaquinto, for the person of a knight was held to be inviolable. The "prince" (see note 230) and two of his counsellors were sentenced to death and hanged, along with ten others. Additionally, ten other men were mutilated. This effectively purged Bari of its most aggressive rebel element.

246. According to Falco, this was on 5 November 1139.

247. The *Annales Casinenses* reports an earthquake in 1141.

248. It is worth noting that the term *castrum* usually refers to a walled town, or one protected by a castle. Sometimes, however, it refers to a castle outside a village or town.

249. This is the last passage of the *Ferraris Chronicle* that seems to be based on the chronicle of Falco of Benevento.

250. Falco mentions the introduction of the ducat (see the photograph in this volume). Neither Falco nor the monk who wrote *Ferraris* mentions the Assizes of Ariano (1140). There is no part of the narrative dedicated specifically to the year 1141.

251. King Roger did indeed have this authority as Apostolic Legate, a power granted to his father in 1098. An example of the kind of appointment that may have irritated Pope Innocent was the king naming Rosman as the rector of an important church in Sicily (see note 237). Most of the text from this paragraph until the end of the chapter seems to have been taken from the chronicle of Falco of Benevento, probably from a manuscript now lost (see this book's Introduction).

252. Holding the title of *amiratus* (for which see note 274), George of Antioch was the chief advisor to King Roger II, and one of those responsible for bringing Apulia under royal control. A Greek, he was a patron of the church in Palermo now known as the *Martorana*.

253. Guy of [Città di] Castello was one of the cardinals who supported Pope Innocent II at Salerno in 1137 (and is mentioned earlier in the text).

254. Robert of Selby, who was from England, became chancellor in 1131.

255. Cardinal Gerard Caccianemici dal Orso, a confidant of Innocent II, had been present at Salerno in 1137 (and is mentioned earlier in the text). He was elected as Lucius II in March 1144.

256. Marginalia reads *Iste dicitur quod fuit bononiensis,* "He was said to be from Bologna." This note was correct. A related passage reads, "Lucius was destined to be Pope for eleven years and five months."

257. Ceprano was located in the Papal State near the border of the Kingdom of Sicily in what is now the province of Frosinone.

258. This passage refers principally to Alfonso, who died in October 1144. Roger of Apulia, however, lived until May 1149.

259. In fact, Simon, who became Prince of Taranto in 1148, was born outside marriage.

260. This was in a few years later, 1147 during the Second Crusade (see the following chapter), when George of Antioch launched an expedition to Corfu.

261. Bernard of Pisa was the first Cistercian to be elected Pope, hence the chronicler's panegyric. This interlude does not mention that the Second Crusade was undertaken on the initiative of Pope Eugene III (encouraged by Bernard of Clairvaux) to recapture Edessa from the Muslims.

262. Bernard of Pisa was first a subdeacon (as mentioned earlier) and then, from 1133, vicedominus of the entire archdiocese. The latter title, in Italian *visdomino,* should not be confused with the French *vidame,* which was a secular official acting on behalf of a bishop. A vicedominus was a bishop's assistant empowered to administer the diocese day by day. Bernard fulfilled this role when the Archbishop of Pisa, Cardinal Hubert Rossi Lanfranchi, being a supporter of the antipope Anacletus, was forced to leave for several years as Pope Innocent II occasionally resided in the city. Indeed, Bernard was ordained by Innocent.

263. Consisting of a number of letters collected into one work, the "Book of Considerations" espoused many principles. An underlying theme was that the Papacy itself might be reformed (spiritually) if the Pope himself were more spiritual, and that mediation and piety must be the foundations for everything else. Among other things, Bernard apologizes to Pope Eugene for encouraging the Second Crusade. See *Saint Bernard On Consideration* (in Sources).

264. Eugene III died at Tivoli in July 1153.

265. Actually King of Germany and never crowned Holy Roman Emperor; see also note 226.

266. King Roger II did not participate in the Second Crusade, concentrating instead on Tunisia and Greece, with a half-hearted naval attack on Con-

stantinople. According to the chronicler William of Tyre, the ill-fated marriage of Roger's mother, the widowed Adelaide, to Baldwin I of Jerusalem (a bigamous union on Baldwin's part) in 1112 fostered in the King of Sicily a profound resentment of the Franks who ruled Palestine. Politically, the idea of a religious crusade may not have appealed to a king who had many Muslim subjects.

267. From 1152 Frederick I "Barbarossa" was King of Germany; he was crowned Holy Roman Emperor in 1155.

268. Representing a small fraction of Bernard's voluminous writings, these are the accepted English titles of the works mentioned by the chronicler.

269. Roger died in February 1154. He seems to have been ill, or at least weakened, for a month or two prior to his death. His ill-health may have been brought on by exhaustion (according to Hugh Falcandus), but it ended in a terrible fever (Romuald of Salerno). He was crowned King of Sicily in 1130, but he was already Great Count of Sicily since the death of his elder brother, Simon, in 1105. Roger reached the age of majority by 1112 (see manuscripts B and C in Sources).

270. This oak forest was located in the Matese Mountains outside Cerreto Sannita northwest of Benevento not too far from Santa Maria della Ferraria.

271. In the original text a very similar story about William freeing a horse trapped in a hole on a stone bridge is recounted immediately before this passage. That line was deleted.

272. These details and others are drawn from various sources, especially the chronicle of Hugh Falcandus.

273. The Treaty of Benevento in June 1156.

274. This title, which derives from the Arabic *emir* or *amir,* was reserved to the highest official in the kingdom after the king himself. More than a court chancellor, the amiratus was something akin to what nowadays would be a prime minister. His authority was military as well as civil. The title *admiral* may derive from *amiratus,* but the amiratus was much more than an admiral. See also the Introduction and note 252.

275. Most of the allegations against Maio of Bari were untrue (he certainly did not wish to seat himself on the throne) and this description is grossly oversimplified. In any case, the basis for this information is drawn principally from the chronicle of Hugh Falcandus.

276. These Zirid lands included Mahdia, which is never mentioned explicitly in this chronicle. The territory William I lost was essentially what is now Tunisia and Libya, the occupation of which justified the occasional reference to Roger II (and initially William I) as "King of Africa."

277. The Zisa palace, in the Genoard park in Palermo, is mentioned by Romuald of Salerno (see Appendix 5). It is where Joanna of England and her ladies-in-waiting were lodged when they arrived in Palermo in 1177 (See the photograph and note 299).

278. This interesting interpretation differs slightly in tone from the accounts of Falcandus and Romuald. At all events, Mahdia, the most important part of what the chronicler refers to generically as "Africa," fell to the Almohads in January 1160.

279. This passage is generally inaccurate. Maio of Bari was killed after dark on the evening of 10 November 1160 whilst returning home from a meeting with Hugh, Archbishop of Palermo. Matthew of Bonello, to whom Maio's daughter was betrothed, was not related to King William.

280. Simon of Taranto, it may be recalled, was an illegitimate son of King Roger II. Tancred was an illegitimate son of William's elder brother, Roger.

See Table 2.

281. Matthew Bonello's mistress, Clementia of Catanzaro, had taken refuge at Taverna (in Calabria) following the failed revolt, and William did attack the fortress in 1162. By then, however, Bonello was already dead.

282. Matthew Bonello died in prison in 1161.

283. The antipope Octavian dei Crescenzi Ottaviani of Monticelli took the name Victor IV (like the antipope elected in 1138).

284. This occurred in March 1162, although the chronicler gives the year as 1163.

285. This passage is misleading. Alexander III was in France from 1162 until late 1165. Then he visited the *Kingdom* of Sicily.

286. This implies that the monk's reference here is the chronicle of Hugh Falcandus, as Romuald of Salerno, contrarily, gives the date of death as 7 May (see Appendix 5). The *Annales Casinenses,* like Falcandus, gives the date as 15 May.

287. William II was about twelve years old. His regent was his mother, Margaret of Navarre, widow of William I; it was probably on her initiative that certain taxes, notably the redemption money in Apulia, were abolished.

288. The Battle of Monte Porzio took place in May 1167. As the text states, the Papal forces were defeated. Robert of Loritello was present, fighting on the imperial side.

289. Stephen of Perche was Norman, although his father, Rotrou, had held lands in Navarre (most notably the prosperous town of Tudela), a fact which may have given birth to this misperception. Stephen was a cousin of Queen Margaret, for which see the Perche lineage in Table 5.

290. This supposition is grossly corrupted from information reported by Hugh Falcandus; the monk recounts only a small part of what, in reality, Falcandus himself acknowledged was merely a rumour.

291. This succinct account of events is not very accurate. For a lengthier explanation see Alio, Jacqueline, op.cit. (in Sources), pages 168-219, 228-236.

292. The siege, such as it was, had already ended, although the Pope was still constrained to remain outside Rome. By 1169, Frederick's envoy was negotiating a peace with the Papacy, first at Benevento and then at Veroli.

293. This alludes to the Papal *pallium,* Alessandria being named for Pope Alexander III, who enjoyed the support of the Lombard League in its efforts against Frederick I. Chartered as a free commune in 1168 (not in 1169 as the text states), Alessandria, in what is now Piedmont, is situated in an alluvial plain between the Bormida and Tanaro rivers, which historically facilitated the cultivation of arborio rice.

294. Saint John, "the Hermit, of Tufara," was born in a town in Molise and educated in Paris. He founded the monastery of Saint Mary at Gualdo Mazzocca (near Foiano di Val Fortore), mentioned above. He was canonized in 1221.

295. The precise year of death of Richard of Mandra, Count of Molise, is not known.

296. From Alio, op.cit., page 296: In July of 1174, the Sicilian fleet commanded by Tancred [of Lecce] arrived at Alexandria to support the friendly Fatimids in their struggle against the adversarial Ayyubids. Here two unexpected problems presented themselves, and Tancred might have elected to abort the principal assault had he known about either one. In Egypt, Saladin had recently captured and killed the leaders of the Fatimid insurgency; in Palestine, Almaric had unexpectedly died, so no army arrived

from Jerusalem. This left the Sicilians alone. Formidable as the landing force was, it was beaten back, suffering heavy losses. In the end, Tancred had to content himself with some raids along the African coast, and Saladin's acquisition of territory continued unabated.

297. This incident is mentioned in the *Annales Casinenses* (see Sources) for that year, on page 311 of the Pertz edition.

298. A firsthand account of the Treaty (or Peace) of Venice comes to us from the chronicler Romuald of Salerno, who was present as one of the negotiators. A significant result was a peace between the Holy Roman Empire and the Kingdom of Sicily. In his chronicle, Romuald notes that in May 1178 several ambassadors of Emperor Frederick I, their journey delayed somewhat, arrived at Palermo. They confirmed the peace negotiated in Venice, swearing a further treaty with the Kingdom of Sicily for the next fifteen years.

299. For the wedding between William II and Joanna of England, see Alio, op.cit., pages 301-306, 399-408.

300. The Third Lateran Council was held in March 1179.

301. Although this passage is placed under the heading for 1182, the chronicler does not attribute all the events described explicitly to that year; he is ruminating on the pontificate of the late Alexander III. Pope Alexander met Thomas Becket at Sens in 1164, and the latter was murdered late in 1170. It is difficult to imagine that the chronicler did not know this, as Saint Thomas of Canterbury was widely venerated, and mentioned in many works. Becket corresponded with Queen Margaret of Sicily, who gave refuge to his kin, and the first public holy image of the saint is an icon in mosaic (shown in this volume) at Monreale Abbey outside Palermo.

302. Andronikos I Comnenus, who died in 1185 (see Table 7), was a cousin of Manuel I Comnenus.

303. Described by Nicetas Choniates and William of Tyre, the Massacre of the Latins took place in April 1182. For Maria "Porphyrogenita," who was formerly betrothed to William II of Sicily, see the Introduction, Appendix 5 and Table 7.

304. This was none other than Isaac II Angelus (see Table 7), who turned Andronikos over to an angry mob, which dismembered and killed him in September 1185. Isaac's brother ruled as Alexios III.

305. Alexios III Angelus (see Table 7) was deposed in 1203 when soldiers of the Fourth Crusade attacked Constantinople. He died at Nicaea in 1211.

306. From Alio, op.cit., page 326: In 1185, William launched an invasion of the Greek lands to the east of the *Regnum,* something he had been considering ever since the Byzantine massacre of the Latins at Constantinople a few years earlier. Leading this incursion was Tancred of Lecce and an able admiral named Margaritus of Brindisi. The Sicilian advance toward Constantinople was stopped by Emperor Isaac Angelus Comnenus, with whom the King of Sicily made peace four years later.

307. Pope Lucius III died in Verona in November 1185.

308. The Siege of Jerusalem lasted from 20 September to 2 October 1187.

309. Pope Urban III died in Ferrara on 20 October 1187.

310. Pope Gregory VIII reigned from 21 October to 17 December 1187, not the year stated by the chronicler.

311. The lavish nuptials were celebrated at Milan in January 1186. On this occasion, Constance was crowned Queen of Germany as Henry's consort. (See also note 315.)

312. It is true that William II died without heirs, and that his widow, Joanna,

subsequently wed and bore children (by Raymond VI of Toulouse). It is possible that during 1181 Joanna, whilst married to William, gave birth to a child, rumoured to have been named Bohemond and to have died in infancy. However, only one chronicler reports the event, and he was not in Sicily; Robert of Torigni, a Norman, was the abbot of Mont Saint-Michel and godfather to Eleanor, the daughter of Henry II of England. Significant as his chronicles are, Robert's statement about Bohemond is probably divorced from reality. See *The Chronicle of Robert of Torigni* (in Sources), page 303.

313. For the account of this by Romuald of Salerno, see Appendix 5.

314. That is to say, the reigns of William I and Tancred.

315. By most accounts, illegitimate Tancred of Lecce was crowned early in 1190, with the assent of the Sicilian baronage, which did not want to risk the kingdom falling into the hands of the Hohenstaufens. Constance could do nothing about Tancred's coronation, but her husband raised an army to invade the kingdom in her name. The fact that Constance (see note 311 and genealogical tables 1 and 2), the posthumous daughter of Roger II, was the childless William's designated successor (heiress as queen regnant) is confirmed by the chroniclers Richard of San Germano and Roger of Howden, as well as the author of the *Annales Casinenses* (who provides a fairly detailed account of events under the entry for 1190).

316. Conrad of Wittelsbach (son of Count Otto IV of Wittelsbach and brother of Otto I of Bavaria) was Archbishop of Mainz and also Archchancellor of Germany. For more on Henry of Kalden, identified in the chronicle by his nickname as *Henrico Testa,* see note 365.

317. Richard I "Lionheart" of England and Philip II "Augustus" of France arrived at Messina in September 1190 on their way to the Third Crusade. Tancred had imprisoned Richard's sister, Queen Joanna, the widow of William II, failing to pay the money due her by virtue of her dower (see

Alio, op.cit., pages 402-407). King Richard, who Tancred had not expected to appear in Sicily, demanded that Joanna be freed and provided with her just inheritance. She was released, but the paltry sum she was given angered Richard. Meanwhile, the crusader troops behaved arrogantly towards the local men and freely with the women; that, and the occupation of a monastery, provoked a revolt by the locals and a crisis for Tancred, who feared that Richard might decide to stay and conquer Sicily. Despite the diplomatic protests of Philip and a Sicilian delegation, Richard's troops burned and plundered part of Messina. A truce was reached in November. Tancred signed a treaty with Richard and Philip guaranteeing money to Joanna who, in the end, actually received very little.

318. The Siege of Acre ended in July 1191. It was a pivotal victory for the crusaders and a setback for Saladin's forces.

319. Cyprus was seized from Isaac Comnenus (not to be confused with a Byzantine Emperor of the same name), who had imprisoned Joanna, Richard's sister (see note 317), and Berengaria of Navarre, his fiancée, when the women were shipwrecked on the island.

320. Saladin destroyed much of Ascalon to prevent it from falling into the hands of the crusaders. Richard then took control of it and erected a citadel.

321. Henry, who was already King of Germany, was crowned Holy Roman Emperor in April 1191 as Henry VI, succeeding his father, Frederick I, who died in June 1190 whilst fording a river in Asia Minor during the Third Crusade.

322. The "pestilence" was probably malaria. Henry VI raised the siege of Naples in late August of 1191. The region was defended for Tancred by Richard of Acerra, his brother-in-law. Constance remained at Salerno with a garrison, but she was imprisoned by Tancred's partisans and taken to Messina and then Palermo, to be released on the Pope's orders in 1192.

323. This was Berthold, Duke of Merania, who ruled coastal lands in Istria and Dalmatia. Otto I of Wittelsbach, Duke of Bavaria, who died in 1183, was Berthold's kinsman through his mother, Hedwig.

324. These events are recounted at greater length, and more accurately, in the *Annales Casinenses* (codices 4 and 5) under the entries for 1191, 1192 and 1193, which seems to be the source for this information.

325. Roger predeceased his father, Tancred, in December 1193; his widow, Irene Angelina, later wed Philip of Swabia, brother of Henry VI, a fact mentioned in the text. Emperor Isaac II Angelus Comnenus (see note 304) died in 1204; here the chronicler may be referring to his deposition and imprisonment in 1195 (see notes 305 and 334).

326. Henry VI burned Salerno as a punishment because he had not forgotten that the city had permitted Constance to be turned over to Tancred.

327. This passage is a highly abbreviated account of events. King Tancred died of natural causes in February 1194, the same month Henry VI released Richard "Lionheart" from captivity in Trifels Castle for a ransom to finance the Sicilian campaign. Tancred's wife, Sibylla of Acerra, and young son, William (who had been crowned as William III), were granted "safe conduct" to the German lands but the boy was apparently killed.

328. Constance gave birth to Frederick II at Iesi, near Ancona, on 26 December 1194 while Henry was in Palermo. At Bari, she was crowned Queen of Sicily. Although Henry VI ruled in her name *jure uxoris,* some of Constance's charters were issued with her own name and seal as queen regnant (see manuscript E in Sources).

329. The execution of Richard of Acerra, Tancred's brother-in-law (30 November 1196) is mentioned in the *Annales Ceccanensis* and by Richard of San Germano. He was punished for having fought against Henry and capturing Constance.

330. Here the chronicler may be given to exaggeration, but it is true that Henry did much to irritate the Norman nobility in Sicily; this spurred a revolt around Catania that, according to some sources, may have been supported briefly by Constance herself (see Jamison, *Admiral Eugenius of Sicily,* pages 157-159). Markward of Anweiler, Margrave of Ancona and Molise, who had served at the court of Frederick Barbarossa, was imperial seneschal.

331. See note 325.

332. This passage is anachronistic insofar as Saladin died in 1193. However, it is true that he captured Jerusalem a few years earlier (in 1187) and died at Damascus. Moreover, Conrad of Mainz (see note 316), Henry's archchancellor, went to Palestine in September 1197 as a Papal envoy, though (obviously) not to visit Saladin.

333. The text refers to *Massimutius,* corrupting *Masmuda.* Abu Yusuf Yaqub al Mansur was the third Almohad caliph, ruling from 1184 to 1199.

334. Isaac II Angelus Comnenus was deposed by his elder brother, Alexios III Angelus (see note 305) in 1195.

335. Henry VI died at Messina, where he was preparing a crusade, on 28 September 1197. The cause of death was probably malaria but some historians suggest it was poisoning.

336. There was indeed a lunar eclipse that was briefly visible in Italy on 5 March 1197. See Espenak, op.cit. (in Sources).

337. Richard of San Germano describes this at some length. The *Annales Casinenses* (codex 3) refers to it under the entry for 1196.

338. In this claim Markward was opposing the authority of Constance, as queen regent, following Henry's death; the margrave's ambitions (and ego)

grew after Constance was gone, when he sought power over young Frederick II. Frederick II had been crowned King of Sicily during his mother's lifetime, in May 1198.

339. Shortly before her untimely death, Constance had appointed Pope Innocent III as the guardian of Frederick II, and acting regent for the boy and the kingdom. The unrest described by the chronicler continued for a few more years, until Markward's death (which is not noted) in 1202. Markward of Anweiler, whose exploits are described in some detail by Richard of San Germano, enjoyed the rare distinction of being excommunicated by two popes, Celestine III and then Innocent III. For the events of this period, such as Frederick's coronation and Constance's marginalization of Markward, as well as the Pope's position, see the series of decrees published in *Historia Diplomatica Frederici Secundi* (in Sources), volume 1, part 1, pages 9-40.

340. Dipold (Dietpold) von Schweinspünt received the County of Acerra after capturing its previous holder, Richard, who was hanged (see notes 322 and 329). Richard of San Germano notes Dipold's attack on San Germano (Cassino) occurring on the night of 9 March 1200, and he describes the great suffering of the people of the town. In 1198, according to codex 3 of the *Annales Casinenses* (and also Richard of San Germano), Dipold had promised not to attack this region.

341. Thaddeus would serve as abbot until 1227, cultivating a friendship with Frederick II.

342. Elvira and her mother, dowager Queen Sibylla, had found refuge in France. (Sibylla, who died in 1205, had six children by Tancred: Roger III, William III, Elvira, Constance, Medania, Valdrada.) The pontifical invitation to Walter of Brienne, who was traveling through Italy on his way to the Fourth Crusade, was part of an effort to oust the Hohenstaufens from the Kingdom of Sicily.

343. Richard of San Germano reports that this battle at Capua, which forced Dipold's retreat, was fought on 10 June 1201.

344. This refers to a battle at Cannae, near Barletta.

345. Based on the *Catalogus Baronum,* Peter of Celano had enough fiefs (and therefore knights) to make him one of the most important vassals in the kingdom. He was present at Constance's coronation at Bari in 1195 and initially loyal to her and to Henry VI. As early as 1199, Pope Innocent was providing Peter funds to take up arms against Markward. In a move typical of the times, Peter of Celano eventually returned the fold, betrothing his daughter to one of Dipold's sons.

346. Like the word *Latins* in the previous section (where it referred to the Normans and Lombards in Italy before the arrival of Henry VI), *Franks* is a term that varies somewhat according to context. Here it denotes Europeans of the western (Roman Catholic) church, be they French or not, beyond the Byzantine and Slavic lands.

347. Prince Alexios (later Alexios IV) was disinherited and imprisoned when his father, Isaac II, was deposed, blinded and jailed by Alexios III (see Table 7) in March 1195. Six years later, the prince was freed by Italian traders and taken to Germany, where his sister, Irene Angelina, was married to Philip of Swabia (see Table 3), younger brother of Henry VI. For the Byzantine emperors mentioned thus far, see notes 305, 306, 325, 334.

348. Volumes have been written about the infamous Fourth Crusade. The pretext for its diversion to Constantinople was support of young Prince Alexios (later Alexios IV), son of the recently-deposed Byzantine Emperor Isaac II, in an internecine feud. The reigning emperor, Alexios III, was a brother of Isaac II (and so uncle of Prince Alexios). He had overthrown and imprisoned Isaac (note 334), but Prince Alexios managed to escape to the German court of Philip, the brother Henry VI. (Philip, as stated earlier in the text, was married to Prince Alexios' sister, Irene Angelina.) Crusaders

initially intending to reach Jerusalem via Egypt were taken by Venetian ships to Constantinople for what was proposed as a "side trip" to restore Isaac II and his son to power before continuing onward to Palestine. Instead, they perpetrated all manner of atrocities at Constantinople, with rather few knights making their way to Jerusalem. Pope Innocent III was appalled at news of the slaughter, effectively a ruthless "crusade" against fellow Christians that put to rest any hope of restoring unity between the churches of east and west separated since 1054. The so-called "Latin Empire of Constantinople" established in the wake of this genocidal conquest survived in some form until Byzantine Greek forces reclaimed the city in 1261. Eight centuries after the Fourth Crusade, Pope John Paul II apologized to the Patriarch of Constantinople for this crime against humanity. (The *Ferraris* account of the Fourth Crusade is, of course, much abbreviated and highly simplified, and should not be considered a chief source of information on that topic.) For the Comnenus parentage see Table 7.

349. This refers to the money promised by Alexios to the Venetians for transporting the crusaders and pilgrims to Constantinople.

350. A witness to these events was the historian (and logothete) Nicetas Choniates.

351. Alexios IV Angelus was murdered in February 1204.

352. This refers to an attack by Henry of Flanders.

353. This is probably the icon of the *Theotokos* in Venice known as the *Madonna Nicopeia*.

354. Mourtzouphlos was killed (probably near Mosynopolis) in November 1204, when he was captured by a crusader force commanded by Thierry of Loos.

355. Matthew 12:25. "Every kingdom divided against itself will be ruined,

and every city or household divided against itself will not stand."

356. Alexios III Angelus was ransomed and sent to Asia Minor, where, confined to a monastery, he died in 1211. Boniface of Montferrat was one of the leaders of the Fourth Crusade and then King of Thessalonica, one of the short-lived states founded in the wake of the fall of the Byzantine Empire; he died in 1207.

357. Thomas Morosini was the Latin Patriarch of Constantinople from 1204 until 1211, the year of his death. The chronicler fails to mention that Pope Innocent did not initially accept the legitimacy of Morosini's election, regarding it as uncanonical.

358. See note 356. Most of the Montferrat region was located in what is now Piedmont and Liguria.

359. Walter of Brienne was assassinated at Sarno in June 1205.

360. Walter of Palear (or Palearia), whose family held Manoppello near Pescara, was the chancellor since the reign of Queen Constance, and is mentioned as such in various documents; see, for example the charter conserved in Palermo, extracted in *Friderici II Diplomata* (in Sources), volume 14, part 1, pages 50-52. In the year cited in the chronicle (1206) he was Bishop of Troia, and in 1208 he became Bishop of Catania. The *Annales Casinenses* dates the arrival of Dipold in Palermo to November 1206, whereas Richard of San Germano tells us that in 1207 (not 1206 as the *Ferraris* text states) Dipold arrived at Palermo with a fleet, taking command of the royal palace and custody of young Frederick. Then Dipold's forces were overpowered by Walter's men and Dipold himself was captured, only to escape in the night and make his way back to the mainland.

361. This refers to the fees charged by notaries and scribes in Pope Innocent's jurisdiction, but it was a problem throughout Italy. In the Kingdom of Sicily, it was a form of corruption addressed by Stephen of Perche in

1167 as recounted by Hugh Falcandus. From Alio (op.cit.), page 179: To discourage future incidents of this kind, the chancellor fixed a limit on what notaries could charge for specific services. Finding the profession a closed caste, he permitted the licensing of a number of new notaries, opening the ranks of this profession to many qualified men who, until now, had been unjustly excluded.

362. This is also recounted at length by Richard of San Germano and in the *Annales Casinenses* (the entry for 1208).

363. Richard was Count of Aquila and also Fondi. For Peter see note 345.

364. There was indeed a lunar eclipse visible in Italy on 29 July 1208. See Espenak, op.cit. (in Sources).

365. This was Philip of Swabia, the brother of Henry VI (and uncle of Frederick II). Following the death of Henry VI, Philip was crowned King of Germany in 1198. As mentioned earlier (see notes 325 and 348), he was married to Irene Angelina Comnenus, who bore him four daughters but no surviving sons. Otto VIII, Count of Bavaria, who assassinated him (for motives still debated by historians) in June 1208, was declared an outlaw and killed by Henry of Kalden in 1209.

366. Constance was the widow of Emmerich (Imre) of Hungary, by whom she bore a son, Ladislas, in 1199. Following Emmerich's death in 1204, she was regent for young Ladislas III until the boy died (in exile in Austria) at a very young age the next year. Constance then returned to Aragon.

367. Philip's death (see note 365) opened the door for Otto IV of Brunswick (of the Welf dynasty opposed to the Hohenstaufens), who then wed Philip's sister, Beatrix, to claim the German crown and, with the support of Pope Innocent III, become Holy Roman Emperor. As we shall see, however, Innocent did not condone Otto's overt attempt to control

the Kingdom of Sicily ruled by young Frederick (which would have contravened Papal intentions of avoiding the concentration of power throughout most of Italy in a sole ruler or dynasty).

368. Otto was thus usurping Innocent's authority, as Spoleto and Ancona were in the Papal State.

369. Innocent had excommunicated Otto (late in 1210) before the incursion into the Kingdom of Sicily, in response to a series of affronts to pontifical authority, including the occupation of Papal territory.

370. Richard of San Germano mentions Frederick arriving at Gaeta, where he was joined by Richard of Fondi and other barons. The monarch issued a charter there in March 1212; see *Friderici II Diplomata,* book 14, part 1, pages 303-304. Charters were also issued by Frederick during his stay at Rome in April; ibid. pages 305-321.

371. Frederick was at Genoa by May and into July 1212; see *Friderici II Diplomata,* book 14, part 1, pages 322-328. He was at Verona by August; ibid. pages 329-331. He was in Basel in September; see *Friderici II Diplomata,* book 14, part 2, pages 1-10. By October he was at Hagenau, on the Rhine; ibid. pages 10-17. In November he was in Toul; ibid. pages 17-18. He reached Worms, Mainz and Speyer, in the German heartland, in December, ibid. pages 19-28.

372. This matter is somewhat more complex than it may seem, and it reflected changing circumstances. Frederick had just had his young son, Henry, crowned King of Sicily in March 1212 (it was not unusual for an heir to be crowned during his father's lifetime), a gesture that, at least in theory, might reassure Pope Innocent of Frederick's willingness to separate the thrones of Germany and Sicily.

373. The Battle of Las Navas de Tolosa, or Al-Uqab, was fought on 16 July 1212.

374. There were probably fewer than thirty thousand Moors and around fourteen thousand Christians.

375. Ubeda was taken years later and the "Goliza" of the text is not readily identified. This paragraph is essentially an apocryphal account.

376. Raymond VI, Count of Toulouse, initially tolerated the Cathars. After a Papal envoy (Peter of Castelnau) sent to investigate was assassinated in 1208, Raymond was excommunicated.

377. Here we see the monk's bias, which has already been expressed about Muslims as well as Greek Orthodox Christians.

378. Arnald Amalric's bloody crusade was, in fact, highly successful in exterminating heresy and heretics. To this cleric is attributed the infamous command: "Kill them (all), for the Lord will know his own."

379. Frederick was elected King of Germany at Frankfurt in December 1212. There were a number of military engagements before Otto withdrew to the Brunswick region late in 1214 (see also note 380).

380. The Anglo-French War resulted in the permanent loss of Normandy by King John. An extended development in this conflict was John's alliance with Otto (who was his nephew) against Frederick and the French. The English king also had to confront domestic problems such as the baronial unrest that led to the Magna Carta, and a dispute with Pope Innocent over archiepiscopal appointments, leading to John (like his allies Otto of Brunswick and Raymond VI of Toulouse) being excommunicated. Frederick benefited immeasurably from the fact that the military campaigns prosecuted against his French allies by John and Otto were poorly coordinated, and that the English king, like his German nephew, went to war in France lacking the knight service of many barons who simply refused to support him. John was soon back in England fighting a civil war (the First Barons' War) while Otto, lacking sufficient support from the German no-

bles, had given up any hope of defeating Frederick, who was crowned King of Germany (again) at Aachen in July 1215. Supported by the Scots and the rebel barons of England, Prince Louis of France invaded Britain (and was even proclaimed King of England at London in June 1216), but the tide turned against him after King John's death in October 1216, and the next year he was forced to withdraw to France. Frederick issued several decrees at Aachen; see *Friderici II Diplomata,* book 14, part 2, pages 284-305. A detailed account of the wars of King John against the French and his own barons (and the granting of the Magna Carta) is given by an English chronicler; see *Roger of Wendover* (in Sources), pages 293-377.

381. Aldobrandino of Este, Lord of Ferrara, was a staunch supporter of Frederick II and Innocent III. Unfortunately, he met an early death in 1215, possibly from poisoning.

382. This probably refers to the abbey of the Holy Spirit at Ocre, which was subsequently refounded in 1248.

383. An eclipse visible in Italy occurred on 17 March 1215. See Espenak, op.cit.

384. This refers to the Fifth Crusade. Its costs, like those of the Fourth Crusade, were defrayed partly through a tax. Innocent issued two bulls calling for the Fifth Crusade, *Quia maior* in 1213 and *Ad liberandam* in 1215.

385. Many theologians regard the Fourth Lateran Council as the most significant council of its kind held during the Middle Ages, as it addressed a great many issues and firmly asserted the position and power of the Catholic Church while infallibly defining certain beliefs (like transubstantiation). Its seventy canons consider faith and heresy, penance, order and discipline, clerical morality, juridical procedures, tithing, simony, the relationship to Jews and Muslims, and other matters.

386. Following this passage is a short, illegible line about the Emperor Otto.

387. This abbey near Rome was first erected for the Benedictines. It was rebuilt for the Cistercians beginning in 1203, with work completed in 1217.

388. Here the chronicler's bias brings us a simplification of the essential facts. Promising the coastal territory to the Venetians, Peter took a Venetian fleet to conquer Durazzo (Durres), in what is now Albania. When this effort failed, he continued on towards Constantinople by land. Along the way, he was captured by Theodore Comnenus Doukas, the Despot of Epirus, who ruled one of the regions that had constituted the Byzantine Empire when it was under Greek control (until 1204). Peter died in prison in 1219.

389. See note 380. Henry III was destined for a long reign, until 1272. William Marshal, Earl of Pembroke, acted as Henry's regent until his death in 1219 at around seventy-two years of age. See Crouch, David, *William Marshal* (in Sources).

390. Otto IV, deposed Holy Roman Emperor, died at Harzburg Castle (of which little remains), on 19 May 1218. He rests in Brunswick Cathedral.

391. The chronicler refers to the fact that many crusaders died from disease.

392. Saint Leonard of Noblac, commemorated 6 November.

393. The siege of Damietta and its aftermath were much more complex than what is described here (although a few more details are presented later). Forced to confront not only an invasion but a conspiracy to kill him, the Ayyubid sultan al Kamil abandoned the city and withdrew to a position up the Nile. Insolent Cardinal Pelagio Galvani (Galvão), the leader of the crusade, refused any kind of compromise (as ambassador to Constantinople a few years earlier he infamously tried to close the Orthodox churches and imprison Greek priests). As shall be seen, Kamil returned to Damietta in 1221 after the crusaders suffered a series of military setbacks along the

Nile. He released his prisoners in exchange for an eight-year truce. The chronicler subsequently mentions the restoration of Damietta to Kamil. Several contemporary chronicles address the Damietta details at far greater length; see, for example, *Roger of Wendover* (in Sources), pages 405-413. In 1223, John of Brienne betrothed his daughter, Yolanda (Isabella), to Frederick II, who married her at Brindisi in November 1225 and then claimed the crown of Jerusalem through her by *jure uxoris,* effectively deposing John. However, if Frederick wanted more than a symbolic title, he would have to take Jerusalem from the Muslims. For Pelagio, see Donovan, Joseph, op.cit. (in Sources).

394. This is an important Benedictine abbey near Avellino.

395. Frederick II was crowned Holy Roman Emperor at Rome on 22 November 1220.

396. Indeed, Frederick issued numerous decrees from Montemario, the highest hill in Rome, and other places around the city, before arriving in Sutri at the end of the month. See *Historia Diplomatica Frederici Secundi,* volume 2, part 1, pages 19-53.

397. This passage is misleading in its omission of any reference to the Assizes of Capua, the legal code of December 1220 that revised these existing laws. With the Assizes of Messina (in 1221), this was a prelude to the enlightened Constitutions of Melfi of 1231. Richard of San Germano, who may have been present with Frederick, mentions the Assizes of Capua, even noting that these consisted of twenty statutes.

398. This was a flotilla led by Henry of Malta in 1221 in response to Damietta having fallen (an event described in the following paragraph).

399. There is not much reason to doubt this account (significant because it relates to an occasion when the chronicler probably met Frederick II), for which the correct day of the week is given by the monk. Teano and

the Ferraria monastery are between Capua and San Germano (Cassino); Frederick's journey through the region is confirmed by charters issued at Capua in January and San Germano in February 1223; see *Historia Diplomatica Frederici Secundi,* volume 2, part 1, pages 294-309, 313-318. Richard of San Germano also mentions Frederick's presence. For King John (Brienne) of Jerusalem see note 393.

400. At Ferentino in March 1223, Frederick promised the Pope to go on a crusade (within two years) in view of the fall of Damietta and the general failure of the recent Fifth Crusade, and he formally accepted the betrothal of Yolanda (Isabella), daughter of King John of Jerusalem.

401. This was Lesser Armenia, the kingdom along the southern coast of Asia Minor near Antioch (see the map).

402. As noted in the Introduction of this volume, the monk reported this story a few years before Roger of Wendover, who mentions it around 1228. See *Roger of Wendover* (in Sources), pages 512-514.

403. The deportation of many Sicilian Muslims to Lucera and other cities in Apulia and Calabria took place over the course of decades, not in a single year as both the monk and Richard of San Germano imply. Following the execution of the Muslim rebel leader Morabit, in 1222, thousands of Muslims from the Iato area revolted with their leader Ibn Abbad (Benaveth). By then, most of Sicily's Muslims had already accepted baptism and were integrated into Sicilian society as Arab Catholics, some already for two or three generations. It seems that after the first deportation there remained a few Muslims in the west of the island, particularly at Mazara and Mount Saint Julian (Erice), and there may still have been a few mosques in Palermo, but this mass transfer to Apulia marks the effective end of the widespread practice of Islam in Sicily. This was not Frederick's only move against Muslims. He sent a fleet against Jerba, off the coast of Tunisia, whose pirates were supporting the forces fighting against the crusaders to the east.

404. As the chronicler states at the beginning of this chapter (albeit refer-ring specifically to lodging fit for a king), there may have been a dearth of houses to provide hospitality for travelers such as the many pilgrims passing through Italy. Interestingly, Richard of San Germano states that in 1223 Frederick ordered the destruction of castles built illegally, citing a provision expressed in the Assizes of Capua a few years earlier.

405. Richard of San Germano states that some taxes imposed around this time (specifically in 1223) were intended chiefly to defray specific costs, such as "a certain sum to pay knights and soldiers who had fought the Muslims who rebelled in Sicily, for which a certain judge Urban of Teano collected three hundred gold ounces from the Benedictine lands around San Germano."

406. *Caesar* refers to the emperor; there may also be a reference to Matthew 22:21, "Give to Caesar what belongs to Caesar, and give to God what be-longs to God."

407. Pope Honorius III died on 18 March 1227.

408. Thomas of Aquino (Aquinas), Count of Acerra, was a justiciar in Terra di Lavoro who had fought against Dipold; in 1212 he met Frederick at Gaeta (see note 370). Some ships did indeed set sail for the crusade in September 1227 (see note 409); Thomas of Aquino probably went to Syria with this group. According to Richard of San Germano, Frederick, whilst at Barletta, received a letter from Thomas, sent from Syria, on Easter (2 April) in 1228.

409. In late summer 1227, Frederick's fleet departed from Brindisi but most (though not all) of the ships soon returned due to an epidemic among the troops; this is what the chronicler refers to as Frederic being "seriously ill." (See also note 408.) Frederick was excommunicated shortly afterward.

410. Incredibly, there were skeptics who cynically suggested that Frederick

had merely feigned illness; see *Roger of Wendover* (in Sources), pages 492-493.

411. "Lesser Armenia" (see the map of regions in 1200) was located in the southern part of Asia Minor, bordering the Kingdom of Antioch, to the immediate north of Cyprus.

412. A formal coronation rite does not seem to have been used, Frederick still being in a state of excommunication. This however, was an era when monarchs accorded ever less importance to such Papal tools as excommunication and interdict.

413. Conrad succeeded Frederick II as King of Sicily in 1250. By then, with the holy city again lost, being King of Jerusalem was a largely symbolic status.

414. See *The Liber Augustalis* (in Sources).

415. The chronicler Matthew Paris famously recorded: "Frederick, peerless wonder of the world, died in Apulia on Saint Lucy's Day." *Obiit insuper stupor mundi Fredericus, die Sanctae Luciae, in Apulia.*

416. See Schmeidler, op.cit (in Sources).

417. This is the author's translation; this part of Romuald's chronicle has not been published in a book in English.

418. See Stubbs, William, *Gesta Regis Henrici* (in Sources), page xii.

419. Gwenyth Hood advanced a widely-supported theory that Falcandus was Hugh Foucault, Prior of Saint-Denis and Argenteuil, whose surname, sometimes *Foucaud,* is readily latinized to *Falcandus.* For this see Hood, Gwenyth, "Falcandus and Fulcaudus" (in Sources), pages 1-41. Evelyn Jamison cogently argued in her *Admiral Eugenius of Sicily* (see Sources) that Falcandus may have been Eugenius of Palermo.

SOURCES AND BIBLIOGRAPHY

Manuscript Sources

A) Biblioteca Comunale di Bologna: Manuscript A44 (formerly 16,b.II,10). Manuscript of the chronicle written at Santa Maria della Ferraria. (For the first publication see *Monumenti Storici* below.)

B) Archivio di Stato di Palermo, Tabulario dei Monasteri di San Filippo di Fragalà e di Santa Maria di Maniace: Manuscript 7 (TSFF 7). Charter of October 1112 in Greek endowing the monastery on Adelaide's initiative.

C) Archivio di Stato di Palermo, Tabulario dei Monasteri di San Filippo di Fragalà e di Santa Maria di Maniace: Manuscript 12 (TSFF 12). Charter of November 1112 in Greek endowing the monastery with reference to Roger I.

D) Archivio di Stato di Palermo, Tabulario dei Monasteri di San Filippo di Fragalà e di Santa Maria di Maniace: Manuscript 17 (TSFF17). Charter of 27 November 1171. Unsealed copy of a charter by Queen Margaret; recorded in Greek and Latin, confirms privileges of Roger II protecting said monasteries, exempting them from the obligation to provide timber and livestock, lodge men-at-arms, and so forth, effectively exempting them from local civic authority.

E) Tabulario della Cattedrale di Palermo: Manuscript 29. Charter of April 1196. Queen Constance's assignment of some serfs, formerly under the feudal jurisdiction of the late Archbishop Walter of Palermo, to the authority of the notary Rainaldo. Bears seal of Queen Constance.

Primary Sources in Print (includes some translations)

Acta Imperii Inedita Seculi XIII et XIV. Collection. Edited by Winkelmann, Eduard (1880).

Alexiad of Anna Comnena. Translated by Sewter, Edgar Robert Ashton (1969).

Annales Beneventani, in *Monumenta Germaniae Historica,* volume 3. Edited by Pertz, Georg (1839).

Annales Casinenses, in *Monumenta Germaniae Historica,* volume 19. Edited by Pertz, Georg (1866).

Annales Cavenses, in *Monumenta Germaniae Historica,* volume 3. Edited by Pertz, Georg (1839).

Annales Ceccanenses, in *Monumenta Germaniae Historica,* volume 19. Edited by Pertz, Georg (1866).

Annales Siculi, in *Rerum Italicarum Scriptores*, volume 5. Edited by Muratori, Lodovico (1774, reprint Bologna 1928).

Book in Honor of Augustus by Pietro da Eboli. Translation and notes. Hood, Gwenyth. (2012).

Catalogo Illustrato del Tabulario di Santa Maria Nuova in Monreale. Garufi, Carlo Alberto (1902).

Catalogus Baronum. Jamison, Evelyn (1972). See also Del Re's *Cronisti,* volume 1, below.

La Chanson d'Antioche. Edited by Graindor de Douai (1862).

Chronica Majora of Matthew Paris, volumes 1-5. Edited by Luard, Henry (1872-1880).

Chronica Monasterii Casinensis, in *Monumenta Germaniae Historica* series, volume 34. Edited by Hoffmann, Hartmut (1980).

The Chronicle of Robert of Torigni. Edited by Howlett, Richard (1889).

Chronicon Vulturnense de Monaco Giovanni, 3 volumes. Edited by Federici, Vincenzo (1925-1938).

O City of Byzantium: Annals of Nicetas Choniates. Translation. Magoulias, Harry (1984).

Codex Diplomaticus Cavensis. Compilation. Morcaldi, Michele, chief editor (1893).

Codice Diplomatico di Sicilia sotto il Governo degli Arabi. Airoldi, Alfonso (1790).

Constantiae Imperatricis et Reginae Siciliae Diplomata, in *Codex Diplomaticus Regni Siciliae,* series 2, part 1. Compilation. Koelzer, Theo (1983).

Cronica Fratis Salimbene de Adam Ordinis Minorum, in *Monumenta Germaniae Historica,* volume 32. Edited by Pertz, Georg (1913).

Cronisti e Scrittori Sincroni Napoletani, volume 1 ("Normanni"), edited by Del Re, Giuseppe (Naples 1845); pages 5-71 and 559-563 (Romuald of Salerno); pages 82-156 (Alexander of Telese); pages 157-276 (Falco of Benevento); pages 277-391 (Hugh Falcandus); pages 405-439 (Peter of Eboli); pages 571-616 (Catalogus Baronum).

Cronisti e Scrittori Sincroni Napoletani, volume 2 ("Svevi"), edited by Del Re, Giuseppe (Naples 1868); pages 5-100 (Richard of San Germano); pages 101-200 ("Nicholas Jamsilla"); pages 201-408 (Saba Malaspina); pages 409-627 (Bartholomew of Nicastro).

The Deeds of Frederick Barbarossa. Translation of the *Gesti Friderici Imperatoris* of Otto of Freising. Mierow, Charles (1953).

I Diplomi della Cattedrale di Messina. Compilation of the Antonino Amico index. Starrabba, Raffaele (1876-1890).

I Diplomi Greci ed Arabi di Sicilia Pubblicati nel Testo Originale, Tradotti ed Illustrati (2 volumes). Cusa, Salvatore (1868).

I Documenti Inediti dell'Epoca Normanna in Sicilia. Compilation. Garufi, Carlo Alberto (1899).

The Ecclesiastical History of England and Normandy. Translation and notes of the *Historia Ecclesiastica* of Orderic Vitalis. Forester, Thomas (1854-1856).

Epistolae Sancti Thomae Cantuariensis. Compilation. Giles, John (1845).

Das Falkenbuch Friedrichs II. Photography and notes of Vatican codex *Pal. Lat 1071.* Walz, Dorothea, and Willemsen, Carl (2000).

Friderici II Diplomata, in *Monumenta Germaniae Historica* (book 14, parts 1 and 2). Compilation. Koch, Walter (2002, 2007).

Gesta Francorum et aliorum Hierosolimitanorum. Parallel Latin/English text. Hill, Rosalind (1967).

Gesta Regis Henrici Secundi Benedicti Abbatis (formerly attributed to Benedict of Peterborough), in *Rerum Britannicarum Medii Aevi Scriptores,* volume 1. Stubbs, William (1867).

Gesta Roberti Wiscardi of William of Apulia. Mathieu, Marguerite (1961).

The Gesta Tancredi of Ralph of Caen: A History of the Normans on the First Crusade. Translation. Bachrach, Bernard (2016).

Historia Diplomatica Frederici Secundi. Compilation. Huillard-Bréholles, Jean (1852-1857).

The Historical Works of Ralph de Diceto, Dean of London (2 volumes). Stubbs, William (1876).

A History of Deeds Done Beyond the Sea, by William, Archbishop of Tyre. Translation and notes. Babcock, Emily, and Krey, August (1943).

History of the Lombards by Paul the Deacon. Translated by Foulke, William (1907), edited by Peters, Edward (1975).

Italia Pontificia, volumes 1 (Rome), 2 (Lazio), 3 (Tuscany), 8 (Campania), 9 (Molise, Apulia, Basilicata), 10 (Calabria and islands). Compilation. Kehr, Paul (1906-1975).

Kitab al-masalik w'al-mamalik. Mohammed ibn Hawqal, in *Bibliotheca Geographorum Arabicorum* (Leiden 1873).

Das Kitab surat al-ard des Abu Gafar Muhammad ibn Musa al-Huwarizmi. Translation. von Mzik, Hans (1926).

The Liber Augustalis or Constitutions of Melfi. Translation and notes. Powell, James (1971).

Materials for the History of Thomas Becket, Archbishop of Canterbury (7 volumes). Compilation. Robertson, James (1877).

Monumenti Storici, series 1 ("Cronache"), *Ignoti Monachi Cisterciensis: Sancta Mariae de Ferraria Chronica et Ryccardi de Sancto Germano Chronica Priora.* Edited by Gaudenzi, Augustus (1888).

Petri Blesensis Opera Omnia (volume 1), Letters of Peter of Blois. Giles, John (1847).

De Rebus Gestis Rogerii Calabriae et Siciliae Comitis et Roberti Guiscardi Ducis Fratris Eius of Godfrey Malaterra, *Rerum Italicarum Scriptores,* volume 5, part 1. Pontieri, Ernesto (1928).

Robert the Monk's History of the First Crusade: Iherosolimitana. Translation. Sweetenham, Carol (2006).

Roger of Wendover's Flowers of History, volume 2. Translation. Giles, John (1849).

Rogerii II Regis Diplomata Latina (Codex Diplomaticus Regni Siciliae), Diplomata Regum et Principum e Gente Normannorum (series 1). Brühl, Carlrichard (1987).

Rollus Rubeus: Privilegia Ecclesie Cephaleditane, a Diversis Regis et Imperatoribus Concessa, Recollecta et in hoc Volumine Scripta. Mirto, Corrado (1972).

Saint Bernard On Consideration. Translation by Lewis, George (1908).

Sancti Bernardi Abbatis Primi Claraevallensis ("Vita Prima"), volume 2. Edited by Mabillon, Jean (1690).

Tabularium Regiae et Imperialis Cappellae Collegiatae Divi Petri in Regio Palermitano Palatio. Garofalo, Luigi (1835).

The Life and Letters of Thomas à Becket (2 volumes). Documents in translation. Giles, John (1846).

St Thomas of Canterbury: An Account of His Life and Fame from the Contemporary Biographers and other Chroniclers. Hutton, William (1899).

The Travels of Ibn Jubayr. Translation. Broadhurst, Ronald (1952, 2008).

Vita Sancti Thomae by William Fitzstephen and Herbert of Bosham, in *Materials for the History of Thomas Becket,* volume 3 (see above).

L'Ystoire de li Normant of Amatus of Montecassino. *Storia dei Normanni.* Parallel French/Italian text. Tamburrini, Alberto (1999).

Secondary Literature

Abulafia, David. "The Crown and the Economy under Roger II and his

Successors," *Dumbarton Oaks Papers,* number 37 (Washington, DC, 1983), pages 1-14.

Abulafia, David. *Frederick II: A Medieval Emperor* (1992).

Abulafia, David. *The Two Italies: Economic Relations Between the Norman Kingdom of Sicily and the Northern Communes* (1977).

Agius, Dionisius. *Siculo Arabic* (1996).

Agnello, Giuseppe. *L'Architettura Sveva in Sicilia* (1935).

Alio, Jacqueline. *Margaret, Queen of Sicily* (2016).

Amari, Michele. *Storia dei Musulmani di Sicilia* (1854).

Aziz, Ahmad. *A History of Islamic Sicily* (1975).

Barber, Richard. *Henry Plantagenet* (1964).

Bates, David. "The Representation of Queens and Queenship in Anglo-Norman Royal Charters," *Frankland: The Franks and the World of the Early Middle Ages* (2008).

Bonardi, Giovanna. *La Cronaca di Santa Maria di Ferraria 741-1228: Struttura, fonti e contesto storico di una cronaca del Regno* (2001); National Library, Florence.

Bowie, Colette. "To Have and Have Not: The Dower of Joanna Plantagenet, Queen of Sicily," *Queenship in the Mediterranean: Negotiating the Role of the Queen in the Medieval and Early Modern Eras* (2013), pages 27-50.

Bradbury, Jim. *The Routledge Companion to Medieval Warfare* (2004).

Brandileone, Francesco. *Il Diritto Romano nelle Leggi Normanne e Sveve del Regno di Sicilia* (1884).

Bresc, Henri. *Palermo al Tempo dei Normanni* (2012).

Brühl, Carlrichard. *Urkunden und Kanzlei König Rogers II von Sizilien* (1978).

Bucaria, Nicolò. *Sicilia Judaica: Guida alle Antichità Giudaiche della Sicilia* (1996).

Cahen, Claude. *Le Régime Féodal de l'Italie Normande* (Paris 1940).

Canning, Joseph. *A History of Medieval Political Thought 300-1450* (1996).

Caperna, Umberto. *Cronaca Santa Maria della Ferraria* (2008).

Caravale, Mario. "La Feudalità nella Sicilia Normanna," *Atti del Congresso Internazionale di Studi sulla Sicilia Normanna* (Palermo 1974), pages 21-50.

Caspar, Erich. *Roger II und die Gründung der Normannische-sicilischen Monarchie* (1904).

Chalandon, Ferdinand. *Histoire de la Domination Normande en Italie et en Sicile* (Paris 1907).

Chappuys, Gabriel. *L'Historie du Royaume de Navarre* (1616).

Cilento, Adele and Routt, David. "Foundation of a Monastery in Byzantine Calabria 1053/54" *Medieval Italy: Texts in Translation* (2009), pages 506-507.

Clarke, Peter, and Duggan, Anne (editors). *Pope Alexander III 1159-1181: The Art of Survival* (2012).

Columba, Gaetano. "Note di Topografia Medievale Palermitana," *Archivio Storico Siciliano* (Palermo 1910), pages 325-350.

Coulton, George. *From St Francis to Dante: Translations from the Chronicle of the Franciscan Salimbene 1221-1288* (1907).

Crouch, David. *The Birth of Nobility: Constructing the Aristocracy in England and France 900-1300* (2005).

Crouch, David. *William Marshal: Knighthood, War and Chivalry 1147-1219* (2002).

Cuozzo, Errico. *Catalogus Baronum: Commentario* (1984).

Curtis van Cleve, Thomas. *The Emperor Frederick II of Hohenstaufen, Immutator Mundi* (1972).

D'Angelo, Edoardo. *Pseudo Ugo Falcando: De Rebus circa Regni Siciliae Curiam Gestis* (2014).

Delogu, Paolo. *I Normanni in Italia: Cronache della Conquista e del Regno* (1984).

Demus, Otto. *The Mosaics of Norman Sicily* (1950).

Di Giovanni, Vincenzo. "Appendice alla Topografia Antica di Palermo," *Archivio Storico Siciliano* (Palermo 1899), pages 379-396.

Donovan, Joseph. *Pelagius and the Fifth Crusade* (1950).

Drell, Joanna. "Cultural Syncretism and Ethnic Identity: The Norman 'Conquest' of Southern Italy and Sicily," *Al-Masaq: Journal of the Medieval Mediterranean,* volume 25, issue 3 (London 1999), pages 187-202.

Duggan, Anne. *Thomas Becket* (2004).

Earenfight, Theresa. *Queenship in Medieval Europe* (2013).

Edbury, Peter. *The Conquest of Jerusalem and the Third Crusade: Sources in Translation* (1998).

Egidi, Pietro. *La Colonia Saracena di Lucera e la Sua Distruzione* (1912).

Espenak, Fred, and Meeus, Jean. *Five Millennium Canon of Lunar Eclipses,* NASA Technical Publication TP-2009-214172 (2009).

Enzensberger, Horst. "Il Documento Regio come Strumento del Potere," *Potere, Società e Popolo nell'Età dei Due Guglielmi* (Bari 1981), pages 104-138.

Enzensberger, Horst. "Chanceries, Charters and Administration in Norman Sicily," *The Society of Norman Italy* (Leiden 2002), pages 117-150.

Epifanio, Vincenzo. "Ruggero II e Filippo di Al Mahdiah," *Archivio Storico Siciliano* (Palermo 1905), pages 471-501.

Fazello, Thomas. *De Rebus Siculus* (1558-1560).

Ferrari, Angelo. *Feudi Prenormanni dei Borrello tra Abruzzo e Molise* (2007).

Fodale, Salvatore. *Comes et Legatus Siciliae: Sul privilegio di Urbano II e la pretesa Apostolica Legazia dei Normanni in Sicilia* (1970).

Freed, John. *Frederick Barbarossa: The Prince and the Myth* (2016).

Fried, Johannes. *Charlemagne* (2016).

Fuhrmann, Horst. *Germany in the High Middle Ages c. 1050-1200* (1986).

Gabrieli, Francesco. "Ibn Hawqal e gli Arabi in Sicilia," *L'Islam nella Storia: Saggi di storia e storiografia musulmana* (1966), pages 57-67.

Garufi, Carlo Alberto. "Monete e Conii nella Storia del Diritto Siculo dagli Arabi ai Martini," *Archivio Storico Siciliano* (Palermo 1898), pages 11-171.

Giordano, Nicola. "Nuovo Contributo alla Determinazione dei Rapporti tra Stato e Chiesa in Sicilia al Tempo dei Normanni," *Archivio Storico Siciliano* (Palermo 1916), pages 25-48.

Giunta, Francesco. *Bizanti e Bizantinismo nella Sicilia Normanna* (1950).

Goskar, Tehmina. "Material Worlds: The Shared Cultures of Southern Italy and Its Mediterranean Neighbours in the Tenth to Twelfth Centuries," *Al-Masaq: Journal of the Medieval Mediterranean,* volume 23, issue 3 (London 2011), pages 189-204.

Granara, William. "Ibn Hawqal in Sicily," *Alif: Journal of Comparative Poetics,* number 3, (Cairo, 1983), pages 94-99.

Hanley, Catherine. *Louis: The French Prince Who Invaded England* (2016).

Haskins, Charles. "England and Sicily in the Twelfth Century," *English Historical Review,* number 26 (Oxford 1911), pages 641-665.

Haverkamp, Alfred. *Medieval Germany 1056-1273.* Translation (1992).

Herrin, Judith. *Byzantium: The Surprising Life of a Medieval Empire* (2009).

Hoffmann, Hartmut. "Die Anfänge der Normannen in Süditalien" *Quellen und Forschungen aus Italienischen Arxhiven un Bibliotheken,* number 49 (Tübingen 1969), pages 95-144.

Hood, Gwenyth. "Falcandus and Fulcaudus Epistola ad Petrum liber de Regno Sicilie: Literary Form and Author's Identity," *Studi Medievali (*June 1999), 3rd Series, XL, pages 1-41.

Houben, Hubert. *Roger II von Sizilien* (1997).

Howard-Johnston, James. "The Chronicle and Other Forms of Historical Writing in Byzantium," *The Medieval Chronicle,* number 10 (Leiden 2015), pages 1-22.

Hurlock, Kathryn, and Oldfield, Paul, eds. *Crusading and Pilgrimage in the Norman World* (2015).

Ingraiti, Gaetano. "Sulla Legittimità della Legazia Apostolica in Sicilia," *Atti del Congresso Internazionale di Studi sulla Sicilia Normanna* (Palermo 1974), pages 460-466.

Jamison, Evelyn. *Admiral Eugenius of Sicily: His Life and Work and Authorship of the Epistola ad Petrum and the Historia Hugonis Falcandi Siculi* (London 1957).

Jamison, Evelyn. "Alliance of England and Sicily in the Second Half of the Twelfth Century," *Journal of the Warburg and Courtauld Institutes,* volume 6 (London 1943), pages 20-32.

Jamison, Evelyn. "Judex Tarentinus: The Career of Judex Tarentinus *Magne Curie Justiciarius* and the Emergence of the Sicilian *Regalis Magna Curia* under William I and the Regency of Margaret of Navarre, 1156-72," *Proceedings of the British Academy,* volume I, iii (London 1968), pages 289-344.

Jensen, Frede. *The Poetry of the Sicilian School* (1986).

Johns, Jeremy. *Arabic Administration in Norman Sicily: The Royal Diwan* (2002).

Johns, Jeremy. "The Norman Kings of Sicily and the Fatimid Caliphate," *Anglo-Norman Studies XV* (1995), pages 133-159.

Johns, Susan. *Noblewomen, Aristocracy and Power in the Twelfth-Century Anglo-Norman Realm* (2003).

Joranson, Einar. "The Inception of the Career of the Normans in Italy: Legend and History," *Speculum,* number 23 (July 1948), pages 353-396.

Jordan, Edouard. "La Politique Ecclésiastique de Roger I et les Origines de la Légation Sicilienne," *Le Moyen Age* (1922), volume 2, pages 237-273.

Kantorowicz, Ernst. *Friedrich der Zweite* (1927).

Kapitaikin, Lev. "The Daughter of Al-Andalus: Interrelations between Norman Sicily and the Muslim West," *Al-Masaq: Journal of the Medieval Mediterranean,* volume 25, issue 1 (London 2013), pages 113-134.

Kehr, Karl Andreas. "Ergänzungen zu Falco von Benevent," *Neues Archiv der Gesellschaft für ältere deutsche Geschichtskunde,* number 27 (Hannover and Leipzig, 1902), pages 445-472.

Kitzinger, Ernst. "The Mosaics of the Cappella Palatina in Palermo," *Art Bulletin,* number 31 (New York 1949), pages 290-319.

Kreutz, Barbara. *Before the Normans: Southern Italy in the Ninth and Tenth Centuries* (1996).

Krönig, Wolfgang. "Sul Significato Storico dell'Arte sotto i Due Guglielmi," *Potere, Società e Popolo nell'Età dei Due Guglielmi* (Bari 1981), pages 292-310.

La Mantia, Giuseppe. "Su l'Uso della Registrazione nella Cancelleria del Regno di Sicilia dai Normanni a Federico III d'Aragona 1130-1377," *Archivio Storico Siciliano* (Palermo 1908), pages 197-209.

Larner, John. *Italy in the Age of Dante and Petrarch 1216-1380* (1983).

La Via, Mariano. "Le Così Dette 'Colonie Lombarde' in Sicilia," *Archivio Storico Siciliano* (Palermo 1899), pages 1-35.

Levtzion, Nehemia. "Ibn-Hawqal, the Cheque, and Awdaghost," *Journal of African History,* volume 9, number 2 (Cambridge 1968), pages 223-233.

Licinio, Raffaele. *Castelli Medievali: Puglia e Basilicata dai Normanni a Federico II e Carlo d'Angio* (1994).

Loewenthal, Leonard Joseph Alphonse. "For the Biography of Walter Ophamil Archbishop of Palermo," *English Historical Review,* volume 87 (Oxford 1972), pages 75-82.

Loud, Graham. "The Genesis and Context of the Chronicle of Falco of Benevento," *Anglo-Norman Studies IV: Proceedings of the Battle Conference 1992* (1993).

Loud, Graham. "History Writing in the Twelfth-Century Kingdom of Sicily," *Chronicling History: Chroniclers and Historians in Medieval and Renaissance Italy* (2007).

Loud, Graham. *The Latin Church in Norman Sicily* (2007).

Loud, Graham. *Roger II and the Creation of the Kingdom of Sicily* (2012).

Lupo, Carmelina. "I Normanni di Sicilia di Fronte al Papato," *Archivio Storico Siciliano per la Sicilia Orientale,* volume 20 (Catania 1924), pages 1-74.

Magdalino, Paul. *The Empire of Manuel I Komnenos 1143-1180* (1993).

Makdisi, John. "The Islamic Origins of the Common Law," *North Carolina Law Review,* volume 77, number 5, June 1999, pages 1635-1737.

Mallette, Karla. *The Kingdom of Sicily 1100-1250: A Literary History* (2005).

Marongiu, Antonio. "La Legislazione Normanna," *Atti del Congresso Internazionale di Studi sulla Sicilia Normanna* (Palermo 1974), pages 195-212.

Martorana, Pierluigi. La Monetazione Aurea in Sicilia (2007).

Massetti, Marco. *Zoologia della Sicilia Araba e Normanna 827-1194* (2016).

Matthew, Donald. *The Norman Kingdom of Sicily* (1992).

Maurici, Ferdinando. *Palermo Araba: Una sintesi dell'evoluzione urbanistica 831-1072* (2015).

Maurolico, Francesco. *Sicanicarum Rerum Compendium* (1562).

Mazzarese Fardella, Enrico, "La Condizione Giuridica della Donna nel Liber Augustalis" in *Archivio Storico Siciliano,* Series 4, Volume 21-22 (Palermo 1997).

Mendola, Louis. *Sicily's Rebellion against King Charles* (2016).

Metcalfe, Alexander. *The Muslims of Medieval Italy* (2009).

Meyendorff, John. *Orthodoxy and Catholicity* (1966).

Morris, Marc. *King John: Treachery and Tyranny in Medieval England, The Road to Magna Carta* (2015).

Morrison, James Cotter. *The Life and Times of Saint Bernard, Abbot of Clairvaux* (1877).

Morso, Salvadore. *Descrizione di Palermo Antico* (1827).

Moshe, Gil. "The Jews in Sicily under Muslim Rule in the Light of Geniza Documents," *Italia Judaica 1* (1983), pages 87-134.

Neville, Leonora. *Anna Komnene: The Life and Work of a Medieval Historian* (2016).

Niccolini, Giovanni Battista. *Storia della Casa di Svevia in Italia* (1873).

Omodei, Filoteo. "La Versione Italiana della Historia di Ugo Falcando,"

Archivio Storico Siciliano (Palermo 1898), pages 465-477.

Orlando, Diego. *Il Feudalismo in Sicilia* (1847).

Palmarocchi, Roberto. "Sul Feudo Normanno," *Studi Storici* (Pavia 1912), pages 349-376.

Paoli, Sebastiano. *Codice Diplomatico del Sacro Militare Ordine Gerosolimitano, oggi di Malta* (1733).

Paratore, Ettore. "Esame delle Varianti dei Codici Vaticano e Cassinense delle Leggi," *Atti del Congresso Internazionale di Studi sulla Sicilia Normanna* (Palermo 1974), pages 477-479.

Parker, John, "The Attempted Byzantine Alliance with the Sicilian Norman Kingdom 1166-1167," *Papers of the British School at Rome* (London 1956).

Pennington, Kenneth. "The Birth of the Ius Commune: King Roger II's Legislation," *Rivista Internazionale del Diritto Comune,* number 17 (Enna 2006).

Perla, Raffaele. *Le Assise de 'Re di Sicilia* (1881).

Pieri, Piero. "I Saraceni di Lucera nella Storia Militare Medievale" *Atti del Terzo Congresso Storico Pugliese,* number 6 (1953), pages 94-101.

Powell, James. *Innocent III: Vicar of Christ or Lord of the World?* (1963).

Re, Edward. "The Roman Contribution to the Common Law," *Fordham Law Review,* number 447 (New York 1961), pages 447-494.

Reston, James. *Warriors of God: Richard the Lionheart and Saladin in the Third Crusade* (2002).

Riley-Smith, Jonathan. *The First Crusade and the Idea of Crusading* (1986).

Runciman, Steven. *Byzantine Civilisation* (1933, 1969).

Runciman, Steven. *The Eastern Schism: A Study of the Papacy and the Eastern Churches during the XIth and XIIth Centuries* (1955).

Runciman, Steven. *A History of the Crusades* (1951).

Russo, Rocco. *La Magione di Palermo negli Otto Secoli della Sua Storia* (1975).

Santoro, Rodolfo. "Architettura Castellana della Feudalità Siciliana," *Archivio Storico Siciliano,* Series 4, Volume 7 (Palermo 1981), pages 59-113.

Sapio Vitrano, Francesco. *Il Nummarium Islamico e Normanno della Biblioteca Comunale di Palermo* (1975).

Sayers, Jane. *Innocent III: Leader of Europe 1198-1216* (1994).

Scaduto, Mario. *Il Monachesimo Basiliano nella Sicilia Medievale: Rinascita e Deca-*

denza (1947).

Scandone, Francesco. *Santa Maria di Ferraria* (1908).

Schmeidler, Bernard. "Ueber die Quellen un die Entsttehungszeit der Cronica S. Mariae de Ferraria," *Neues Archiv der Gesellschaft für ältere deutsche Geschichtskunde,* number 31 (Hannover and Leipzig, 1906), pages 13-57.

Sentis, Franz Jacob. *Die Monarchia Sicula* (1869).

Seward, Desmond. *The Monks of War: The Military Religious Orders* (1972).

Simonsohn, Shlomo. *Between Scylla and Charybdis: The Jews in Sicily* (2011).

Siragusa, Giovanni Battista. *Il Regno di Guglielmo I in Sicilia* (1885, 1929).

Spahr, Rodolfo. *Le Monete Siciliane dai Bizantini a Carlo I d'Angio 582-1282* and *Le Monete Siciliane dagli Aragonesi ai Borboni 1282-1836* (1959).

Spata, Giuseppe. *Le Pergamene Greche Esistenti nel Grande Archivio di Palermo Tradotte ed Illustrate* (1862).

Spiegel, Gabrielle. *The Past as Text: The Theory and Practice of Medieval Historiography* (1999).

Starrabba, Raffaele. "Del Dotario delle Regine di Sicilia," *Archivio Storico Siciliano* (Palermo 1874), pages 7-25.

Stern, Horst. *Mann aus Apulien: Die privaten Papiere del italienischen Staufers* (2015).

Stevenson, Jöseph. *The Chronicles of Robert de Monte* (1991).

Strauss, Raphael. *Die Juden im Königreich Sizilien unter Normannen und Staufen* (1910).

Takayama, Hiroshi. *The Administration of the Norman Kingdom of Sicily* (1993).

Taylor, Julie Anne. *Muslims in Medieval Italy: The Colony at Lucera* (2003).

Testa, Francesco. *De Vita, et Rebus Gesti Guilelmi II, Siciliae Regis, Monregalensis Ecclesii Fundatoris,* 4 volumes (1705-1773).

Thompson, Augustine. *Francis of Assisi: A New Biography* (2012).

Tramontana, Salvatore. "Gestione del Potere, Rivolte e Ceti al Tempo di Stefano di Perche," *Potere, Società e Popolo nell'Età dei Due Guglielmi* (Bari 1981), pages 79-101.

Tramontana, Salvatore. *L'Isola di Allah* (2014).

Travaini, Lucia. "La Monetazione del Regno di Sicilia al Tempo di Tancredi" *Tancredi, Conte di Lecce Re di Sicilia* (2004), pages 193-206.

Tronzo, William. *Intellectual Life at the Court of Frederick II* (1994).

Van Cleave, Rachel. "Rape and Querela Law in Italy: False Protection of Victim Agency," *Michigan Journal of Gender and Law,* volume 13, number 273 (January 2007).

Vetere, Benedetto. "Tancredi di Lecce nella Storiografia Medievale," *Tancredi, Conte di Lecce Re di Sicilia* (2004), pages 1-32.

Weiler, Björn. *Henry III of England and the Staufen Empire 1216-1272* (2006).

White, Lynn Townsend. *Latin Monasticism in Norman Sicily* (1938).

Williams, Watkin Wynn. *Saint Bernard of Clairvaux* (1935).

Wolf, Kenneth. *Making History: The Normans and their Historians in Eleventh-century Italy* (1995).

Zanfagna, Gerardo. *Vairano tra Storia e Leggenda* (1986).

Zecchino, Ortensio. *Le Assise di Ariano: Testo Critico, Traduzione e Note* (1984).

INDEX